# The
# NEW AMERICAN
# HOMESTEAD

## Sustainable, Self-Sufficient Living in the Country or in the City

John H. Tullock

WILEY

John Wiley & Sons, Inc.

Howell Book House
Published by John Wiley & Sons, Inc., Hoboken, New Jersey

No part of this publication may be reproduced, stored in a retrieval system or transmitted in any form
or by any means, electronic, mechanical, photocopying, recording, scanning or otherwise, except as
permitted under Sections 107 or 108 of the 1976 United States Copyright Act, without either the prior
written permission of the Publisher, or authorization through payment of the appropriate per-copy fee
to the Copyright Clearance Center, 222 Rosewood Drive, Danvers, MA 01923, (978) 750-8400, fax
(978) 646-8600, or on the web at www.copyright.com. Requests to the Publisher for permission should
be addressed to the Permissions Department, John Wiley & Sons, Inc., 111 River Street, Hoboken, NJ
07030, (201) 748-6011, fax (201) 748-6008, or online at http://www.wiley.com/go/permissions.

Wiley, the Wiley logo, Howell Book House, and related trademarks are trademarks or registered trademarks of John Wiley & Sons, Inc. and/or its affiliates. All other trademarks are the property of their
respective owners. John Wiley & Sons, Inc. is not associated with any product or vendor mentioned in
this book.

The publisher and the author make no representations or warranties with respect to the accuracy or
completeness of the contents of this work and specifically disclaim all warranties, including without
limitation warranties of fitness for a particular purpose. No warranty may be created or extended by
sales or promotional materials. The advice and strategies contained herein may not be suitable for every
situation. This work is sold with the understanding that the publisher is not engaged in rendering legal,
accounting, or other professional services. If professional assistance is required, the services of a com-
petent professional person should be sought. Neither the publisher nor the author shall be liable for
damages arising here from. The fact that an organization or Website is referred to in this work as a
citation and/or a potential source of further information does not mean that the author or the publisher
endorses the information the organization or Website may provide or recommendations it may make.
Further, readers should be aware that Internet Websites listed in this work may have changed or disap-
peared between when this work was written and when it is read.

For general information on our other products and services or to obtain technical support please contact
our Customer Care Department within the U.S. at (877) 762-2974, outside the U.S. at (317) 572-3993
or fax (317) 572-4002.

John Wiley & Sons, Inc., also publishes its books in a variety of electronic formats and by print-
on-demand. Not all content that is available in standard print versions of this book may appear or be
packaged in all book formats. If you have purchased a version of this book that did not include media
that is referenced by or accompanies a standard print version, you may request this media by visiting
http://booksupport.wiley.com. For more information about Wiley products, visit us www.wiley.com.

Library of Congress Control Number: 2011945555
ISBN: 978-1-118-02417-1 (pbk); ISBN: 978-1-118-18231-4 (ebk);
ISBN: 978-1-118-18322-9 (ebk); ISBN: 978-1-118-18323-6 (ebk)

Printed in the United States of America

10  9  8  7  6  5  4  3  2  1

Book production by John Wiley & Sons, Inc., Composition Services

# Contents

*To Jerry Yarnell and everyone else who works*
*hard and refuses to give up on their dreams.*

# Acknowledgments

Fifty years of growing, reading, and sharing with others have informed the text of this book, and thanking everyone who had a part is simply an impossible task. My grandparents, Clarence and Faye Boswell, played the greatest role in developing my interest in and love for both the natural world and the controlled spaces of farm and garden. In school, some special teachers, including in particular the late Mildred Luttrell, encouraged me to exercise my creativity and to communicate my thoughts through the written word. And throughout the lifelong adventure of gardening I have been privileged to encounter people from every state and several countries that share my enthusiasm for growing plants and enjoying them in every way from the purely aesthetic to the deliciously practical. Standouts among them are the late Sidney Arnold, Barry Glick, Monte Stanley, Lisa Stanley, Terry Richman, Scott Morrell, Graham Byars, Dr. Ken McFarland, Dr. Dave Etnier, Liz Etnier, Pat Rakes, J.R. and Peggy Shute, and the late Dr. Jack Sharp. Thanks are also due to the many people who send their gardening questions to me each month through *Tennessee Gardener* magazine. By helping you, I add to my own knowledge of gardening and the challenges it can sometimes pose.

Special appreciation goes to my agent, Grace Freedson, and to John Wiley & Sons acquisitions editor Pam Morouzis, for encouraging me to develop my original concept of a "cooking from the garden" book into a more comprehensive guide to sustainable living in the modern urban/suburban environment. To my project editor, Suzanne Snyder, thanks for your patience, your enthusiasm, and your well-crafted adjustments that make this a much better book than I began with. Kudos to the production team for the attractive design and helpful illustrations.

# The Principles of Permaculture

I am sitting cross-legged on the luxuriously soft grass beneath a spreading sugar maple. The shade tempers the 80-degree heat of June. A faint breeze now and then stirs the humid air and shakes the blousy white flower clusters of the hydrangea bushes like a cheerleader's pom-poms. Beside me in a white-painted lawn chair made of hand-shaped wooden slats sits my grandmother, breaking beans into a bowl. She grasps each bean by the little piece of stem attached to one end and bends it sharply backward, snapping off the tip and removing the string along one side of the pod. Then she quickly breaks the pod into pieces and drops them into the bowl.

Supposedly, I am helping her with this chore, but my bowl is filling at a rate half that of hers. I have trouble concentrating on bean breaking. Too much else is going on. All around me, lush foliage glows shades of green in the morning sunshine. Near the house, the hydrangeas, orange daylilies, and a climbing rose dapple the green with summer colors. Raspberries slowly ripen on their thorny canes that always look cold and wet like a glass of iced tea. Green tomatoes the size of tennis balls hang from their vines, caged in sheep wire as if they might somehow escape the garden. And long, long rows of deep green corn promise roasting ears. Soon. Maybe by the Fourth of July. The syrupy smell of fallen apples reaches me from the orchard, and I can hear the drone of insects and the calls of a dozen kinds of birds, all following the scent to an easy meal. In a sunny spot of lawn, apple slices lie drying between sheets of gauzy fabric. Earlier in the season, that same cloth shielded tender tobacco seedlings from frosty nights,

1

tobacco being the main cash crop hereabouts. Shaded by the apple trees, chickens cluck and flutter, separated from the vegetable and strawberry patch by a wire fence. Beyond the orchard, the railroad separates the house and four acres surrounding it from the rest of my grandfather's farm. A tangle of small trees, vines, and numerous kinds of wild plants stretches along the right-of-way. Orange and purple milkweeds, dusty-pink Joe Pye weed, bright purple ironweed, and Queen Anne's lace are all seemingly placed there for the swallowtail and monarch butterflies, the fritillaries and skippers that visit them repeatedly, a kaleidoscope of color and movement as long as the sun is up.

It was, in short, a perfect June day, the first day of summer, in 1963. I would soon be 12 years old. I was growing up, getting more serious about school and chores, but on that day I was still a little boy, basking in the warmth of the sun, the sights, sounds, and smells of my grandmother's gardens, and her reassuring presence beside me, quietly breaking beans. Neither of us had any inkling of the tragedy coming in November.

The assassination of President Kennedy might be considered a milepost along the pathway to the dramatic changes wrought on American society during the decades that followed. While Vietnam and race relations were creating rips in the social fabric, small family farms like ours began disappearing at an unprecedented rate. In 1960, just under 9 percent of America's population lived on a farm, and the average farm size was slightly more than 300 acres. By 1990, only 1.1 percent of Americans were living on farms, while the average farm size had ballooned by 52 percent to 461 acres. Industrial agriculture was displacing the family farm. Other demographic trends, such as suburbanization around city centers, rendered land more valuable for residential development than for agriculture.

As fewer and fewer people came to live on small farms, the skills that my grandparents depended on for meeting their daily needs began to be lost. When my generation is gone, I worry that few will remain who know how deeply satisfying life can be when lived in tune with the rain, the sun, and the seasons.

We denizens of the modern Western world have allowed our lives to become compartmentalized. We live in one place, drive to work at another, and obtain most of what we need from still other places, to which we also drive. We spend countless hours and significant amounts of money just getting around. We ignore the change of the seasons, indeed the separation of day and night, warming and illuminating our working and living spaces where and when we choose. The fuel we consume to accomplish all this also fuels climate change and international political conflagrations. Isn't it about time we thought about making some changes?

It should be apparent to anyone that we could reduce the number of those trips, not to mention save money, by sourcing more of our needs from home. The Internet has made telecommuting possible, along with e-shopping and the ability to see or to hear any conceivable form of entertainment. Why shouldn't home also directly provide some of our basic needs, especially food?

Anyone can apply the basic techniques needed to achieve a greater level of self-sufficiency. All that is required is a new attitude toward your home and its environs. Your space in the sun is a resource that can help feed you, cure some of your health problems, provide supplemental income, and calm your frazzled nerves at the end of a trying day.

# Rethinking Residential Landscapes

Fortunately for society and the planet, interest in growing one's own food and achieving a greater level of self-sufficiency is enjoying a resurgence. Four major influences have shaped this trend.

The first is *locavorism*, or eating food produced as close to one's home as possible in the interest of saving fuel, supporting the local economy, improving nutrition, and fostering good community relations.

The second influence is *sustainable living*, conducting one's affairs to utilize available resources in a way that does not jeopardize their potential for use by future generations. The greatest threat to future generations is climate change. Sustainable living, therefore, often boils down to reducing one's carbon footprint, along with wiser, more responsible use of resources such as water and soil. It also means working to reduce the impact of human activities on the other species with which we share the planet.

The third influence is the *economic impact* of the Great Recession of 2009. People began to realize (as I am sure my grandparents did in 1929) how old-fashioned skills like making pickles or keeping chickens make hard times easier to survive. During the Great Depression, my mother and her brother sometimes lacked shoes, but food was always on the table. My father's family, who lived in the city, occasionally went hungry.

The fourth major influence can only be described as *spiritual growth*. All across America, more people every day recognize the need to reconnect themselves with the rest of the ecosystem. Not literally to go tramping out to the wilderness to hew out an existence—that is a romantic fantasy few will ever achieve and arguably is less sustainable than staying put and making some serious changes to the way we live. But we need the experience of nature, the sights, the sounds, and the smells of vibrant life humming away, filling our consciousness with the sense of being well and truly alive and connected to the vast panoply of life, as it did for me that lovely June day so long ago.

Each day more of us are discovering how growing food and living in greater harmony with the natural world reduces our stress level. War, terror, and bitter hatreds, all the details and images, the arguments pro and con, the acrimony and the diplomacy, can be read, viewed, heard, and commented on from wherever you are by using a device you carry in your pocket. In the garden, among the bees and butterflies and blooms, one can find harmony and peace, not to mention delicious food, and leave the tweeting to the birds.

The purpose of this book is to help you find inner peace, natural harmony, and greater satisfaction by teaching you the skills you need to become more self-sufficient. You can join the new breed of American homesteaders with a different concept of "living well" in a city, a town, or a suburb, a concept based not on consumption but efficiency, not on profligacy but thrift, and not on the rat race so much as on, perhaps, the catnap.

Imagine sitting among a fragrant display of vanilla-scented flowers. Monarch butterflies seem to bounce on air as they float from umbel to umbel, probing each blossom for nectar. Satiated, the females repeatedly visit a nearby milkweed plant to deposit their eggs. Shaded by the glossy green foliage of two potted Meyer lemon trees, you bite into a perfectly ripe strawberry just picked from the raised bed near the corner of your house. Close your eyes and leave the day's cares behind you. Tonight you will dine on golden carrots and emerald snap peas seasoned with freshly snipped French thyme. Thus, you reap the rewards of a beautiful garden of flowers, foliage, and food, closely integrated with both your lifestyle and your surroundings.

The idea of *permaculture,* which began as a set of design principles for small farms, has evolved into a philosophy of sustainable living encompassing rural, suburban, and urban lifestyles. At the level of the urban or suburban home, permaculture encompasses growing food, restoring local ecosystems, and nourishing your spirit from the space available. Ironically, as a passion for food gardening takes hold among America's suburbanites, the disappearance of family farming as a way of life leaves two generations almost wholly ignorant of how to go about it. Understanding the crops themselves is but half the battle. Urban and suburban homesteaders, like their rural ancestors, must also function as engineers, meteorologists, and craftspeople. They must solve problems stemming from the intersection of the ecological requirements for plant growth and the impediments presented by

## The Principles of Permaculture

The meaning of the term *permaculture*, coined by combining *permanent* with *agriculture*, has evolved since the concept originated with Australians Bill Mollison and David Holmgren. In his book, *Permaculture: Principles and Pathways Beyond Sustainability*, Holmgren enumerates twelve permaculture principles, including:

- Obtain a yield
- Produce no waste
- Use and value diversity

I have applied these principles to the guidelines presented here. Readers are encouraged to learn more about the theory and practice of permaculture at www.permacultureprinciples.com.

circumstances of limited space, inadequate exposure, legal red tape, social demands, and other requisites of high-population-density living.

As a lifelong gardener and advocate for a more sustainable approach to modern living, I want to teach you how to make wise choices in the design, the planting, and the maintenance of your residential space, regardless of its size or location. You will learn how to produce at least some of your food yourself. You will also discover how to integrate vegetables, herbs, and fruits with native species that contribute to the restoration of your local ecosystem. You will acquire a deeper understanding of the continuously evolving *livingscape* that you create for yourself, and of its relationship to the planet that nourishes and sustains all life.

Rethink the way you utilize your space in light of the advice in this book, and you will be on your way to creating your new American homestead.

# 1

# The Earth and You

Think the world's problems—climate change, extinctions, poverty, hunger—are too large to be affected by individual action? Think again. You can start right now to reduce your household's impact on the environment by learning a few simple skills that were known and practiced by almost everyone in an earlier time in our country's history. Remember that our ancestors survived in the untamed New World because they understood how to feed themselves without reliance on technology much beyond a hoe and a bucket.

We are exposed daily to countless messages urging us to consume more of everything. In the United States, the economy has shifted over the past few decades from production and manufacturing to financing these activities in other countries. Americans actually make or do very little, collectively, apart from moving money from place to place. Nevertheless, we consume a far greater proportion of the planet's resources than anyone else. We live in a world of factory farms and industrial agriculture. We shop at 24/7 big box retailers offering a dazzling array of cheap gadgets imported from China. We face unprecedented environmental challenges: climate change, vanishing species, massive oil spills. As we are subjected to economic uncertainties unheard of for decades, all of us search for new ways to save money.

Small wonder that every day, more people look for ways to produce more of what they need themselves, to make do with less, and to find joy in a simpler way of life that resonates in harmony with the rest of the planet. Home food gardens have never been more popular. City ordinances around the country are being modified to allow people to keep backyard chickens. Farmers' markets pop up like mushrooms after a rain.

---

### ⊔ Self-Sufficiency Is Good for You!

The benefits derived from becoming increasingly self-sufficient and sourcing more of your needs close to home reach well beyond financial gains. Those who pursue a more sustainable and self-sufficient lifestyle typically discover that their lives have become much less stressful. Exercise, outdoor activity, improved nutrition, and a sense of personal satisfaction all combine to make the practice of homesteading in the city or suburbs a positive and rewarding experience.

---

Each step toward a new American homestead, whether on a rooftop in Boston or a dozen acres in Missouri, helps ever so slightly to compensate for the damage wrought upon the planet by two centuries of plunder and pollution by agriculture and industry.

Make no mistake, however. Homesteading on any scale requires commitment. Most of us who embark on the project have to contend with limited space, uncooperative neighbors, bureaucrats, and the demands of a day job. Today's urban or suburban "wilderness" can be no less daunting than the rugged landscape confronting the settlers of the American West in their covered wagons. Therefore, it makes sense to arm yourself with *knowledge and a plan before setting out on your personal journey to the new American homestead of your dreams. Let us begin with knowledge.*

## How the Earth Works

In the unfathomable past of 2.5 billion years ago, single-celled organisms in the sea developed the ability to harness the energy of sunlight, permitting them to combine molecules of carbon dioxide and water to produce sugars. We know this process as *photosynthesis*. Perhaps most important for us, these primitive, plant-like organisms began to liberate gaseous oxygen into their surroundings. As carbon dioxide was removed from the primitive atmosphere and oxygen was added to it, conditions on the planet began more and more to resemble what we experience today. The atmosphere contains about 20 percent oxygen and less than 1 percent carbon dioxide. The availability of abundant oxygen made possible the development of ever more complex life forms, from single-celled protists that could swim and eat the photosynthetic algae to multicellular animal life in a vast array, first in the sea and later on land. The process ultimately gave rise to us.

At every step in this process, the ecosystem has remained wholly dependent on photosynthesis to gather the energy needed to build forests and meadows, coral reefs and seaweed beds. Photosynthesis captures an estimated 100 trillion watts of the sun's energy each year, or roughly six times the total power consumption of all of the Earth's human inhabitants.

As each generation of organisms lived, grew, and died, it participated in biogeochemical cycles (cyclical movement of water, minerals, and energy through the ecosystem) that continue to the present day. Among the most important of these is the carbon cycle.

# How We Impact the Earth

Removal of carbon dioxide from the atmosphere results from photosynthesis. About 100 trillion grams—call it 2 billion metric tons—of new biomass are formed by this process each year. When photosynthetic organisms (terrestrial plants or seaweeds and phytoplankton in the ocean) are consumed by other organisms, some of the carbon dioxide returns to the atmosphere as a result of the consumers' respiration, thus completing the cycle from air to plant to animal to air again. Not all of the original carbon returns. The rest becomes incorporated into the body of the animal or is present in uneaten dead plant matter that eventually accumulates at the sea bottom, in river deltas, and so forth. The consumer, too, will someday die, adding its carbon to the pile. In most cases, dead organic matter slowly decomposes, and large amounts of carbon are recycled by means of bacteria, fungi, and other single-celled organisms. Sometimes, however, organic remains become trapped underneath sediments that shut out oxygen and inhibit the decomposition process. When this happens, the remains are transformed over millions of years into deposits of coal and petroleum.

For centuries, humans have been digging up the carbon stored in fossil fuel deposits and burning it, along with wood from the forests that once covered much of the planet. Combustion produces the heat needed to run our industrialized society, but it also releases enormous volumes of carbon dioxide into the atmosphere. From the beginning of the Industrial Era to the present day, atmospheric carbon dioxide has steadily increased. Since 1900, the level has risen from 290 parts per million to almost 400 parts per million today.

Increasing the amount of carbon dioxide in the atmosphere poses a significant problem: climate change. The blanket of carbon dioxide traps the sun's heat, with the result that the planet is becoming warmer. This is the *greenhouse effect*. The atmosphere prevents heat from escaping in a manner analogous to the way glazing on a greenhouse retains heat. Over the past 100 years, the average surface temperature of the planet has increased by 1°F. However, this average does not tell the whole story. In some northern regions, for example, the temperature increase has been as high as 4 to 7°F in the past half century. One result of increasing temperatures at high latitudes is melting of the polar ice caps, observable in satellite photos taken over the past several decades.

The litany of current and potential problems associated with climate change includes extinctions, disruption of natural cycles of animal migration and feeding, changes in ocean currents, abnormal and severe weather, redistribution of rainfall patterns, and likely social upheaval on a scale not previously seen. The worldwide scientific consensus is that we must change our patterns of behavior or the consequences for future generations will be dire indeed.

Carbon dioxide and other greenhouse gases such as methane are byproducts of almost everything we do to maintain our technologically sophisticated lives. Industry, electric power generation, agriculture, and transportation are the main culprits in the production of these gases. Consider all the things you need and use throughout the course of a day that require an expenditure of energy. The food you consumed yesterday probably required the use of petroleum-based fertilizers and pesticides in its production, together with gasoline and diesel fuel for its cultivation, harvest, processing, and transportation to your local market. If you drove or took the bus to the market, the trip used more fuel, and you burned either natural gas or electricity when you cooked the food. Washing the dishes ate up more energy for heating the water and for the purification of the water itself by your local utility. If you add up all the energy your household consumes directly or indirectly each day, you begin to realize the size of your home's *carbon footprint*. A carbon footprint is the total set of greenhouse gas emissions caused by an organization, event, product, or person. The number is usually expressed in tons of carbon dioxide emitted per year. Arriving at an exact estimate of your household carbon footprint, while an interesting exercise, is not necessary to realize that the less fossil-based energy your activities consume, the smaller your carbon footprint will be. Reducing the carbon footprint of whole societies will be needed to halt and reverse climate change.

## Changes We Can Make

Shrinking the household carbon footprint requires some effort, and that work should be preceded by careful thought and planning. Few of us want to give up *all* of our creature comforts, and not all possible changes—for example, to the design of your house—are feasible. Replacing the windows can greatly improve energy efficiency, but there may not be room in the budget for such a major overhaul. In chapter 9, I suggest some relatively simple, low-cost solutions to managing household energy needs.

Upgrading insulation and similar projects will dramatically reduce the direct energy consumption of your house. Changing your driving habits can reduce gasoline consumption. These strategies will result in additional energy savings and a consequent reduction in your family's carbon footprint. Nevertheless, one of the most important steps you can take to reduce household energy dependency is to produce as much of your own food as possible, and to source the rest close to home.

Any activity that utilizes present resources or materials in such a way as to permit continued utilization for generations into the future is a sustainable activity. Digging up fossil carbon to burn as fuel is not a sustainable activity because it contributes to climate change, jeopardizing the future stability of the entire biosphere.

To create more sustainable patterns of production, movement, and utilization of food and related products, we can employ concepts of planning and design that are anchored in three basic ideas:

- Locavorism
- Permaculture
- Eco-urbanization

Although, for example, an herb garden can also provide remedies for health problems, the primary product of concern is food at the household level. For that reason, many of the skills needed on the new American homestead are those associated with food production and food preservation.

## Locavorism

*Locavorism* is a word of recent vintage referring to the idea of obtaining your food from sources as close as possible to your home. Estimates place the amount of energy required to grow, process, and ship the typical American meal at about 7 calories for each food calorie placed on the plate. This number drops dramatically as the distance from field to plate decreases. The shortest possible distance, obviously, is between the backyard garden and the kitchen door. Besides reducing the demand for energy, home food gardening has other benefits. Freshly picked vegetables taste better than the stale specimens on the grocer's shelves. Nutrients that would be lost during storage and shipment remain intact by consuming produce within hours of harvest. Homegrown is better, period.

Not everyone, of course, has the room, time, climate, or resources to cultivate enough food for an entire family year-round. Once you try it, though, you will be amazed at how much you can produce. As your skill and soil improve and the plantings of perennials, such as fruit trees, mature, your homestead will become more productive with each passing year. Nevertheless, you will probably have to "import" some of your food supply. By seeking out local producers—for example, via a farmers' market—you can enjoy products you cannot produce on your own. Reach out a bit farther via the Internet and you will surely discover regional producers offering food products you would have scarcely thought about, all within a short distance of your community.

### Eat Mostly Plants

In one of the foundational books of the locavore movement, *In Defense of Food*, author Michael Pollan urges us to "Eat food. Not too much. Mostly plants." Locavorism does not automatically imply vegetarianism, but reducing your household's meat consumption is a good idea for several reasons. Not the least of these is the oft-repeated advice of nutritionists to obtain a greater proportion of our calorie needs from plant sources in the interest of better health. Add to that the considerable effort required for meat production, not only for accommodating the needs of the animals as they grow but also for the messy and unpleasant tasks of slaughtering and butchering. The energy expenditure required to produce, process, and transport meat is greater than for a caloric equivalent amount of vegetables and fruits. Eating more meat therefore increases your carbon footprint, while eating less meat reduces it.

## "Exotic" Is Becoming "Local"

I love to cook Asian food. The two most important seasonings in that cuisine are garlic and ginger. I can grow plenty of garlic in Tennessee, but ginger is tropical. Would I have to give up Asian food to be a locavore? Then I discovered Alabama-grown ginger for sale in Tennessee. Soy sauce brewed in Kentucky from Kentucky-grown wheat and soybeans is another staple in my Asian pantry. One of the best ways to discover new local and regional foods is to join one of the numerous online groups that share information about producing, finding, and preparing the best foods your area has to offer. Locavorism has swept the country, with no sign of abating.

## Eat Seasonally

Prior to the development of modern transportation, all fresh food was seasonal in its availability. Indeed, the oldest processed foods—such as cheese, beer, and salt cod—all provide examples of methods developed by early civilizations to preserve foods beyond their natural seasons. Even as society became more industrialized, food seasonality remained as it had for centuries, owing largely to the lack of cost-effective refrigerated transportation methods. Thus, oranges and celery continued to be regarded as Christmas treats in many parts of the country until after World War II.

> When I was growing up in the 1950s and 1960s, we anticipated the arrival of each summer fruit: strawberries and cooking apples in June, blackberries and cherries in July, peaches in August, pears and more apples in September. Mechanical refrigeration and air transportation, each of which consumes vast quantities of fossil fuels, now bring us blackberries and cherries in the dead of winter, and pears in spring.

Although it is possible to produce both plant and animal foods in the confined quarters of a suburban backyard, not everyone will be ready to add chickens or goats to the household. Therefore, in subsequent chapters, I will first tackle the techniques for home production of vegetables, herbs, and fruits, then turn to animal husbandry. After that, I will explore the many ways of preserving the bounty in your home kitchen.

## Permaculture

Permaculture embodies the notion that humans cannot continue indefinitely to practice food production utilizing methods that exhaust limited resources such as oil, soil fertility, and irrigation water.

Home-based permaculture relies on several basic concepts and techniques, each of which will be elaborated upon in subsequent chapters. These include:

- Organic horticulture
- Composting
- Water management
- Native plant restoration

I can remember when an American farm was a thing of beauty, a patchwork of green and brown surrounding a house and a cluster of outbuildings, the whole thing bedecked with the colors of blooms, butterflies, and birds, changing and evolving with the progress of the seasons, quietly thrumming with the rhythm of life itself. Modern factory farming relies on petroleum-fueled machines to cultivate and harvest acres of a single crop such as corn or soybeans, sustained by fertilizer and showered with pesticides, both also derived from oil. It is an activity devoid of any discernible connection to the land that harbors it.

## Organic Horticulture

Backyard food production should always follow organic methods. In a nutshell, this means avoiding chemical pesticides while using ecologically sound techniques to improve soil fertility and enhance productivity. Fertilizers should be natural products, such as cottonseed meal or green-sand. Management techniques should include crop rotation, companion planting, and composting.

## Composting

There is no such thing as "garden waste." American households generate an astonishing 20 million tons or more of grass clippings, pruned branches, and so forth each year, with as much as two-thirds of it entering landfills. Once there, it not only takes up space but also contributes to methane gas production. (Methane is a greenhouse gas more potent in its heat-trapping effects than carbon dioxide.) Municipal programs to capture the methane, the primary component of natural gas fuel, have been launched in several localities. Other cities have composting programs that turn collected wastes into mulch. But the most efficient way to handle such material is via *home* composting. Instead of wasting fuel to truck crop residues to a landfill or mulching facility, we should be reusing them at home and reducing our carbon footprint.

Composting simply takes advantages of the natural process of bacterial and fungal decomposition of plant matter to produce a superior soil amendment. Nutrients once locked up are quickly freed for use by growing plants, while complex molecules that break down slowly contribute to a desirable soil structure for crop production.

By setting up a composting system for grass clippings, garden trimmings, kitchen waste, and certain other household materials, you can practice the "ultimate" in recycling. When the finished compost is returned to the garden as mulch or a soil amendment, it improves soil structure while contributing nutrients. Those nutrients had originally been absorbed from the soil by the now-dead plants in the compost. When you harvest a crop grown in that soil, the cycle is completed.

Composting is fundamental to plant cultivation on the new American homestead and will be discussed in detail in chapter 2.

### Water Management

Food production at any level requires water. Minimizing your use of the municipal supply will save money and reduce demand on the system. Collect rainwater from your roof in barrels for watering. Direct surface runoff to areas where it will do the most good. Capture water in a pond. Ideas for better water management on your property appear in chapter 9.

### Native Plant Restoration

Not every plant in your garden needs to be a food producer. You will want flowers, not only for their delightful appearance but also to attract beneficial insects. When choosing plants for blooms, start with locally native species and their horticultural varieties. These plants will be more adaptable to your conditions and will support local species of wildlife. In chapter 10, I provide recommendations and guidelines for using native flowering plants in a homestead garden.

## Eco-Urbanization

This idea of *homesteading* may conjure up images of a determined family abandoning the suburbs and two city-based jobs to move to the country and live off the land. Although many people have made this drastic lifestyle change with success, for most of us such a move remains an unattainable dream. In fact, if the motivation for developing a more self-sufficient lifestyle results from concerns about the ecosystem and the need to reduce our carbon footprint, then we should stay put in our cities, towns, and suburbs.

As long as we employ appropriate permaculture technologies such as green building, local food production, alternative energy generation, cheap and convenient mass transit, municipal recycling, and greenspace restoration, living in cities and suburbs beats living sparsely distributed across the countryside, in terms of global sustainability. In other words, bloom where you are planted.

Urban and suburban agriculture, if practiced widely enough, can dramatically change our dependence on imported food. The typical suburban lot of about a quarter acre or less should be able to generate at least half the fruits and vegetables needed by a family of four. With ingenuity and effort, productivity can increase beyond that. You may also be able to add chickens or bees to expand your food production ability.

Despite space limitations, urban apartment dwellers also have numerous opportunities to live more sustainably by applying homesteading techniques. Purchasing fresh produce in season at the local farmer's market and preserving it at home, for example, or growing fresh herbs on the balcony, provides homegrown taste and nutrition along with cost savings. And anyone, of course, can switch out their lightbulbs to save electricity.

## Seize the Moment

Enormous challenges confront everyday Americans. At the top of most lists would be economic uncertainties, powerful motivation for making every dollar count, and achieving as full a measure of self-sufficiency as possible. Larger concerns, from climate change and the future of the planet to the global politics of petroleum, can be addressed by the collective effect of individual action, each person seeking to lower his or her carbon footprint. The tools presented in this book and through the other channels suggested in the resources section provide a palette of choices from which you can select the ones appropriate to your particular circumstances.

Start now, today. Put into practice some of the basic suggestions to be found in the pages that follow. Start living the good, green life on the new American homestead.

# 2

# Earth-Friendly Gardening Basics

G rowing great food at home requires comprehension of how plants grow and how to provide for their needs. Understanding the natural cycles of water, nutrients, and plant growth from seed to flower helps you garden successfully wherever you are.

## The Original Green

*Photosynthesis* is the process by which plants take carbon dioxide from the air and combine it with water to manufacture sugar. The energy for this process comes from sunlight. To construct their bodies and carry out the biochemical processes that photosynthesis entails, plants require minerals. If the farmer supplies all these elements consistent with the plant's needs, the plant can complete its life cycle. The plant's life cycle is complete when it bears a crop. By the same token, imbalances among these essentials can produce a reduction in productivity and, in extreme situations, crop failure.

## Fire, Water, Air, Earth

Ancient humans recognized four basic elements: fire, water, air, and earth. Thinking in terms of these four elements (with the sun's energy taking the place of fire) is a simple way to understand the basics of any form of agriculture.

## Sunlight (Fire)

Because sunlight provides all the energy for plant productivity, it is the most important factor in the equation. Vegetables must have more than six hours of full sun exposure a day, and much more if possible. While in some areas afternoon shade is preferable for certain heat-sensitive crops, as a rule growing areas should receive no shade. You can provide no economical substitute for sunlight. Therefore, its availability should be your first consideration in locating your vegetable bed, berry patch, and herb garden. You can import water, soil, and nutrients, but not the sun.

## Water

Water availability is of crucial importance. Crop production requires prodigious quantities of water, approximately 1 inch per week of precipitation or the equivalent irrigation. One inch of rain over 1,200 square feet of growing area equals 100 cubic feet, or 750 gallons of water. Irrigation can be a significant expense. In some regions, it is the major cost associated with farming.

The most obvious water management consideration for a homestead should be avoiding the use of water you must pay for, and instead achieving better management of the rainfall you receive. Chapter 9 covers various means of accomplishing better water management.

## Air

Air is free, so your plants will be able to get all the carbon dioxide they need without much in the way of your help or expense. Nevertheless, permitting air circulation around plants is an important consideration. Crowding plants encourages pests such as fungi to gain a foothold. Assuming that productivity can be increased simply by closer spacing is a common mistake. Crowding is more likely to have the opposite effect, lowering productivity. Researchers have developed optimum spacing guidelines for the majority of crops. The same spacing that works for broccoli is not the best for bell peppers. Adhere to the guidelines in the individual crop descriptions elsewhere in this book to avoid many kinds of problems.

## Earth

Discussions of plant nutrient ratios, micronutrients, and trace elements can be daunting, especially for beginners. Plants require three major elements: nitrogen (N), phosphorus (P), and potassium (K). Of these, the one in shortest supply is nitrogen.

## Nitrogen

Until recently, humans had to depend on natural sources of nitrogen, such as decomposed plant debris and animal manure, to supply the needs of agriculture. During the past century, chemical processes that rely on inputs of energy obtained from fossil fuels have been able to convert nitrogen into plant-friendly form. Industrially produced nitrate is incorporated into the chemical fertilizer formulations you see lining the shelves of garden centers.

> Chemical fertilizer was invented in the nineteenth century by the German chemist Justus von Liebig (1803–1873). He maintained that plants need only N, P, and K, and his ideas encouraged pursuit of the chemical-based agriculture that now dominates food production.

## Phosphorus

Phosphorus is a key component of what might be called a plant's "energy currency" and contributes to healthy root development. Most soils contain phosphorus minerals, but not always. Phosphate rock, mined from natural deposits, is the most widely available natural source, when a soil test indicates a need for additional phosphate. Eggshells and banana peels also contain phosphorus. Adding either one to compost is a great idea. Another widely used source, bone meal, is a byproduct of meat production.

## Potassium

A necessary component of the process regulating the uptake of water and nutrients by plant cells, potassium has long been associated by gardeners with flowering and fruit production. Soluble potassium may be plentiful in some soils or can be added if a soil test indicates the need. Greensand, a mineral, is one natural source. Kelp meal also contains significant amounts of potassium, as do wood ashes. If you burn wood for any reason, add the ashes to the compost.

## Other Nutrients

A growing plant does not "care" whether its nutrients come from natural sources or a factory. For the health of your soil and the planet, however, you should improve fertility by adding compost, rock powders, cottonseed, blood and bone meals (unless you object to the use of these slaughterhouse byproducts), and wood ashes. These products also contain varying amounts of minor and trace elements that plants require in relatively small quantities.

## How to Compare Fertilizers by Cost of Nitrogen

Commercial fertilizer products, whether chemical or organic, must by law be labeled with the percentages by weight of nitrogen (N), phosphorus (P), and potassium (K) they contain. While all of these components are essential for plant growth, phosphorus and potassium are abundant and cheap, while nitrogen in a suitable form is comparatively rare and costly. Therefore, you can make a cost comparison between two fertilizer products by calculating how much just the nitrogen in each one costs per pound.

Because the label tells you the percentage by weight of nitrogen and how much the bag weighs, you have all the information you need to calculate cost.

Let's say a 5-pound bag of 6-3-3 organic fertilizer costs $8.00. Six percent of the weight is nitrogen. Therefore:

$$5 \text{ pounds} \times 0.06 = 0.3 \text{ pounds of N}$$
$$\$8.00 \div 0.3 = \$26.67 \text{ per pound of N}$$

Similar calculations will enable you to compare a range of products.

Adding compost also helps soils maintain a healthy population of beneficial microorganisms. Soil is itself an ecosystem. Its bacteria, fungi, worms, and insects interact with each other and with plants. The teeming population of subterranean life also helps to keep harmful organisms at bay, so plants growing in healthy soil are less affected by pathogens and pests.

As you practice organic gardening, the soil becomes better and better able to sustain life over time. Consequently, crop health improves and productivity increases.

# Composting

Making compost from garden and kitchen waste and then using it to grow food is the ultimate in household recycling. Every experienced gardener seems to have his or her preferred recipe for making compost, but it's really a straightforward procedure. All compost needs three ingredients:

- ❧ Brown organic matter
- ❧ Green organic matter
- ❧ Water

*Brown organic matter* consists of dry, woody materials like tree bark and branches, dead flower stems, cornstalks, and shredded paper. *Green organic matter* includes wet stuff like vegetable peelings, coffee grounds, grass clippings, weeds, eggshells, and overripe fruit. As a rule, you want equal amounts of green and brown matter in your compost pile, along with enough water on a regular basis to keep the decomposition process going.

Make sure to chop or shred everything you add to the compost pile. You can chop kitchen waste in a food processor before placing it in the compost. Use a lawnmower with a bagging attachment to shred branches up to about half an inch in diameter, along with leaves and plant debris. Larger materials, such as a tree limb, call for a more powerful chopper made for the purpose. For the quantities small gardens are likely to produce, chopping compostable material with a machete or hoe is feasible. If it is necessary to deal with a large limb, you could consider burning it, then adding the ashes to the compost. If your house has a fireplace or wood-burning stove, so much the better.

> Besides kitchen wastes, compost can also include household trash, such as newsprint, cardboard, and office paper. Once shredded, these components can be added to a compost pile or used as mulch.

### ⊔⊔ Caution

Be careful about incorporating uncomposted organic matter—such as coffee grounds, for instance—directly into your growing beds. Doing so can be counterproductive unless you add enough extra nitrogen to support the growth of beneficial bacteria. The bacteria responsible for decomposition need nitrogen just as the crops do. When raw organic material is added directly to a garden bed, bacterial activity ramps up and the growing microbes will out-compete your crops for the available nitrogen. Therefore, it is best to produce compost in a separate pile or bin and then add it to the growing space when the decomposition process is complete.

## A Simple Compost Pile

The simplest approach to starting a batch of compost is to pile everything up, hose it down, and cover it with a tarp. Keep adding materials as you have them available, trying always to maintain equal parts green and brown. (This is not crucial to the success of the project, by the way, so don't fret about keeping too precise a balance.)

When adding green material to the pile, mix it in, burying it beneath 8 to 10 inches of the existing compost. Doing so not only helps speed the decomposition process but also avoids attracting insects.

Each time you add to the pile, moisten it. Try to keep the pile evenly moist but not wet, as if it were already growing a vegetable crop. Depending on how often you turn the pile, what you add to it, and other factors, the compost will be ready in a couple of months to a year or more. When the finished compost at bottom of the pile becomes dark and crumbly and develops a "woodsy" aroma, it is ready to use in the garden.

## Faster Results with a Compost Bin

If you want a regular supply of compost and are willing to put forth a little extra effort, you can use a compost bin. I purchased a plastic bin that holds over 100 gallons of compostable material, and have found that I can use it to make good compost faster than by just piling everything up. You can go this route or build an enclosure, using treated wood and hardware cloth, that will hold as much material as you like. A three-sided pen, 4 feet square, built of 2-by-4s and covered with quarter-inch galvanized steel mesh, will hold nearly 500 gallons of household and garden wastes for composting.

As with the compost pile method, make sure everything that goes into the bin is chopped or shredded. Aim for pieces no more than an inch in length or diameter, preferably smaller.

1. Start by placing 6 inches of brown material in the bottom of the bin or enclosure.

2. Next, add 3 inches of green material. Top this with a shovelful of your best garden soil. If this soil includes some earthworms, so much the better.

3. Mix the soil and greens into the bottom layer of brown. (I use a garden fork, fireplace poker, or small hoe for mixing. You can buy a gizmo made just for the purpose if you are so inclined.)

4. Finally, add another 3 inches of brown material and water until everything is well moistened. Cover and leave undisturbed for a week.

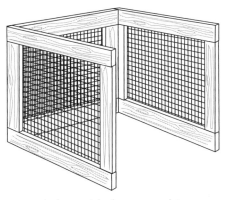

A three-sided compost bin.

Turn the pile on a weekly basis, and add new material on top as you have it available. As you proceed, try to add roughly equal volumes of green and brown material. After the first week, the pile should heat up from bacterial activity. You may see steam rising if you turn the mixture on a cool morning. As you turn the compost, try to keep the materials uniformly mixed. Add water if the mass begins to dry out too much. Once the compost stops heating up after turning, it is done. That should take anywhere from one to four months.

## Indoor Composting

If you live in an apartment or otherwise lack space for an outdoor compost pile, you can make compost indoors. If maintained properly, an indoor compost bin will not attract vermin and produces no odor.

You can buy a bin made for indoor composting, but it is easy and cheap to make one. You will need two plastic containers, one of which easily fits inside the other. For example, you could use a 30-gallon plastic garbage can with a 5-gallon plastic bucket. On a smaller scale, a 3-gallon bucket inside a 5-gallon bucket would also work. Just make sure the outer container is leak proof and has a snug-fitting lid.

1. Drill the inner container full of half-inch holes, spacing them about 2 inches apart each way. This need not be a professional quality job. You want liquids to drain easily from the smaller container and to admit air to the compost.

2. Put a brick or large flat stone in the bottom of your outer container, and fill in with a layer of absorbent material. This can be garden

soil, wood chips (the kind sold for pet bedding, for example), or shredded newspapers.

3. Set the smaller container on top of the brick and start adding your compostable materials. Remember to add equal volumes of greens and browns, stir every few days, and add water if the compost begins to dry out.

Keep the composter in a warm place, such as an inside closet. If you must place it in the garage or on the porch, insulate the outer container in some way. You could wrap it with fiberglass batting, or place it in a large cardboard carton and surround with Styrofoam shipping peanuts or shredded paper. Or simply cover it with old blankets. The idea is to retain heat. After two weeks to a month, you should have compost.

## Creating Healthy Soil

A great garden begins with great soil. This oft-repeated advice recognizes that soil is a living ecosystem. Besides being the source of plant nutrients, soil holds water and air while providing a stable support for plant roots. The best garden soil contains roughly equal parts of sand, compost, and whatever the local soil happens to be. Adding components to your existing soil is called *amending* the soil. Amendments can include lime to raise the pH of an acidic soil. Compost is an amendment that supplies organic matter and micronutrients.

In addition to homemade compost, you may find it necessary to add purchased materials such as horticultural peat, partially composted pine bark, perlite, vermiculite, sand, and/or calcinated clay, especially if you are creating a container planting mix. Choose these materials with care, and use only what you need to achieve good soil structure. Perlite, vermiculite, and calcinated clay are all produced from minerals by the application of heat, and are less sustainable than plain sand dredged from river bottoms. Partially composted pine bark is a byproduct of the forestry industry. Properly managed, pine forests are also renewable.

Don't confuse horticultural peat with sphagnum peat moss. The latter is harvested from bogs formed by slow-growing sphagnum mosses. Harvested instead from bogs created by fast-growing sedges, horticultural peat is considered a renewable resource.

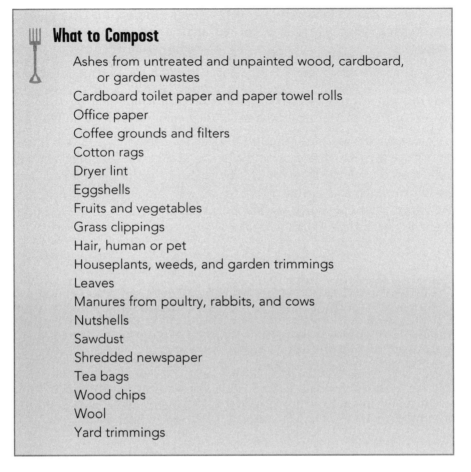

## What to Compost

Ashes from untreated and unpainted wood, cardboard, or garden wastes

Cardboard toilet paper and paper towel rolls

Office paper

Coffee grounds and filters

Cotton rags

Dryer lint

Eggshells

Fruits and vegetables

Grass clippings

Hair, human or pet

Houseplants, weeds, and garden trimmings

Leaves

Manures from poultry, rabbits, and cows

Nutshells

Sawdust

Shredded newspaper

Tea bags

Wood chips

Wool

Yard trimmings

## Encourage Earthworms

The lowly earthworm not only helps to break down plant residues but also allows the penetration of air and water by tunneling through the soil. Earthworm poop, consisting of soil particles and partially digested plant matter, is an excellent organic source of plant nutrients. Some professional specialty growers swear by it. You can buy packaged earthworm "castings," but why not produce your own? Each shovelful of soil from your vegetable patch should contain earthworms. If not, adding compost will help attract earthworms during warm weather.

During the winter, you can improve growing beds for the following season by inviting earthworms to move in. Scatter fruit and vegetable peelings, crushed eggshells, and coffee grounds on the surface of the bed. Incorporate this material into the top 2 inches of soil with a hand spade, or

## What Not to Compost

Black walnut tree leaves or twigs
*Why?* Contain natural chemicals that inhibit growth in other plants.

Weeds that have gone to seed or have perennial rootstocks
*Why?* Might distribute more weeds around the garden.

Coal or charcoal ash
*Why?* Contain arsenic and other toxic chemicals.

Dairy products and eggs
*Why?* Odors, plus attractive to rodents and flies.

Diseased or insect-ridden plants
*Why?* Diseases or insects might survive and be transferred back to other plants.

Cooking fats
*Why?* Same problems as with dairy and eggs.

Meat or fish bones and scraps
*Why?* Same problems as with dairy and eggs.

Dog feces, pig feces, soiled cat litter
*Why?* Might contain harmful parasites, bacteria, or viruses.

Horse manure
*Why?* May contain harmful chemicals from horse feed components.

Anything treated with chemical pesticides
*Why?* Pesticide residues can kill beneficial composting organisms and/or be transferred to garden soil.

add a thin layer of finished compost on top. This step helps to prevent rodents or pets from investigating the bed. Cover the bed with a layer of lightweight mulch, such as autumn leaves or wheat straw. You can either wait for earthworms to find the food or you can add earthworms from a bait shop or a friend's garden. Stray worms can often be found searching for higher ground after a rain. Help them out by moving them to your well-drained garden beds.

The best time to start an in-ground earthworm "farm" is in the fall, before the ground freezes. By spring, the bed should be teeming with worms and ready to receive seeds or transplants of early vegetable crops. If you are farming earthworms in aboveground containers, the best time to begin is after the hard freeze date in early spring. Adding earthworms to any growing space will benefit the plants, and composting will proceed at a faster rate with worms in the composter.

## Grow Green Manure

*Cover cropping* is the simple technique of following up a harvested crop with a planting designed to restore soil fertility. Cover crops are sometimes called "green manure" because they are incorporated into the soil rather than being harvested. For example, after closing down a growing bed, you could plant winter ryegrass. This annual grass grows quickly and tolerates winter cold. In early spring, the grass is tilled under to enrich the soil for a crop of vegetables. Legumes such as clover are frequently used as cover crops because of the nitrogen-fixing bacteria associated with legume roots. Besides providing nutrients, cover crops shade out slower-growing weed seedlings, thus making weeding less of a chore. Deep-rooted cover crops can actually "mine" minerals such as calcium from soil layers unreached by cultivation. When the cover crop is tilled in, these minerals become available in the surface soil. Some cover crops are even thought to produce compounds that help to prevent subsequent weed growth.

## Other Nutrient Sources

Rock powders (lime, rock phosphate, greensand) can be added to soil as sources of calcium, phosphorus, and potassium, respectively. Animal byproducts such as bone meal (calcium, phosphorus), blood meal (nitrogen), and fish emulsion (nitrogen, phosphorus, potassium, micronutrients) can be used to improve soil fertility. Plant-based materials, including cottonseed meal (nitrogen) and seaweed extracts (nitrogen, phosphorus, potassium, micronutrients), provide fertilization options for those who do not wish to use animal-derived products.

### ⑴ Overwintering Earthworms

Earthworms survive cold by burrowing deeper into the soil to avoid freezing temperatures. The depth required for overwintering depends upon the climate. Aboveground containers are probably too exposed to protect the worms where winters are cold.

## Tea Time

Water-based fertilizers are often desirable for their quick absorption by growing crops. Diluted fish emulsion or seaweed extract can be used for this purpose. These are commercial products not practical to produce at home. Vegetable-based "teas," however, offer another option. The principle behind making fertilizer tea is simple: You extract the water-soluble nutrients from a mass of compost or other plant material in the same manner tea is made from tea leaves. For example, compost tea can be made by steeping a shovelful of compost in a 5-gallon bucket of water for a couple of days and then pouring off the water for application to the growing area.

The herb comfrey *(Symphytum officinale)* is sometimes grown specifically for making a nutrient-rich organic fertilizer tea. Comfrey leaves can be repeatedly harvested from a single planting. They quickly break down, releasing nutrients into the tea, which can then be used to water crops. Comfrey may also be dug into the soil, added to a compost pile, or used as mulch.

## Test Your Soil

It is impossible to know which soil amendments will provide the level of fertility necessary for crop production without testing your soil. For a nominal fee, your local agricultural extension agent will perform soil tests and make recommendations for amendments. Check with the agency first regarding sample collection.

### ⦚ Chemical Fertilizers

Chemical fertilizers are cheap and convenient. The positive effect they have on plant growth, when properly applied, is undeniable. The trouble is that their manufacture consumes large amounts of fossil-based energy. If you cannot bring in a crop any other way, however, using a small amount of fertilizer probably has less of an impact on the environment than hauling the same crop from a distant farm. Don't feel guilty if you cannot produce enough compost in the first spring to meet the needs of your vegetables. Apply organic methods and have patience. By all means avoid disrupting your soil's ecology with pesticide. In time, your soil will improve, your compost bin will be producing a steady supply, and you can avoid synthetic fertilizer thereafter.

DIY soil test kits work just like swimming pool tests. A sample is mixed with chemicals and the resulting color is compared to a chart that gives an estimate of the pH, nitrogen, phosphate, or potassium content of the sample. Home test kits are not as accurate as a professional test, but the cost is nominal.

Depending on the results of the test, you then add specific amendments to render the soil more satisfactory for crop production. The timing of such additions can be important. For example, adding limestone to correct the pH should be done far enough in advance of the growing season to allow the lime three months to take effect. Greensand and rock phosphate need time to break down and should be applied in the fall to benefit crops the following spring. A fall-planted cover crop will be ready to till under in early spring. Amendments rich in soluble nutrients such as cottonseed, bone and blood meals, or wood ashes should be added to the planting area only a week or so before planting time. Otherwise, rainfall may wash nutrients out of the soil before the plants are up and growing.

# Integrated Pest Management

Integrated pest management (IPM) offer the means to control crop pests without applying synthetic chemical pesticides. "Pest" in this sense includes any external biological threat to plant health, including diseases such as blights and wilts. IPM involves taking advantage of the pest's natural enemies and/or aspects of its life cycle to minimize crop losses. Burning blight-infected plant residues rather than composting them, for example, reduces the likelihood of the blight returning next season. Once you start looking, you will find that you have an ample arsenal at your disposal for controlling garden pests.

## Use Proper Culture Technique

As a first principle, remember that pests and diseases typically attack plants that are under stress. Providing the appropriate growing conditions, healthy soil, adequate water, and absence of weed competition is the first line of defense against insect pests and plant diseases. Plants under stress actually produce chemical signals that act like a beacon to herbivorous insects.

## Barriers

Sometimes it is enough simply to prevent a pest from gaining access to your crops. A deer fence, or in a suburban setting perhaps a fence designed to keep the neighbors' pets at bay, is a good example of this strategy. Deer can easily jump over the average garden fence, requiring either an expensive chain-link or board fence over six feet tall, or a more modest fence equipped with repellents. Deer repellents can range from common household products such as soap to commercial preparations that smell to the deer like a predator. Rabbits and groundhogs will not be deterred by a fence that does not extend at least a foot below ground level, and will simply burrow under a standard garden fence. Dogs generally respect a fence, but cats cannot be excluded unless you enclose everything. Keep cats from digging in your garden beds by laying narrow sticks or lengths of bamboo across them at varying angles, spacing the sticks about six inches apart. Arrange them so that they will roll a bit if disturbed, and cats will soon learn that your garden is off limits.

To block access to crops by insect pests, a floating row cover—a fabric designed to be draped over growing plants—thwarts various kinds of pests, including squash borers and cabbage butterflies.

A snail and slug "fence" is another example of a barrier technique. Copper works as an effective barrier for these molluscan pests. The metal apparently reacts chemically with the slime exuded by snails and slugs, generating an electric shock that deters them from crossing the barrier. A greenhouse may sometimes suffer a plague of slugs. Wrap several turns of uninsulated 12-gauge copper electrical wire around each of the bench legs and slugs won't climb up to get to your plants.

For raised beds outdoors, two or three parallel rows of the same wire along the top of the bed frames works well. Copper flashing, cut into strips and attached with small nails, can be used also. A fence of copper screen or flashing can be installed around an in-ground bed, buried to a depth of 4 inches, and extending above the soil surface by about the same amount. The goal is to create a continuous barrier of copper enclosing the growing area. Young cabbage transplants attract slugs like a magnet. Short lengths of copper pipe bent into a circle can be set around the base of each plant needing protection.

## Natural Pesticides

Also known as *botanicals*, natural pesticides are derived from plant extracts concentrated into commercially available forms that do the same thing in your garden that they did in nature: deter or kill insects that visit the plant to feed. Shaped by millennia of evolution, natural pesticides offer advantages over their synthesized counterparts. Insects appear less able to develop resistance to these products, for example.

Pyrethrum, obtained from a type of chrysanthemum, is a quick-acting poison that affects the insect nervous system. Neem, another natural pesticide, contains extracts from an Asian tree. Neem acts both to repel insects and to disrupt their growth cycles. It also appears to be effective in controlling some forms of fungal diseases. Spinosad, derived from bacterial fermentation, kills thrips, flea beetles, and caterpillars.

Use cayenne pepper and other products based on hot pepper to control the ubiquitous gray squirrel. Squirrels have become accustomed to humans; if you bury something, a squirrel may dig it up. They can do significant damage to a planting. To deter them, liberally pepper the area when you plant. Squirrels usually stop digging after one or two encounters with the hot pepper, thus limiting the damage. Replenish the cayenne after a rain.

## Traps

If you have marauders such as raccoons, you may need a professional's help to trap and remove them. But traps are not just for critter control. Sticky traps that lure flying insects to immobilization on glue-coated surfaces can be remarkably effective in some instances. The devices can trap aphids, whitefly, fungus gnats, and cucumber beetles. To make your own trap, coat anything yellow with anything sticky, or purchase a commercial coating product made for the purpose. The longer the trap remains sticky, the more effective it will be.

Certain types of traps can be counterproductive. Japanese beetle traps, for example, may lure more insects to your property. Unless you have a severe infestation, trapping may be unwise. Handpicking is a better option when the infestation is spotty. A biological agent best controls Japanese beetles, as discussed later in this chapter.

Living crops can also function as traps. Planting one crop that is sacrificed to pests, thus protecting the main crop, is a technique sometimes used in commercial production. To protect melons from cucumber beetles, use a trap crop of cucumbers, for example. Nasturtiums will lure cabbage butterflies away from the broccoli patch. A good trap crop must be more attractive to the pest than the main crop. Trap crops can be interplanted with the main crop, planted around it to create a living fence, or planted at a distance from the main crop to lure pests aside. The best method depends on the crop being protected. On smaller properties, trap crops may take up too much growing space to be practical.

## ⫿ Slug and Snail Bait

Use a slug and snail bait containing iron phosphate rather than methaldehyde as the active ingredient. Methaldehyde is highly poisonous if ingested and is particularly dangerous for dogs, which are sometimes attracted to the commercial pellet form of slug bait. Iron phosphate, on the other hand, is used as a nutritional supplement in human food and is considered completely safe when employed to control snails and slugs.

The effectiveness of iron phosphate can be enhanced by mixing it with coffee grounds, to which slugs appear to be easily attracted. Three rounds of baiting spaced about two weeks apart in early spring will keep slugs and snails under reasonable control in my garden for the remainder of the season.

## Insects as Biological Control Agents

Biological pest control agents include beneficial insects. Eliminating the use of chemical pesticides will help preserve the natural predators that probably already live in your garden. Spiders, for example, prey on insects of all types, and their presence should be encouraged. Various beneficial insects including praying mantises, ladybugs, lacewings, and parasitic wasps help to control garden pests.

### Praying Mantis

The praying mantis is an insect predator that sits motionless on plants to await the arrival of prey. Mantises will take beneficial species along with garden pests, but on balance are desirable garden denizens. You can purchase mantis egg cases in the fall and winter. Attach them to fences or shrubs about 3 feet above ground level. Baby mantises will hatch the following spring to feed voraciously. In many areas, it is possible to establish a permanent mantis population in your garden. Bear in mind that the mantis may be of minimal help in combating an overwhelming infestation by a single species of insect pest.

### Ladybugs

The most widely used biological control insect is the ladybug. The insect's value to the garden was greatly appreciated in earlier times. The name *ladybug* probably refers to "Our Lady," the Virgin Mary. Farmers' prayers for relief from crop-damaging insects were often answered by the appearance of ladybugs.

Ladybugs gather in great numbers to spend the winter protected from the harshest weather in a sheltered spot. They reemerge in spring hungry for prey, feeding primarily on aphids, and on various other insect pests. After building up their energy reserves, they mate. The eggs hatch into larvae that attack other insects with the same voracity as their parents. Thus, several generations can be produced before the onset of winter.

Buy ladybugs for release into your garden, or better yet, attract a natural population. They prefer the flowers of parsley, carrots, cilantro, fennel, dill, and other members of the carrot family and are attracted to cosmos and scented geraniums. Other plants that bloom in late summer and early fall attract adult ladybugs looking for pollen. You can purchase ladybugs at some well-stocked garden centers, but whether they remain in your garden will depend on them finding adequate food and shelter.

### Lacewings

Adult lacewings are vegetarians, feeding on nectar, pollen, and honeydew (the sweet excrement of aphids and some other insects). Their larvae, on the other hand, are fearsome predators of the tiny, pesky aphid and a wide array of other small insect pests. In a garden well planted with flowers to provide nectar for the adults, lacewings can establish themselves. They are easily recognized by their gossamer wings and golden eyes, often hovering around outdoor lights on warm evenings.

### Parasitic Wasps

Certain wasps lay eggs in the eggs or bodies of other insects. For example, several species of *Trichogramma* wasps attack cabbage loopers and corn earworms. Many parasitic wasps are small and pose no threat of harm to humans. Wasp predation on other insects may be nonspecific. For example, the female mud dauber stings a grub to paralyze it, and then places it in her egg chamber as living food for her offspring. Other wasp varieties behave in similar fashion, including several species of paper wasps that can deliver a painful sting. Some of them are territorial and will angrily leave the nest to sting you if you merely approach too closely or too quickly. Nests that appear near doors and windows, therefore, should be destroyed immediately. However, unless someone in your household is allergic to the stings, leave wasps unmolested when they nest away from your domicile. Unless provoked, they pose no threat and will kill insects that otherwise might damage your crops.

# Soil Organisms as Biological Control Agents

Soil is a teeming jungle of interacting organisms where "eat or be eaten" is the rule of the day. Certain beneficial soil organisms can help control pest insects. These organisms can be deliberately introduced or encouraged to develop on their own by practicing organic culture methods.

## Nematodes

These tiny roundworms live by the billions in soils worldwide. Several are cultivated for their value as biological pest control agents for cucumber beetles, squash beetles, cutworms, and other insects with soil-dwelling larvae. You can purchase these products via mail order. All work by taking advantage of the natural ecology of nematodes, certain bacteria, and insects. Some nematode larvae crawl around to locate prey; others lie in wait for prey to come to them. If the nematode encounters its preferred host, it enters through one of the insect's body openings. Then it releases its bacterial partners, like soldiers emerging from a Trojan horse. Quickly multiplying bacteria kill the insect. When the bacteria further decompose the corpse, they release nutrients. These in turn feed the nematode, enabling it to multiply and invade still more insect hosts. You could hardly find a better example of how the existence of a diverse soil ecology benefits the gardener.

## Bacteria

Bacterial diseases of insects have been used in attempts to control crop pests for decades. One approach to this technique involves collecting a handful of the target pests. You then purée them in a blender with some water and spray the resulting liquid on infested plants. Naturally occurring pathogens will then presumably spread among the pest population. Sometimes this works, and sometimes it doesn't.

*Bacillus thuringiensis*, better known as "Bt," was identified as an insect pathogen in the early 1900s and first became available in commercial form in 1938. Products containing Bt consist of the living spores mixed with a carrier. Bt produces a fatal disease in many kinds of insects, including cabbage butterflies, mosquitoes, and Colorado potato beetles.

Another widely used bacterial control is milky spore. This product, which produces a fatal disease in Japanese beetles and related insects, is applied to turf or other areas not subject to regular cultivation. When used according to package directions, it provides effective control of beetles by attacking the larva, or grub, which spends its life underground feeding on plant roots. Because closely related native insects such as the June bug are equally affected, do not use milky spore unless the level of infestation warrants its use.

> ## ⫿ The Old One-Two
>
> Hitting pests with two or more of the above-mentioned tech-
> niques simultaneously can be highly effective. We once rescued
> our tomato crop from disaster with applications of both neem
> and Bt coupled with trapping white flies on sticky traps. During a
> particularly bad spate of weather, the plants had become targets
> for multiple pests. In the case of broccoli, which is not easy to grow
> in the hot, humid climate where I live, we use a combination of row
> covers and applications of Bt to keep cabbage butterflies from
> ruining the crop.

## Common Sense Pest Control

Always try the simplest approach first when dealing with insects in the garden.
Don't overlook the benefits of simply picking insects off your plants. You can
quickly dispatch them by dropping them into a pail of water with a few drops
of liquid dish detergent added. Learn to identify the common pests of your
crops. A wealth of helpful identification guides with images can be found
on the Internet. Does the insect lay distinctively colored eggs, for instance?
Learn to recognize the egg mass and destroy each one you encounter.

### Soap

Soapy water can be used as a general-purpose insect spray and is particularly effective against aphids. Special insecticidal soap is commercially
available that won't damage plants.

### Diatomaceous Earth

Chewing insects can sometimes be controlled with an application of diatomaceous earth. This is a mineral powder composed of the silica shells of
countless microscopic algae. When ingested, the glasslike silica does fatal
damage to the insect's digestive tract. Diatomaceous earth is basically very
fine sand, so wear a particle mask when using it. Spray plants lightly with
water to help the powder stick to leaves. The particles are too small to harm
wildlife or pets if ingested. It is available in garden centers.

### Solarization

Insects that spend some part of their life cycle in the ground can be thwarted
by simple cultivation, which exposes the dormant insects to winter cold or
desiccation in summer heat. Insects, fungal pathogens, and some weeds can

be killed by solarization. This is a good way to clean up a bed in which you have had problems in the past. Cover the bed with black plastic film. Secure the edges of the film tightly to the bed by covering them with a thin layer of soil. Try to do this a time when you can expect several days of good sunshine. The plastic will absorb the sun's heat, warming the soil underneath. As the soil warms, weeds begin to sprout, and insects to emerge from dormancy. Trapped underneath the plastic, they die. The sun heats the soil to a temperature beyond which the pests cannot survive.

### Mulch

Mulching plants can protect them from soil-borne pathogens. Mulch prevents rain from splashing soil up on the leaves, bringing with it harmful fungi and bacteria. Mulch also helps create a microclimate favorable to the natural enemies of plant pests.

# Plant Genetics

One of the best tools for avoiding crop pest problems lies in plant genetics. Within each plant species, natural variability exists with regard to any particular trait. If you plant the seeds of a single tomato, you can easily observe this variation in the offspring. Some will have tougher skins, or the flavor may be different from the parent's, or one will be weak and spindly and die young. Humans have been selecting plants' offspring for preferred traits ever since our first ancestors decided to replant the biggest, fattest seeds of wheat's ancestor. The extent of variability within a species can be appreciated when you consider that one species, *Brassica oleracea*, has given rise to broccoli, Brussels sprouts, cabbage, cauliflower, collards, kale, and kohlrabi.

You can preserve desirable characteristics in a line of cultivated plants by two methods. The first, *selection*, involves choosing the seedlings that best exhibit the combination of traits you want and allowing only these to produce seeds for the next crop. The vast majority of heirloom varieties are selections. Seeds from selected plant varieties are said to be *open-pollinated*, meaning that they were naturally pollinated via wind or insects, or in some cases self-pollinated. Serious seed-saving efforts require keeping one variety separated from another, the distance depending on the specific plant. As the seed crop matures, it also becomes necessary to practice *rouging*, or removal of any individual plants that do not behave true to type. Doing so will maintain the desired traits through subsequent generations.

The second major plant breeding methodology is *hybridization*. This involves combining two plant varieties, or even two different species, to obtain offspring in which traits from each parent are expressed. Natural hybridization, for example, has given rise to many of the 5,000 cultivated varieties of potatoes. The Sugar Snap pea was developed by Dr. Calvin Lamborn through crossing the snow pea variety Mammoth Melting Sugar with a natural mutant of the shelling pea Dark Skinned Perfection. Hybridization has introduced resistance to disease to many varieties of tomatoes and cucumbers.

The problem with hybrid plant varieties, from the homesteader's point of view, is that the seeds produced by the hybrid will not necessarily give rise to offspring with the desired traits. Rather, most of the seeds will revert to types more resembling the hybrid's parents. In other words, the hybrid must be re-created each season to maintain the target traits within the line. Doing so is usually impractical for home gardeners, so we must return to the garden center each year to purchase our seeds. Often a given hybrid performs so well we gladly buy its seeds. One example in my garden is the tomato Celebrity. It has multiple disease resistance and bears many uniform fruits on compact plants. The fruits arrive all at once, making it useful for canning. The flavor is excellent.

> It is worth noting that hybrid plant varieties are not genetically modified organisms (GMOs) in the sense that this term is usually applied. GMOs are derived through laboratory methods that permit the introduction of wholly unrelated genetic material into the breeding line. Bacterial genes have been inserted into fish, for example. This is not the same thing as crossing two related peas to obtain something more useful.

Vegetables, herbs, fruits, and flowers have all been subjected to various levels of hybridization and selection over the centuries, resulting in the many cultivated varieties, or *cultivars*, now available for nearly any plant you'd care to name. Although herb, berry, and fruit tree cultivars are seldom propagated by seed, the principles behind obtaining the first individual of a given strain are the same as for seed-propagated plants. Once a superior form is recognized, it is vegetatively propagated—that is, via cuttings, grafting, or division.

# Planting and Maintaining a Garden

If you have never grown a food garden before, start small. What looks good on paper in December can become chaos by July. Use the information presented in subsequent chapters covering vegetables, herbs, and fruits to determine candidates appropriate to the conditions you can provide. Then develop a crop plan outlining where and when you will plant everything.

## Site Selection

Locate the garden in full sun, or as sunny a location as possible. Choose a location sheltered from prevailing winds, which can enhance the effects of low temperatures and do physical damage to crops. Because the wind in my region blows mostly from the west, my garden is on the southeast side of the house. A garden enclosed by walls or other structures, such as might be found in a city courtyard, can provide a microclimate several degrees warmer than the surrounding open spaces, thus permitting cultivation of out-of-season crops.

Drainage is important as well. No crop thrives in constantly wet soil. Ideally, the land will gently slope away from the garden area but not at so steep an incline as to encourage erosion. Among other benefits, raised beds can provide improved drainage where the natural topography is unsuitable. (For more information on raised beds, see the section later in this chapter.)

If you wish to include perennial vegetables and herbs, a berry patch, a grape arbor, or a couple of fruit trees in the garden design, first decide where they will go and how much space they will require when mature. Then allocate the remaining space to annual crops. Finally, be sure to leave room in your plan for flowers. Purely ornamental plantings make gardening a joy and offer ecological benefits by contributing to the overall diversity of your property. Flowers also attract pollinators that will visit your squash and cucumbers.

## Crop Rotation

Your crop plan and the layout of growing spaces should take into account the need for systematic rotation of annual crops among different growing areas. Growing the same crop in the same spot year after year will result in a depletion of soil nutrients and the establishment of disease organisms in your garden. Learn to think of vegetables as groups of similar crops. Follow one group with another group, not another member of the same group. The most important vegetable groups are:

- Potatoes, tomatoes, and peppers
- Broccoli, cabbage, cauliflower, and kale
- Beans and peas

Cool Weather (Spring)

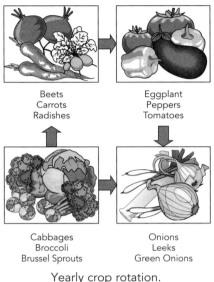

| Beets | Eggplant |
| Carrots | Peppers |
| Radishes | Tomatoes |

| Cabbages | Onions |
| Broccoli | Leeks |
| Brussel Sprouts | Green Onions |

Yearly crop rotation.

- Lettuce, spinach, and other leafy greens
- Cucumbers, squash, and melons
- Beets, radishes, turnips, and carrots

A simple garden plan would involve three beds, each home to two groups for a season. In the first season, for example, you might grow peas and spinach in one bed, cabbage and beets in the second bed, and potatoes in the third bed during cool weather. In early summer, replace the peas with the cucumbers and the spinach with the carrots. Follow the cabbage and the beets with tomatoes and peppers. Plant beans where the potatoes grew. This scheme demonstrates one possible pattern of crop rotation together with another important principle, that of succession planting.

## Seeds or Transplants?

Some vegetables and herbs do best if the seeds are sown directly into the ground. While all plants can theoretically be started this way, some fare better if the seeds are started under controlled conditions and the small plants transplanted to the garden (see "Starting Seeds," later in this chapter, for more information on starting seeds indoors and then transplanting them to your garden, raised bed, or container).

## ⊥⊥⊥ Succession Planting

You can get more food from a given amount of space by following one crop with another. Sometimes, this means you need some auxiliary growing space to get a jump on the season. For example, you can plant a fast-maturing crop like radishes or arugula several times during early spring, sowing a small amount of seeds each week. If you are prepared with a tray of small green onion plants, you can poke a clump of onions into the ground each time you pull a few radishes or a bunch of arugula. Just make note of the days to maturity for each crop and plan accordingly.

As a general rule, the following crops are seeded directly:

| | |
|---|---|
| Beans | Lettuce |
| Beets | Melon |
| Carrots | Okra |
| Corn | Scallions |
| Cucumber | Spinach |
| Greens | Squash |

The following vegetables are generally started from transplants:

| | |
|---|---|
| Artichokes | Garlic |
| Asparagus | Leeks |
| Broccoli | Onions |
| Cabbage | Peppers |
| Celery | Potatoes |
| Eggplant | Tomatoes |

Lettuce, spinach, and other leafy greens may be either direct seeded or transplanted.

Early Summer

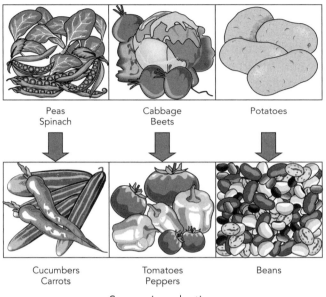

| Peas Spinach | Cabbage Beets | Potatoes |

| Cucumbers Carrots | Tomatoes Peppers | Beans |

Succession planting.

## Companion Planting

Certain crops grow well together. Companion planting takes advantage of this phenomenon. Guidelines for growing all the vegetables mentioned are given in the following two chapters. To save space, "brassicas" has been used to represent all members of the cabbage family.

Because they compete with one another or attract the same pests, some plants are poor companions. Fennel and sweet potatoes seem always to do best when planted alone.

### Vegetable Companions

| Crop | Companion Vegetables |
| --- | --- |
| Asparagus | Tomato |
| Bean | Brassicas, carrot, cucumber, eggplant, pea, potato, Swiss chard |
| Beet | Bean, brassicas, garlic, lettuce, onion |
| Brassicas | Beet, cucumber, garlic, lettuce, onion, potato, spinach, Swiss chard |
| Carrot | Bean, lettuce, onion, pea, pepper, tomato |

| | |
|---|---|
| Cucumber | Bean, brassicas, lettuce, tomato |
| Eggplant | Bean, pepper |
| Lettuce | Beet, brassicas, carrot, garlic, onion |
| Melon | Pumpkin, squash |
| Onion | Beet, brassicas, carrot, lettuce, pepper, Swiss chard, tomato |
| Pea | Bean, carrot, cucumber, turnip |
| Pepper | Carrot, eggplant, onion, tomato |
| Potato | Bean, brassicas, eggplant, pea |
| Spinach | Brassicas |
| Squash | Melon |
| Tomato | Asparagus, bean, carrot, cucumber, onion, pepper, turnip, pea |

## Herb and Edible Flower Companions

| Herb/Flower | Vegetable Companions |
|---|---|
| Basil | Pepper, tomato |
| Bee balm | Tomato |
| Borage | Bean, squash, tomato |
| Calendula | Asparagus, tomato |
| Chamomile | Brassicas, onion |
| Chive | Carrot, lettuce, tomato |
| Dill | Brassicas, lettuce, onion |
| Garlic | Beet, brassicas, lettuce |
| Lovage | Bean |
| Marigold | Bean, cucumber, eggplant, melon, potato, squash |
| Mint | Brassicas, tomato |
| Oregano | Bean |
| Parsley | Asparagus, tomato |
| Rosemary | Bean, brassicas |
| Sage | Brassicas, carrot, tomato |
| Thyme | Brassicas, carrot, eggplant, tomato |

## Poor Companions

| Vegetable | Avoid Planting Near |
|---|---|
| Bean | Chive, garlic, leek, onion, shallot |
| Beet | Pole bean |
| Brassicas | Kohlrabi, nasturtium, pole bean, tomato |
| Carrot | Dill |
| Cucumber | Potato, sage |
| Fennel | Most other vegetable crops |
| Pea | Chive, garlic, leek, onion, shallot |
| Potato | Cucumber, squash, tomato |
| Sweet potato | Most other vegetable crops |
| Tomato | Dill, kohlrabi, potato |

## Irrigation

In the most fortunate circumstances, rainfall would supply all of the water your garden needs. Indeed, my grandfather grew many vegetable crops without irrigating his fields. When natural rainfall is not enough, however, or the weather is hot and arid, you will need to supply extra water to bring in a successful crop. The simplest tool available for this purpose is the old-fashioned 2-gallon watering can. Mine was handed down from a family member, but you might find a good one at a yard sale, and garden centers sell them in all sizes.

If carrying water from the tap seems like too much of a chore, the next step is a good garden hose. Make sure you get one long enough to reach all the places you might need to water. Better quality hoses can last a lifetime and are a good investment. Look for heavy brass fittings, reinforced tubing, and a "no-kink" guarantee. Hose attachments and fittings should be solid brass. They cost more but will outlast plastic or soft metal products.

To meet all the watering needs in my garden, I have a mister attachment, several Y valves permitting two hoses to be connected to the same tap, a watering wand about 2 feet long that allows easy access to hanging baskets or plants in the back of the bed, a trigger sprayer for specialized tasks like washing out flowerpots, and brass thumb control valves for controlling the flow rate.

Watering by hand is more efficient than using an area sprayer. You can direct water at the plant's roots, avoid wetting foliage (which can encourage disease in some cases), and even knock out an infestation of aphids with a well-aimed water jet.

Irrigating a larger area can call for additional equipment. One of the most water-friendly methods available is drip irrigation. In a typical system, a timer controls the water tap, which is connected to a feeder hose. From the feeder hose, smaller hoses tipped with emitters carry water to the base of each plant in the row. Timer settings and the water pressure can be adjusted to keep the roots at just the right moisture level automatically. Such systems work well for beds, containers, or in-ground rows, but the larger the growing area, the greater the initial investment in equipment. Indoor growing spaces seem ideal spots for this type of system because splashes and splatters are minimized. Only you can decide whether this makes sense in your situation.

Overhead spray irrigation equipment wastes a lot of water and should be avoided where possible. This method also deposits much of the water on foliage, which can encourage fungal disease.

## Fertilization

Despite having healthy soil, you will often find occasions when additional fertilizer makes sense. For example, after you remove a nitrogen-hungry crop like spinach, you may want to replenish the nitrogen for a follow-up planting of squash. Adding a few tablespoons of cottonseed meal to the growing area serves the purpose nicely. Some crops benefit from feeding while they grow. Onions, for example, need nitrogen while the green tops are being produced. Spreading cottonseed meal along the row for this purpose is called *side dressing.* You also can side dress with liquid fertilizers such as compost tea or diluted fish emulsion when you want to give plants a quick boost. (See "Tea Time," earlier in this chapter, for instructions on how to make compost tea.)

## Weeding

By competing with your crops for sunshine, water, and nutrients, weeds can reduce yield by more than half. Learn to recognize the common weeds that appear in your garden and take steps to minimize their impact. Perennial weeds, such as dandelions, must be dug out root and all or they will sprout right back. Never allow perennial weeds to attain any size; dig them out as soon as you see them. Annual weeds require a different approach. The key to controlling them is to prevent the current crop from making seeds for a future crop. Annuals can be pulled by hand, killed by shallow cultivation, and/or smothered with an organic mulch.

Many annual weed seeds, such as grasses, fireweed, mullein and wild lettuce, are capable of lying dormant in the soil for years. When the ground is cultivated, they respond to even minimal exposure to sunlight by germinating. Therefore, a second round of cultivation becomes necessary to destroy the young sprouts. That, in turn, may expose additional seeds, creating a vicious cycle. Therefore, try to keep out the light by laying mulch around your crop plants.

Beware, however, of laying mulch before the ground has warmed up. Otherwise, you may slow down crop development. In my garden, early crops like lettuce typically receive hand weeding, and we start mulching about the time we plant the beans.

Another method to control annual weeds in open beds is by using a germination inhibitor or an organic herbicide. These products contain weak organic acids that break down quickly in the soil and pose no harm to soil organisms, pets, or people. A commonly used organic germination inhibitor is wheat gluten, available in a variety of commercial preparations.

Unfortunately, some weeds are so pernicious that a large patch of them may require professional assistance and possibly the application of chemical herbicide to control. As long as this application is done with proper attention to dosage rates and timing, the soil can recover. After the weeds are dead, the soil can be amended with compost or other organic materials, covered with a heavy mulch and allowed to lie fallow for a year before using it for growing flowers. After a couple of seasons of blooms, you can use the plot for vegetables or fruits.

One of the benefits of growing in raised beds is that weeds become less and less of a problem as the beds are used season after season.

## Starting Seeds

Seed starting is one of the most valuable skills you can learn as a modern homesteader. For your very first attempts at vegetable growing, buy started plants at the garden center. Once you feel you have mastered the basics of vegetable gardening, you can save money and expand your palette of plant varieties by starting your own transplants indoors.

## Some Common Weeds and Their Control

| Name | Annual/Perennial | Spreads By | Control |
|---|---|---|---|
| Dandelion | Perennial | Wind-blown seeds | Dig, root and all, as soon as noticed. Do not allow to flower. |
| Pokeweed | Perennial | Bird-carried seeds | Dig, root and all, as soon as noticed. Do not allow to flower. |
| Nutsedge | Perennial | Bird-carried seeds, underground runners | Pernicious; may require professional help to achieve control. |
| Wild radish | Annual | Explosive seed capsule | Germination inhibitor, pull before seed sets. |
| Common Bedstraw | Annual | Sticky seeds carried by animals, including pets | Germination inhibitor, pull before seed sets. |
| Bittercress | Annual | Explosive seed capsule | Germination inhibitor, pull before seed sets. |
| Wild lettuce | Annual | Wind-blown seeds | Germination inhibitor, pull before seed sets. |
| Spurge | Annual | Abundant tiny seeds are carried by wind and water | Germination inhibitor, pull as soon as noticed. |
| Fatua | Annual | Abundant tiny seeds set as soon as plants have true leaves | Pernicious; may require professional control. |
| Tree seedlings | Perennial | Both wind and bird-borne | Pull as soon as noticed, do not allow tap root to lengthen. |
| Spanish needles | Annual | Seeds stick to fur of animals and pets | Germination inhibitor, pull before yellow daisy blooms appear. |

## Containers for Seed Starting

You can use almost anything you have around the house that will hold soil for starting seeds, since it typically needs to serve the purpose for only a month or two. Empty egg cartons, food containers of all kinds, and any old flowerpot can serve the purpose. Make sure to poke a few drainage holes in the bottom of the container before filling it with seed-starting mix. To maximize the use of limited space, you may want to invest in plastic nursery trays with small cells for individual seedlings. Larger seedlings, such as those of tomatoes and peppers, grow best in individual pots.

Instead of pots, you may wish to use pre-formed planting disks that swell when you pour hot water over them. They are made from peat, with added components and a binder. Seeds go directly into the moistened disks, and the entire thing is buried with the roots at transplanting time.

You can buy professional-quality pots and carriers that will last many seasons or improvise with paper or plastic cups from the grocery store. Much will depend on how many seedlings you need and how efficiently you wish to manage your indoor growing space. If you plan on producing many plants in as small an area as possible, go with the professional equipment. Cell trays measure 10 by 20 inches and can hold three dozen vegetable starts each. Four of them will fit nicely under two 4-foot fluorescent shop lights or along 4 feet of greenhouse bench. Three- to 4-inch pot carriers measure 18 by 18 inches and handle eighteen or twenty pots.

## Starting Mix

Seed-starting mix consists of nothing more that a good potting mix that has been screened to a uniform mixture of fine particles. Use ordinary window screen attached to a frame to sift your favorite potting mix or purchase a ready-made product. In a pinch, you can use potting mix without sifting for starting all but the most delicate seedlings. Pick out any really large chunks by hand.

## Sowing and Growing

Never ignore the temperature at which seeds prefer to germinate. Many vegetable seeds will rot or fail to germinate if the soil is too cold. If the area where you plan to start seeds does not remain at the required temperature (and frequently a garage or porch is too cool), consider purchasing a heating mat designed to be placed underneath a flat of germinating seeds. As a general rule, seeds are started at a soil temperature of 65°F to 75°F. The air temperature can be 5 to 10 degrees cooler if the soil is warm enough.

Do not bury seeds too deeply. Many seeds, such as lettuce, require light to germinate. Cover them with only a thin scattering of fine growing mix. Other seeds, such as those of peppers and tomatoes, should be buried under about ¼ inch of mix. Follow the instructions given with the descriptions in chapters 3 and 4 for starting the seeds of specific vegetables.

## Hardening Off

Young plants that have luxuriated under ideal growing conditions inside cannot be transplanted directly into the garden. Sudden exposure to bright sunshine and harsh winds will set them back or even kill them. You must first harden them off by gradually exposing them to outdoor conditions. About two weeks before you plan to transplant them, move the new plants to a sheltered, partially shaded spot, such as a porch. Take them out in the morning and bring them inside at night for a week. Then move them to a sunnier location and start leaving them out overnight. After a week of this, they should be ready to go into the garden. The ideal spot for hardening off transplants is a cold frame, which is discussed later in this chapter.

# Growing in Containers

Herbs, many vegetables, and even dwarf fruit trees can be cultivated in containers. Container gardening allows apartment dwellers and others with limited space to produce food on a patio, a balcony, or a windowsill. Anywhere you have at least six hours of daily sun will yield a crop if you select your plants with care. Another application of container methods that makes sense even if you have a large outdoor garden is growing plants not reliably hardy in your climate zone. For example, dwarf citrus trees can remain in a large container for many years if moved to a sheltered spot when frost threatens.

## Potting Mix

The key to successful container growing is to start with a well-drained, water-retentive planting mix. Purchase your growing mix from a nursery supply house, not a garden center, to get the best value. Remember that commercial mixes may contain components, such as sphagnum peat, that are not sustainably produced. Many experienced gardeners rely on their homemade compost, mixed with sand or other components, for container growing. If you do not have enough compost to fill all your pots, you can make a good growing mix by combining equal parts of the following:

- Horticultural peat (also called Canadian peat)
- Sand
- Partially composted pine bark

Horticultural peat, unlike sphagnum peat moss, derives from quick-growing sedges and is considered a renewable resource.

## Containers

Among the cheapest containers available for vegetable gardening are plastic 3- and 5-gallon buckets. They are sometimes available for free from restaurants that receive ingredients packed in them or you can buy them from paint and DIY stores. Drill several holes ¼ inch in diameter in the bottom of each bucket before filling with planting mix. Three gallons is large enough for a crop of Tom Thumb lettuce, chives, or Little Finger carrots. Use a 5-gallon bucket for a Celebrity tomato, a mixed herb garden, or a trellis with White Half Runner green beans. When choosing containers, larger is always better.

> Self-watering containers, with a reservoir that needs only occasional refilling, are designed to maintain the proper level of soil moisture without constant attention to watering. Many gardeners swear by them and report great success, especially with vegetables that are particularly sensitive to proper moisture levels, such as tomatoes and cucumbers.

Remember that a container garden will dry out much faster than one growing in the ground. Daily watering may be necessary in hot weather. Stick your finger into the potting mix. If it feels dry at a depth greater than the first joint of your finger, water. Although some gardeners object to using anything remotely "artificial" for growing vegetables and herbs, I have found that the addition of polyacrylamide gel, sold in dry granular form as a "water saver" for container mix, works extremely well. This product absorbs many times its weight in water and releases it slowly back into the potting mix, thereby reducing the need for frequent watering.

# Raised Beds

Few inventions have made backyard vegetable and herb gardening easier than the raised growing bed. The raised bed is a simple frame or enclosure holding soil or growing mix for crops. Typically a foot deep or more, raised beds can be built of any material that will withstand exposure. Wood, masonry, and metal are all good options, each with its pros and cons.

I use pressure-treated pine for my beds, contrary to the suggestion of many good gardeners to avoid it because it leaches harmful chemicals into the soil to be taken up by plants. I generally use a bed made from new lumber only for growing flowers the first year. In my opinion, this allows rainfall and irrigation water to wash away the major proportion of anything soluble that might escape the lumber. (Manufacturers of pressure-treated lumber suggest waiting 90 days before painting an outdoor structure made from their products to allow time for residual chemicals to be washed away.) I have found this method to be an affordable compromise, because naturally resistant wood, such as cedar or cypress, is too expensive for my budget.

To make a rectangular wood-frame garden bed, do the following:

1. Start with three planks, each 8 feet long. I use nominal 2 by 12 lumber, which is actually 11½ inches wide by 1½ inches thick.

2. Measure and mark the center of one plank, and then use a carpenter's square to inscribe a straight line across the width.

## Brick or Stone Raised Beds

In my view, masonry is the best value in a raised-bed construction material. Stackable landscape blocks are easy to install and last forever. You can create solid construction by gluing the blocks together with a specially made adhesive. It is risky, however, to build a bed deeper than 2 feet in this manner. For a taller wall, use conventional mortar or the structure may collapse.

Laid brick or stone with mortared joints looks beautiful and lasts for decades, too, but requires skill and practice to obtain a professional-looking installation. Either of these options cost considerably more than wood. Masonry is also difficult or impossible to relocate if your needs change. Wooden frames are easy to move.

3. With the line as a guide, cut the board in half using a hand or electric circular saw.

4. Set one of the short pieces on edge, bracing the far end against a solid object, such as the foundation of your house or a fencepost.

5. Line up the end of one of the long pieces with the other end of the short piece and fasten them together. Use either stainless steel or galvanized nails driven into the wood with a hammer, or specially treated exterior screws driven with an electric screwdriver. If you do not have an electric screwdriver, drill a pilot hole before installing the screws with a hand driver. Otherwise, the chore will be, at the very least, exhausting work.

An alternate method of assembly employs galvanized steel corner braces made for construction work. You attach these to the outside of the bed and hold them in place with short screws or special joist hanger nails. Using them results in solid construction that won't separate at the corners, no matter how bad the weather.

6. Attach the opposite end of the long piece to the second short piece in the same manner. Then set the whole thing on a flat surface with the short pieces sticking up and attach the other long side.

Use a carpenter's level to make sure that the top of the bed is level in both directions. Otherwise, it won't drain evenly. You may need to excavate a little if the site is not already level. I always have to remove and redistribute a few inches of soil, even in the apparently flattest spots on my property.

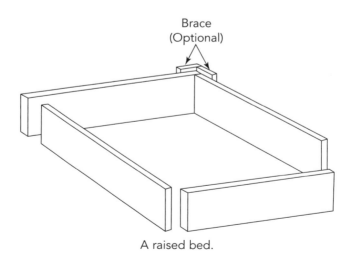

Brace
(Optional)

A raised bed.

# Trellises

A good, sturdy trellis is easily worth its weight in gold, because growing crops vertically protects them from mud, increases yield, lowers rates of disease, and makes the crop easy to pick.

Different crops require different trellis designs. Peas, cucumbers, and melons climb via *tendrils*, specially modified leaves that curl around a support as the plant reaches toward the sun. These plants naturally climb by clinging to small twigs; therefore, wire or nylon netting with openings about 6 inches square works best. The larger openings enable you to reach through the trellis to pick.

In the case of pole beans, the main stems twine around the support. They prefer a wooden or bamboo pole about an inch in diameter. Tomatoes need yet another type of trellis because they do not climb naturally and must be tied to the support.

Installing a trellis when plants are growing is a pain. I prefer to build permanent supports attached to growing beds. These supports can hold different types of trellis, depending on the crop. That allows for flexibility in rotating crops among the beds. A well-built trellis can last many years without replacement.

## John's All-Purpose Trellis

This trellis supports both climbing vines and tomatoes. It is attached to the frame of a raised wooden bed, but you could easily modify my design and install uprights directly in the ground. I use four 8-foot lengths of 2-by-4 lumber and exterior-grade wood screws. First, I attach two uprights at each end of the bed. Then I install a lower crossbar running between them about a foot above ground level. I place the 2-by-4 on its edge for the crossbar. A second crossbar connects the uprights near their top ends.

Attached vertically to the crossbars I place six 1-by-1-inch bamboo poles spaced at 1-foot intervals. This creates a trellis that pole beans can climb or to which I can tie my tomatoes. To make the structure suitable for tendril-climbers, I hang nylon trellis netting on metal hooks screwed into the crossbars.

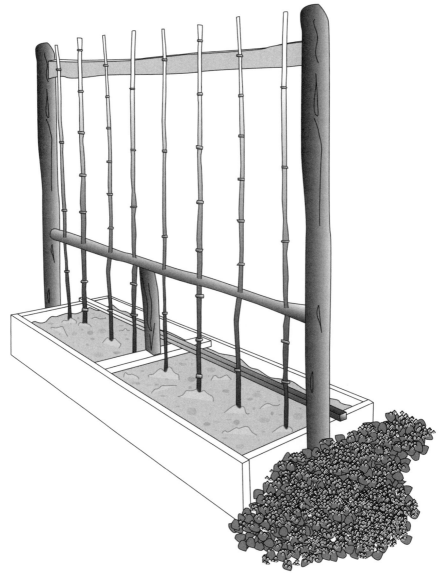

John's all-purpose trellis.

# Season Extenders

Throughout the continental United States, gardeners can add a month or more to the growing season by means of several techniques.

- Row covers
- Cloches
- Cold frames
- Greenhouses
- Indoor growing systems

## Row Covers

One of the simplest ways to protect a growing bed from the cold is to cover it with an old sheet. A better choice of material, however, is a floating row cover, a lightweight fabric made for the purpose. This material provides a few degrees of frost protection and won't crush tender plants. Go a step further and provide support to hold the covering above the bed, and you can gain additional frost protection. Half-inch PVC pipe, generally sold in 10-foot lengths, makes a great support for a row cover. Simply attach one end of the pipe to one side of the bed, bend it in a gentle arc over to the other side, and secure. Attach the pipe to the frame of a wooden raised bed, using exterior-grade wood screws. Alternatively, just stick one end of the pipe into the soil about 6 inches, bend it over the bed and stick the other end into the ground to secure it. (You may have to cut the PVC to obtain the best fit for your growing bed.) Drape a floating row cover over the support, or better yet, use clear plastic film to trap warmth and create a microclimate for growing plants.

## Cloches

A clear plastic row cover on PVC supports is merely a large cloche. Think of a cloche as a portable greenhouse designed to protect just one or a few plants. For example, you can cut the bottoms from clear plastic soda bottles and use the top portion to cover small transplants. Leave the cap off to allow air circulation, but keep it handy in case frost threatens. Garden centers sell cloches for tomato and pepper transplants that allow you to fill the sides of the cloche with water, which helps hold heat in the early days of the growing season. Also, covering a mature plant with a large cloche is a great way to keep it producing well beyond the end of the season.

A cloche's effectiveness can be enhanced with a little added heat. Some gardeners bedeck plants with tiny Christmas lights (not LED lights) before enclosing them in a cloche. The lights provide enough heat to keep the plant from freezing on frosty nights.

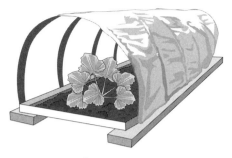

A row cover.

## Cold Frames

Cold frames take the idea of a cloche to the next level. A typical cold frame is designed to protect plants over a long period and give the gardener convenient access. Beyond that, you can go as simple or as fancy as you like.

Four bales of straw and an old window sash or two are all you need to create a makeshift cold frame. Arrange the straw to enclose a rectangle of growing space and place the sash(es) over the top. *Voilà!* You can grow cool-season veggies for at least a month longer.

Many gardeners construct one or more permanent cold frames for winter production. You can purchase a precut kit or find plans online for a cold frame suited to your space and growing needs. Gardeners in Zone 7, for example, can harvest carrots, chard, chervil, cilantro, dill, lettuce, mustards, parsley, scallions, and spinach all winter long from a large cold frame.

For best results, orient the long axis of your cold frame east and west. This means the top is facing south for maximum solar gain. Tilt the top to shed rain and snow. The ideal tilt angle corresponds to the latitude. For example, in my location it is 35 degrees, but any convenient angle will do. Typically, the rear wall of the cold frame is taller than the opposite front wall, thus creating the tilt. You also need a support to keep the top open to ventilate the frame on warm, sunny days. Automatic devices are available for this purpose, or you can simply open the frame by hand, and prop it open with a stick. I can keep track of the temperature in my largest cold frame by means of a wireless thermometer.

While wood is the usual material for backyard cold frame construction, masonry will hold much more heat due to its mass. Therefore, consider a masonry enclosure for a permanent cold frame. You can increase the thermal holding capacity of any cold frame by adding mass. This can be large stones, concrete blocks, or translucent plastic milk jugs (the best choice)

A cold frame.

filled with water. Arrange any of these along the north wall of the frame to help moderate nighttime temperatures.

## Greenhouses

A greenhouse is merely a cold frame with amenities. If the enclosure is large enough to walk inside, it qualifies as a greenhouse, even if it's unheated. An enthusiastic gardener with a small, unheated greenhouse can produce vegetables and herbs all winter long. With a little added heat, the possibilities for crop production expand considerably. Even with a tropical greenhouse, however, the short days of winter will cause plant growth to slow to a crawl. You can always add auxiliary lighting, but the cost of this plus heating can make such a greenhouse impractical. You might as well buy imported fruit!

Before investing in a greenhouse, consult several references regarding design, placement, and energy efficiency considerations. Always make sure any electrical and heating components are rated for outdoor use. Any electrical circuit supplying the greenhouse must be protected by a ground-fault circuit interrupter. Also consider that the greenhouse should have its own water supply. Seek out a professional if you are uncertain about wiring or plumbing issues.

## Indoor Growing Systems

Rather than going to the trouble and expense of a greenhouse, you can take advantage of any available indoor space by growing plants under artificial lights. The advent of compact fluorescent lamps (CFLs) has made fluorescent lighting cheap and convenient to use. An inexpensive fixture with a reflector and a CFL floodlight that consumes about 15 watts will light a corner of the kitchen counter sufficiently to grow herbs.

For a larger light garden, you can use a fixture that holds multiple CFLs or go with an inexpensive shop light outfitted with fluorescent tubes. A 4-foot shop light with two tubes will illuminate 4 square feet of growing space, allowing you to start seeds, carry herb cuttings through the winter, or even produce a little lettuce and parsley. You can expand the lighting system to cover as much space as you have available. Using a timer to keep the light on for twelve hours per day or more will mimic growing-season conditions for your plants.

Serious indoor gardeners can consider metal halide lighting, available at aquarium and DIY stores. These intense illumination systems can provide enough light for tomatoes, but consume a lot of electricity. In fact, electricity consumption is the most serious drawback to any size indoor garden. Weigh the cost of both the equipment and its operation in your decision to go this route. All the safety precautions for greenhouse electrical equipment of course apply to an indoor setup.

## Now, Grow Some Food

With the techniques explained in this chapter, you should be equipped to start a food garden in whatever space you have available. The next four chapters provide specific advice on growing vegetables, herbs, and fruits on the new American homestead.

# 3

# Vegetables: Part One

Deciding which vegetables to grow requires you to consider productivity, ease of culture, and your family's eating preferences. Bear in mind that in a given location, some vegetables do better than others. Locate information specific to your region of the country by visiting the website of your state's cooperative extension service. Find yours at www.csrees.usda.gov/Extension.

## The Onion Family

Members of the onion clan all prefer deep, rich, moist soil; a long growing season; and an absence of competition from weeds. With the exception of scallions grown as annuals, all will do best if planted in a patch separate from other vegetables. Scallions can be started in a container and then tucked into spaces vacated by other crops.

### Perennial Onions

Perennial onions (*Allium cepa* var. *aggregatum*) have never received the press they deserve. Once a bed is established, they will deliver a crop with minimal attention for years. Egyptian, or "walking," onions produce topsets, which are little bulbs appearing at the tip of a long, upright stalk where you would otherwise expect flowers. When the topsets enlarge enough, their weight causes the stalk to bend over, and they plant themselves a short distance from the parent. In this manner, they "walk" all over the place unless you restrain them. That's easy to do; simply remove any offenders, which you can use in the kitchen like shallots (see page 64).

Another perennial onion is sometimes called a "mother," "multiplier," or "potato" onion (*Allium cepa* var. *aggregatum*). Each bulb divides during the growing season to produce several more. By separating and replanting the bulbs, you establish a patch that will produce all the onions you care to dig. Select some to eat and replant the rest.

A third possibility is the perennial leek (*Allium ampeloprasum*). Produced either from seeds or the numerous bulblets formed each year, this leek dies back in summer and resprouts in early fall. The sprouts can be harvested from winter through spring, when they will yield greens early in the season and baby leeks later on. Some, of course, should be saved to continue the patch.

**Culture:** All perennial onions produce well and will grow in all parts of the continental United States. Plant them in rich, sandy soil that has lots of compost dug in. All onions require plenty of phosphorus and potassium. They also require nitrogen during the early part of the growing season. Set the bulbs about 4 inches apart. Keep the bed carefully weeded, as onions do not tolerate competition. Be careful about cultivating because the roots are shallow and can be easily damaged. Mulch well with compost, shredded leaves, or straw to suppress weeds without cultivation. Mulch helps to keep soil moisture even, which onions prefer.

**Harvest and Yield:** Perennial onions may not produce well during the first year as they are becoming established. Thereafter, they should yield well every year. This crop can produce a larger yield per square foot than any other crop except tomatoes. You can harvest green tops anytime after they appear, but wait until late summer or early autumn to harvest the main crop. Potato onions should be sorted by size, the larger ones being retained for the kitchen and the smaller ones replanted for next season. Walking onions can be dug as needed over fall and winter. Leave the smaller ones, produced from topsets this season, to overwinter for next year's crop.

Harvest perennial leeks at the size you desire for cooking. Otherwise, leave them in the ground.

**Storage and Preservation:** Perennial leeks store best in the ground but can be refrigerated for a few days after harvest without damage. Dry bulbs of potato onions and walking onions keep especially well when stored cool and dry in a dark place. Walking onions can remain in the ground until harvest if you need larger bulbs rather than the topsets.

**Uses:** Perennial onions and leeks can be substituted for other types of onions in any recipe.

## Scallions and Bunching Onions

Scallions, or green onions, do not produce an enlarged bulb. They are always started from seed and typically are harvested when about ¼ to ½ inch in diameter.

Bunching onions are scallions that divide to form clumps like the multiplier types. They are perennial where the ground does not freeze deeply and can be protected by a cold frame in areas with harsh winters.

**Culture:** Culture for both scallions and bunching onions is the same as for other members of the family. Plant seeds indoors in cell trays, three to six seeds per cell, beginning in late winter. Sow in succession for a continuous harvest through spring, and then start more in July for fall transplanting. Most types require about sixty days to produce a crop. Transplant whole clumps from cell trays without trimming, spacing them 4 inches apart. Water well.

Bunching onions should be sown in late winter also, but use six to ten seeds and place in a 4-inch pot. Transplant the resulting clumps to the garden in spring, spacing them 10 inches apart. Water and then mulch well to suppress weeds. They should establish themselves easily.

**Harvest and Yield:** Pull all green onions as you need them. Quality suffers in hot weather, so use them before the summer heats up. Harvest bunching onions lightly the first year, and then pull as needed. Divide the clumps every three years.

**Storage and Preservation:** Freshly harvested scallions and bunching onions will keep for about a week in the refrigerator. They are best left in the garden until needed.

**Uses:** Green onions are most often used raw as a garnish or added to salads. Their flavor does not hold up well in cooking.

## Garlic

Every cuisine seems to include dishes that feature the distinct, savory flavor of garlic. Through centuries of cultivation, garlic varieties have adapted to nearly every place on Earth habitable by humans, but all of them fall into two basic groups: softneck garlic (*Allium sativum* var. *sativum*) and hardneck garlic or rocambole (*A. sativum* var. *ophioscorodon*). The softneck varieties are further subdivided into two horticultural groups: artichoke and silverskin types. The most productive varieties are softneck artichoke types.

I have had good luck with garlic from the grocery store, but this practice may introduce diseases into your garlic bed depending on the source of the bulbs. By investigating what is available via mail order, you can find garlic bulbs adapted to your needs and your region of the country. For example, silverskin types do best in the South and Southwest.

**Culture:** Softneck garlic types grow in zones 7–9, while hardneck types are best suited to more northerly climates. Cultivate either type in rich, moist, well-drained soil and keep the patch free of weeds. Plant individual cloves about 4 inches apart, pressing them gently into the soil until the tips are about ¼ inch below the surface.

The best time to plant garlic is in late summer or early fall. The plants will grow over the winter and should be ready to harvest the following summer. "Baby" garlic can be harvested anytime after the shoots appear in spring. It has a mild flavor compared with the mature plant. If you wish, you can plant cloves on a 2-inch spacing and then thin out every other one for baby garlic. Pull all the extras before the plants are more than a foot tall.

**Harvest and Yield:** Harvest garlic when the leaves begin to turn yellow. Pull the entire plant. Allow them to dry thoroughly in a shady, well-ventilated spot for a day or two, and then rub off as much dirt and plant debris as you can, taking care to leave the cloves well protected by their papery skins. Allow the bulbs to cure by placing them on frames covered with wire mesh for maximum ventilation, or do what I do and place the bulbs upside down between the wires of closet shelving or a baker's rack, with the stems hanging down. Space them out so they are not touching.

A pound of starter bulbs will yield anywhere from 3 to more than 10 pounds of harvest, depending on the variety and cultural conditions. Hardneck garlic types are less productive than softnecks.

**Storage and Preservation:** After a couple of weeks of curing, garlic bulbs can be braided and hung up as a decoration, or trimmed of their stems and stored loose in a basket under the kitchen counter. Leave about an inch of stem on each bulb.

## Elephant Garlic

Elephant garlic is a leek variety grown for its swollen bulb containing four cloves. Culture is the same as for regular garlic. It will withstand harsh winters, and the cloves, usually four very large ones per plant, keep for months when stored dry, dark, and cool.

**Uses:** Almost any savory dish will benefit from a little added garlic, and every cuisine has recipes that include it.

## Roasted Garlic

Carefully slice off the top quarter of whole garlic bulbs, revealing all the cloves inside. (The small pieces left in the cut-off portions can be peeled and used in another dish.) Place the cut bulbs on a sheet of aluminum foil and drizzle with a little olive oil. Gather the corners of the foil together and squeeze gently to create a packet. Place the whole thing in a preheated 350°F oven for 1 to 1½ hours or until the cloves are soft. (Carefully open the packet and the middle of a bulb with the tip of a paring knife.) Remove from the oven and allow to cool. Hold the bulb upside down and squeeze. The roasted cloves should pop right out. They can be added to all sorts of dishes or used directly as a spread for toasted bread. Be sure to save the flavored oil in which they cooked. Use it for salad dressing or to add a garlic note to any dish.

## Leeks

The annual leek (*Allium ampeloprasum*) has a delicate, oniony flavor that works well in dishes where regular onions would be overpowering.

**Culture:** Leeks require a long growing season, so it is best to start them indoors in late winter for transplanting to the garden in early spring. To produce enough for home use, sow seeds in a 12-inch flowerpot filled with any good potting mix. Scatter seeds thinly on top of the soil, cover with a layer of fine soil about ¼ inch deep, and water thoroughly. Place a sheet of clear plastic or glass over the pot to retain moisture and set the pot in a warm, sunny window or under lights. As soon as many seedlings have emerged, remove the glass and keep the pot well watered. Feed with liquid fertilizer every two weeks until you are ready to transplant to the garden.

The soil for leeks should be deep, rich, and well drained, with abundant phosphorus and potassium. When ready to transplant, knock the seedling clump out of the pot and separate into individual plants. Don't worry too much about damaging the roots. You should trim them to about 2 inches long anyway. Select the best of the seedlings, or as many as you need, and trim the tops so the whole thing (not counting the 2 inches of roots) is 4 to

6 inches in length. Set the transplants into a narrow trench about 2 inches deep. Space the plants 6 inches apart. Draw soil up around them and firm it with your hands. Water well.

As the leeks grow, hill up the soil around the plants to keep the root ends white and flavorful. They will get 2 feet tall or more, and you want the bottom third to be buried. Side dress with compost and a little cottonseed meal about every two weeks.

**Harvest and Yield:** Harvest leeks when they are the diameter you desire. Depending on the variety, the maximum diameter ranges from 1 to 3 inches. Three-quarters of an inch or so is suitable for most dishes that call for leeks. Leave them in the ground until you need them. Some varieties tolerate cold well and can be left in the ground all winter. However, if the roots freeze, quality suffers considerably.

**Storage and Preservation:** Although leeks can be blanched and frozen, they are best left in the ground and harvested as needed. They also keep well under refrigeration, although after some time the outer portions may decline in quality and require removal. A good candidate for root cellaring, trimmed leeks can be covered with damp sand and refrigerated, mimicking in-garden storage without freezing. This method is most practical where winters are severe.

**Uses:** Leeks can be steamed and eaten as a vegetable with vinaigrette dressing, but they are most often added to savory dishes such as quiches and soups.

## Storage Onions

Bulb-forming storage onions include both *long-day* and *short-day* types. In these, the timing of bulb formation is controlled by the length of the day. This has obvious implications for their cultivation, depending on your latitude. Short-day onions start making bulbs when the days are eleven to twelve hours long. Certain varieties of short-day onions produce unusually sweet bulbs. Low sulfur content in the soil around Vidalia, Georgia, accounts for the special flavor of that region's trademark onions, but sweet onions can be produced anywhere with a sufficiently mild winter and long, warm spring season, generally from Virginia southward. Sweet onions are planted in the fall for harvest around June.

As a general rule, if you live in the South, plant short-day onions in the fall and long-day or day-neutral onions in early spring. If you live in the North, plant long-day or day-neutral onions in the spring.

Long-day onions form bulbs as the days reach fifteen to sixteen hours in length. They are planted in early spring to produce bulbs during the extended days of summer. They are typically grown from sets, tiny bulbs that give rise to larger onions after several months, and are harvested in early fall. Their bulbs contain less sugar and thus keep better in storage than sweet onions do.

Plant breeders have developed onion hybrids, including one called Candy, that are day neutral. These will produce a bulb when the days are twelve to fourteen hours long and are reportedly very popular among home gardeners.

**Culture:** Storage onions require rich, sandy soil that drains well, and must be kept free of weeds. They are heavy feeders. Amend soil with plenty of compost, adding cottonseed meal, bone meal, and wood ashes. Spacing in the row depends on the anticipated size of the bulbs, but 3 inches is about right for most varieties. You can purchase onion sets from garden centers or start from seeds.

Where winters are severe, sow seeds of long-day onions ¼ inch deep in cell trays about sixty days prior to the anticipated last hard freeze. Transplant to the garden in early spring. In mild winter areas, sow seeds in fall in a flowerpot as previously described for leeks. Keep indoors until ready to transplant them to the garden in mid-February. Unlike leeks, however, onions should not have their foliage trimmed back at transplanting time, or yield will be reduced. Culture for short-day onions is identical, except they should be fall planted in the South, which means you will need to start seeds in June or July.

**Harvest and Yield:** Harvest onions when the majority of the tops have fallen over. Each plant, of course, produces one onion bulb. At a 3-inch spacing, you should get forty onions from a 10-foot row. The yield will be determined by the average size of a bulb, which in turn is a function of both the variety and growing conditions. A medium onion weighs about half a pound.

**Storage and Preservation:** After harvest, cure fresh onions in a dry, airy, partially shaded spot for two weeks or until the tops are completely dried. Trim and store in a cool, dry place in the dark. Keeping quality varies with the variety, so read seed catalog descriptions carefully or inquire at your local garden center. Sweet onions do not store as well as the more pungent types.

**Uses:** Innumerable dishes featuring onions are found in every cuisine. Many delicious versions begin with caramelization of raw onions. This is accomplished as follows.

Thinly slice the onions and place them in a large pot with a little oil or butter. Cover the pot, place over medium heat, and sweat the onions until they are soft and translucent. Remove the lid, reduce the heat to low, and continue cooking, stirring occasionally, until the onions take on a rich, golden brown color. Take care not to allow them to burn on the bottom of the pot, or the acrid taste will permeate the dish.

When the caramelized onions are done, they can be used for French onion soup, in an onion tart, or as the basis for an Italian frittata.

## Classic French Onion Soup

3 cups sliced onions, caramelized as described above
2 tablespoons all-purpose flour
4 cups stock (beef, chicken, or vegetable)
Salt and pepper
A few sprigs fresh thyme
Croutons and shredded cheese for garnishing

To the caramelized onions, add the flour and stir until well combined. Add the stock, along with a few sprinkles of salt and pepper, and stir well. Bring the soup to a simmer and add the thyme sprigs. Simmer for 15 minutes. Taste and adjust the seasonings if necessary. Ladle the soup into ovenproof bowls and top with croutons and shredded cheese. Put the bowls under the broiler for a few minutes until the cheese has melted.

Good cheeses for this soup include Gruyere, Swiss, and Parmesan, or a combination.

## Shallots

Shallot varieties are multiplier onion types, such as the potato onions mentioned earlier, that have been selected for their delicate flavor and the keeping quality of the bulbs. They are either elongate and pointed on both ends, or globose like a small onion. The flesh may be white or laced with purple, but the skin is always nut brown. Most keep well and are highly regarded by gourmet cooks.

**Culture:** Shallots are fall-planted. Follow the instructions given earlier for multiplier onions.

**Harvest and Yield:** Harvest shallots in the summer when the tops begin to die back. Each bulb will produce several more. Save the best for storage and replant the others the following fall.

**Storage and Preservation:** Store shallots like other dry bulbs. You can pot them up in the winter and force new growth for greens, but most people will want to grow scallions from seed for this purpose instead.

**Uses:** Shallots add a subtle onion note to many savory dishes. One of my favorite ways to use them is in that Southern staple, pimento cheese.

### Gourmet Pimento Cheese

1 medium shallot, peeled and finely chopped
1 small jar pimentos, partially drained
3 cups freshly shredded Cheddar cheese
Freshly ground black pepper
Hot sauce (such as Tabasco) to taste
Homemade or store-bought mayonnaise

In a bowl, combine the shallots, pimentos, cheese, and several grinds of black pepper. Add a few dashes hot sauce, if you like it. Stir gently, then add the mayonnaise by spoonfuls just until the mixture holds together. Store tightly covered in the refrigerator for up to a week. The flavor improves in storage.

Use pimento cheese as a sandwich spread, a topping for burgers, or a dip for raw vegetables.

---

# Annual Vegetables

By far the majority of commonly grown vegetables are annuals that must be replanted each season. Although this factor would seem to be a disadvantage because of the effort involved, replanting provides several benefits. Annuals mature in a time frame that often permits several crops to be harvested during a single growing season. Crop rotation, a technique that helps control insect and disease problems and avoids the development of nutrient imbalances in the soil, is relatively easy when the crops are annuals, since they have to be replanted each year anyway. In addition, growing annual crops gives you the opportunity to try new varieties.

A convenient way to organize annual vegetables is by their botanical family. Members of the same family tend to place similar demands on the soil, the climate, and the gardener. The three families discussed in the remainder of this chapter, along with the onion clan, are for most backyard growers the most productive and useful of all the vegetables. Additional vegetables are covered in chapter 4.

# The Daisy Family

The daisy family (Asteraceae) has over 22,750 members, yet only one of them, lettuce, is a common vegetable. What appears to be the individual daisy bloom is actually a composite consisting of sterile ray flowers (the ones you pluck off while saying, "She loves me, she loves me not . . .") and the fertile flowers, often yellow in color, clustered at the center of the whole arrangement. These latter ones, when pollinated, produce a special type of seed, the *achene*, that is variously modified to facilitate seed dispersal. Lettuce produces an achene with a fluffy "parasol" to catch the wind, has escaped from gardens countless times, and is a commonplace weed throughout much of the eastern United States.

## Lettuce

Few vegetables reward the grower in so many ways as does lettuce (*Lactuca sativa*). With good culture technique, you can bring in a lettuce crop within six weeks of sowing. Thinnings can be used as baby lettuce.

Hundreds of lettuce varieties exist. Cultivars adapted to specific growing conditions abound. There are summer lettuces, for example, that tolerate much more heat than other types, and varieties specifically bred for winter cultivation under cover. Romaine lettuce, also called "cos" is thought to be the most ancient form of the plant. It is also the most nutritious and is more tolerant of warm weather than other types. Other varieties include looseleaf, bibb, and crisphead lettuce. Looseleaf cultivars like Black Seeded Simpson offer the greatest likelihood of success for the novice gardener. They also resist bolting. Bibb lettuce, also called butterhead, produces a loosely packed head of soft-textured leaves. Crisphead type includes the familiar iceberg lettuce with a tight, rounded head of crunchy leaves. Despite its low nutritional value, it is quite popular. Because it is more difficult to grow than other types of lettuce, it is not recommended for beginners.

Besides the various growth forms, lettuces come in a spectrum of shades of green. There are also red-colored varieties and cultivars with red and green leaf variegation. Leaf shape runs the gamut from simple rounded leaves to elongated ones to frilly ones. Lettuce, therefore, is one of the most decorative edible plants, and should be included whenever the aesthetic appeal of the vegetable bed is an important consideration, such as a curb-side planting in front of your house.

**Culture:** Lettuce seeds can be broadcast directly in the growing bed or you can start them in cell trays. Use cell trays when you want perfect, uniform heads. Use broadcast sowing for "cut and come again" harvesting. Cutting the leaves with scissors and allowing the plants to sprout again from the roots gives you at least two crops from a single planting. The downside, however, is a reduction in plant vigor, and the harvest becomes more perishable.

To start lettuce indoors, fill a 36-cell tray with seed starting mix, water well, and make a small indentation in the surface of the planting mix with a blunt object, such as the eraser end of a pencil. Drop two or three seeds into each indentation. Lettuce needs light to germinate, so do not cover the seeds, but water gently from the top to settle them in. At 75°F, lettuce seeds often germinate within twenty-four hours. They will be ready to transplant when plants have two or three sets of leaves and roots are just beginning to appear in the drain holes of the cells. This can take from two to four weeks depending on the amount of light they receive. Under fluorescent lights, plants take longer to develop than if grown with natural sunlight in a greenhouse.

Avoid exposure to temperatures below 50°F during the first three weeks of growth. Fertilize seedlings with a soluble fertilizer when they are an inch tall. Harden off plants for a week before transplanting. Transplant them on 4- to 6-inch centers—that is, leave 4 to 6 inches between plants in each direction. Water the transplants and side dress with compost. Feed them every two weeks.

Hot weather causes lettuce to turn bitter and bolt, or go to seed. Romaine lettuces are among the most heat-tolerant varieties, as mentioned earlier, but even they generally perform poorly when nighttime temperatures exceed 75°F. In areas with mild winters, lettuce can be produced as a winter crop. It performs well under cover and will tolerate temperatures down to 20°F.

**Harvest and Yield:** Lettuce will be ready to harvest about a month to six weeks after transplanting, depending on the variety and growing conditions. Stagger plantings to have plants maturing every week until the weather becomes too hot. You can either harvest whole heads by cutting them off near the base or pick individual leaves and allow the plant to produce more. An 8-foot long double row should yield thirty to forty mature plants, enough for many salads.

**Storage and Preservation:** As soon as possible after harvest, immerse lettuce in cold water to chill it and remove soil. Repeated washing in two more changes of water should eliminate all debris. Use a salad spinner to dry the leaves thoroughly and store in a plastic zipper bag in the refrigerator. Place a paper towel in the bad to absorb excess moisture or use special perforated vegetable storage bags. Lettuce keeps well for three days when properly stored. If you have a bumper crop, blanch the lettuce in boiling water for 1 minute, followed by a plunge into ice water. Drain well, squeeze dry, and freeze in 1-cup portions. Frozen lettuce can be added to soups.

**Uses:** It would be hard to improve upon a salad of fresh lettuces tossed with a little lemon juice, olive oil, salt and pepper. However, the following soup, which can also be prepared with frozen lettuce, comes close.

## LETTUCE AND FISH SOUP

For two servings
1½ cups chicken stock
1-inch piece of fresh ginger, peeled
2 scallions, trimmed and cut into 1-inch pieces
Soy sauce
2 drops Chinese dark sesame oil
2 cups lightly packed fresh lettuce leaves
¼ pound fillets any firm-fleshed white fish, such as halibut or grouper

Bring the chicken stock and 1½ cups water to a simmer in a large saucepan and add the ginger and scallions. Simmer, partially covered, for 30 minutes. Remove from the heat and discard the vegetables. Taste the soup base and add soy sauce to taste. Return the saucepan to the heat and add the sesame oil. Bring the soup base to a boil and stir in the lettuce. When the water returns to a boil, add the fish. Remove the saucepan from the heat, cover, and allow it to sit for 2 minutes before serving.

    Note: If using frozen lettuce, use only 1 cup, and do not thaw before adding.

# The Pea Family

Members of the pea family (Fabaceae) are known as *legumes*. All add nitrogen to the soil in which they are grown, owing to the presence of symbiotic bacteria living on their roots. Peas and beans belong to this family, along with some other edibles, such as the tropical jicama and tamarind. Many nonvegetable cover crops, such as clover, are legumes.

# Green Beans

Green, or "snap" beans (*Phaseolus vulgaris*) are one of the easiest and most productive crops you can grow and are highly recommended for beginning vegetable gardeners. Bush bean varieties typically mature in two months or less, provide multiple pickings per planting, and can be planted in succession for a long harvest season. Pole bean varieties mature two weeks or so later than bush beans planted at the same time. They form vigorous vines that can grow 6 to 8 feet tall and require a trellis. Picking bush beans can be a tedious, backbreaking task. That is the main reason for the strong preference for pole beans among many gardeners of my acquaintance; they are easier to pick. Pole beans also produce slightly more pounds per square foot than bush beans do.

Green beans come in many cultivars, ranging from tiny pods the diameter of a pencil to big, flat versions as large as a ruler. There are waxy yellow ones and bright purple ones. The former cook quickly and have a smooth texture. The latter turn green when cooked, but they are much easier to see when picking. Gourmet French filet bean types known as *haricots verts* have been bred specifically for "baby" bean production. Available in both bush and pole types, they are a tiny bit more finicky to grow than regular green beans, but their superior flavor when steamed until just barely tender is worth the extra trouble.

> Heirloom beans with names like Greasy Back and Pop's Peanut are highly sought after in my region, and no doubt your neighbors have their favorites as well. Usually well adapted to local conditions and delicious when cooked, heirloom beans reward your efforts at seeking them out. Seed saving is a cinch with beans, as they are self-pollinating. This no doubt accounts for the abundance of local types.

**Culture:** Beans should be planted in mid to late spring when the soil temperature has reached 60°F. In the spring, this will typically be eight to ten weeks after the last freeze. My grandfather planted beans on Good Friday, based on local lore. Despite their frost tenderness, beans grown in cool temperatures have a better flavor, so fall crops taste better than summer crops where summers are hot. Plant fall beans (bush or half-runner types are best for fall) about ten to twelve weeks before the anticipated first frost.

Bean seeds may rot in cool, wet soil. This is more likely if the seeds are light in color. Therefore, plant dark-seeded varieties in spring and light-seeded ones later in the season. Because they are quick to mature, bush beans can be planted in succession about every two weeks. By the time the second crop blooms, the first crop should be finishing up and can come out of the bed. Space seeds about 2 inches apart in rows an inch deep, thinning after true leaves appear to stand 4 inches apart. Row spacing should be about 12 inches in a raised bed, or wider if you will need to walk between the rows to pick.

Beans will grow in almost any soil that is well drained, but they prefer a slightly acidic pH of 6.0. If the soil is nitrogen deficient, you can apply a soluble nitrogen source such as cottonseed meal, but do this only during the first three weeks of growth. Adding nitrogen for a longer period is not desirable, as by then the beans will have developed their nitrogen fixing root nodules and excess nitrogen may actually reduce the crop.

Pole beans need to be planted only once per season, as they bear over a long period. For support, nothing beats a bamboo or rough-sawn wooden pole about an inch in diameter and at least 8 feet tall. Poles should be sunk firmly into the ground spaced about 18 inches apart. Sow four or five seeds around the base of each pole. You can also build a teepee of several long poles, their bases arranged around the perimeter of a circle about 6 feet in diameter. Leave a gap to enter the teepee from the north side. When the vines are mature, you can pick beans in the cool shade of the teepee or perhaps even grow a small crop of summer lettuce or parsley under there. Children love bean teepees, too.

Some bean varieties lie halfway between bush and pole types and are known as "half runners." White-seeded half-runners are among the most popular varieties for home canning and freezing here in the Tennessee Valley. These types need support to a height of about 4 feet, or they will sprawl all over the bed.

**Harvest and Yield:** Harvest beans frequently to keep the vines producing. Although different varieties will mature at different pod sizes, in general all green beans should be picked before the individual beans are discernible

## Soil Inoculants

You can purchase soil inoculants that jump-start development of the legume-bacteria partnership. Use of these products has been shown to increase yield. These products are simply nitrogen fixing bacteria in a dormant state, mixed with a carrier in powdered form. Just before sowing, you combine the inoculant, a little water, and your seeds, coating the seeds with the powder before planting. Inoculant can also be added directly to the furrow.

through the pod. For standard varieties such as Blue Lake, mature pods will be ¼ inch in diameter and about 6 inches long. Italian types such as Romano bear flat pods about ½ inch wide and up to a foot long. French filet beans should be harvested when the pods are smaller than a pencil in diameter. With all green beans, quality suffers if the pods remain on the vine too long.

**Storage and Preservation:** Keep freshly picked green beans cool and dry until you are ready to use them. Wet beans will mold and spoil quickly. Refrigerate them uncovered and use or preserve them within three days. Green beans freeze easily. Trim them, and then break them into pieces or leave them whole as you desire. Rinse well and drop into a large pot of rapidly boiling water. When the water returns to a boil, start timing. After three minutes, drain well, and then plunge the beans into a sink full of cold water to which you have added a tray or two of ice. Drain them thoroughly again and spread them out on kitchen towels. Pat dry using additional towels. Fill labeled freezer containers and freeze immediately.

Green beans can be canned with excellent results, but their low acidity requires the use of a pressure canner. See page 240 for additional information about pressure canning.

**Uses:** Delicious in all sorts of recipes, green beans should first be blanched as just described for freezing. This process allows them to keep well for a few days in the refrigerator and makes further cooking a breeze. Add them to soups or casseroles, or enjoy them on their own.

## SESAME GREEN BEANS

1 tablespoon vegetable oil
1 pound green beans, any variety, blanched and drained
1 clove garlic, minced
2 slices fresh ginger, each about the size of a quarter and ⅛ inch thick
2 teaspoons soy sauce
1 teaspoon dark sesame oil
½ teaspoon sesame seeds

Heat the oil in a large skillet or wok and add the beans, garlic, and ginger. Stir-fry until the garlic is a pale golden color. Add the remaining ingredients, toss to combine, and serve at once.

## Other Bean Varieties

Green beans provide a great combination of versatility, ease of culture, and high productivity. Even with limited space, you can easily grow enough of them to last all year if you freeze the seasonal abundance. If you have room in your garden, you may also want to try some of the many other bean varieties.

**Dry Beans:** Literally hundreds of dry bean varieties exist, some going back centuries to Native American cultures. Any green bean type, if left to mature, can be used as dry beans. Culture is the same as for green beans. The main difference between dry and green beans is that the dry bean pods must fully mature and dry on the vines; therefore, a longer growing season is required. After harvest, separating the beans from the pods can be a chore. When the beans are dry, pick before the rain soaks them, or they may mold in storage.

> Dry bush beans (*Phaseolus vulgaris*) are simply not sufficiently productive to warrant growing them where space is at a premium. High-quality, organically grown dried beans for consumption are widely available.

**Runner Beans** (*Phaseolus coccineus*) do not set pods at temperatures above 90°F. Although the soil must be at least 50°F for germination, this bean does best where summers are cool. It will flower anywhere, though, and makes a great decorative vine. The flowers are edible. Runner beans will overwinter in mild climates. They need plenty of water, especially when flowers begin to develop, but grow as easily as bush beans.

**Lima Beans** (*Phaseolus lunatus*) need warmth; soil temperature should be above 65°F before planting. Limas bear in about eighty days and grow best in sandy loam or raised beds. They perform poorly in heavy clay soils. Although both pole and bush limas are available, most need at least some support. Unlike green beans, limas tolerate low soil moisture until flowering begins. Pick them as the pods just begin to turn yellow for "baby" limas or wait until the pods are dry to harvest "butter beans." Immature green limas freeze well. Prepare them like green beans (see page 71). Butter beans should be shelled, and then stored dry and cold.

**Fava Beans** (*Vicia faba*) can overwinter in mild climates, but more typically are grown like peas as a spring crop. Their sturdy vines need support. Favas will not set seed in hot weather, but can be planted in fall and winter for early spring harvest in hot summer areas. From Zone 5 northward, they can be planted in early spring for harvest before the daytime temperature exceeds 70°F. You can pick pods at 3 inches for use as green beans or allow them to get larger and shell them as for green limas. Or wait until they mature, thresh out, and store them as dry beans. Cooks take note: Fava beans can substitute for chickpeas in hummus and falafel.

**Soybeans** (*Glycine max*) come in two basic varieties: regular and edamame (ee-dah-MA-mee). Regular soybeans are grown as a field crop, harvested when dry, and used to make everything from cooking oil to tofu. Small-scale production of regular soybeans is not practical, but soybeans are easy to grow if you have room. Follow the recommendations for planting bush beans. The other soybean variety, edamame, is popular in Asian cuisine and has been catching on in America. This soybean is eaten green, much like limas, and has a nutty, sweet flavor.

Both types of soybeans mature at 2 to 5 feet, so they require more room than bush beans. However, their sturdy stems do not need poles or a trellis for support. Plant when soil temperature is 65°F or warmer, as seeds will not germinate in cold soil. Space the seeds about 2 inches apart in rows set 18 inches apart in raised beds, or twice that distance if you must walk between the rows. Pick edamame when the pods resemble snow peas and are about 80 percent filled. Do not wait until they turn yellow, or they will be starchy. Count the days from the first appearance of flowers, and check the pods after about a month.

## Peanuts

The peanut is a legume, one that bears its pods of seeds underground, where they are presumably safe from predators (except humans). There are four types: Virginia, Runner, Spanish, and Valencia. The first two are bushy, sprawling, and bear two large seeds per pod, while the others are more upright in habit and have two to five smaller seeds per pod. All types grow in hot summer areas in light, well-drained soil of average fertility. They are planted from April through June, depending on latitude, with earlier planting necessary in northern areas, due to the plant's requirement for a long growing season of 120 to 150 days. They need plenty of water as flowers begin to appear, usually six to eight weeks after planting. Allowing them to dry out at this stage will reduce productivity significantly.

As flowers mature, they bend toward the ground, eventually burying the pod under the surface of the soil. Take care at this stage not to overwater, which can cause the nuts to sprout while still on the parent plant. Water deeply and thoroughly and allow the soil to dry to a depth of 1 inch before adding more water.

Harvest when the top growth begins to turn yellow. Pull up the entire plant and allow to dry in a shady spot for several days (unless you are making boiled peanuts), ideally sheltered from rainfall. Then pull off the nuts and store in a cool, dry place. Peanut yields can be as high as 3,500 pounds per acre, or about 50 to 100 peanuts per plant. Grow twelve plants for each person in the family. Peanuts can be dry roasted, oil roasted, or boiled.

Dry peanuts are best for roasting, but boiled peanuts should be prepared shortly after digging, when the nuts are still soft.

## SOUTHERN STYLE BOILED PEANUTS

1 pound fresh, raw peanuts in the shell
¼ cup kosher salt

Thoroughly wash the nuts in running water and drain well. Combine the nuts, salt, and 1 quart water in a large pot, bring to a boil, and simmer until the nuts are tender. Remove a nut and check for doneness after 2 hours. It can take considerably longer for the nuts to cook, depending on their moisture content and other factors. Some traditionalists cook them from dawn to dusk. Serve from the pot with a slotted spoon. Diners shell them like shrimp, so provide plenty of napkins.

For a delicious variation, add 2 tablespoons Old Bay seasoning, smoked paprika, shrimp boil, or other flavorings to the cooking water.

Refrigerate boiled peanuts in their cooking liquid for up to 2 days. The longer they sit in the water, the saltier they get.

## Peas

Fresh shelling peas can be hard to find at the supermarket. The effort to grow and harvest them requires that their price be equivalent to that of the edible-pod types, but about half the weight is shells. Therefore, frozen or canned shelled peas have taken over, and the only way you are likely to be able to enjoy them freshly picked is to grow them yourself. Shelling peas are sometimes called English peas.

Edible-podded peas come in two varieties—snow peas and snap peas. Snow peas, which have broad, flat pods, are harvested and eaten before the seeds fill out the pods. They have been around a long time and are popular in Asian cuisine. Snap peas are only a few decades old and are one of the best crops developed through plant breeding during the twentieth century. Not only do they have good disease resistance but the productivity per square foot, when compared with shelling peas, is roughly doubled.

**Culture:** Peas of any variety do not perform well in warm weather (above 80°F) and can be planted as early in spring as the ground can be worked. They can also be started in a cold frame in winter for the earliest possible harvest in spring. Fall-sown peas may be damaged by frost. Although the vines resist cold, the pods may be ruined if they freeze. Therefore, time plantings appropriately.

> Well-drained soil with plenty of phosphorus and potassium, but little nitrogen, is ideal for any type of pea. Too much nitrogen will give you lots of vines and few pods. Peas, therefore, can rotate with a nitrogen-demanding crop like spinach.

Sow seeds about an inch deep and an inch apart. Space rows 18 inches apart in a raised bed, or 3 feet apart if you must walk between them. Thin them before they begin to vine, leaving about 2 inches between individual plants. Although several varieties produce dwarf vines, they all need support on a suitable trellis. I prefer nylon netting with 6-inch mesh, stretched on a sturdy wood frame. Peas climb by means of tendrils that prefer to wrap around a thin support. You can also use skinny bamboo stakes or tree limbs with many small branches. Unless the soil is dry as pods are developing, peas seldom need irrigation.

**Harvest and Yield:** Pick shelling peas as soon as the pods are filled out. Snap peas can be picked at any stage of seed development but are best when the pods are about half full. Pick snow peas before the seeds inside are noticeable as bumps on the outer surface of the pod. A well-grown row of shelling peas can produce a pound per foot. Snap peas produce double the usable yield of shelling peas, while snow pea productivity lies between.

**Storage and Preservation:** Although shelled peas can be preserved by canning, they are much better frozen. Process within two hours of harvest for the best flavor, as the sugars in the pod quickly convert to starch after picking. Snow and snap peas can be frozen but taste best when eaten fresh. Snap peas are delicious raw, right from the vine. To freeze any pea type, blanch them in boiling water for three minutes, drain well, and plunge into cold water to stop the cooking. Drain well again and pack into labeled containers.

**Uses:** Snap peas are a wonderful addition to salads. Both snow and snap peas can be steamed or stir-fried. Don't overdo it. Three minutes on the heat is enough. After thawing, reheat frozen snap or snow peas just to serving temperature. Overcooking results in poor texture and loss of flavor. Shelled peas can be added to soups and casseroles. A mixture of shelled and edible-pod types makes a superb version of green pea soup.

## CREAM OF FRESH PEA SOUP

Fresh green peas are one of the spring garden's most valuable treasures. Make this soup when they are at their best. The fresh herbs called for in the recipe are available at the same season. You can use any combination of shelled or edible-podded peas, as long as the total amount is 1 cup.

½ cup chopped scallions
¼ cup chopped celery
2 tablespoons butter
2 cups chicken or vegetable stock
1 dried Thai or Japanese hot chili pepper (optional)
1 cup cream
½ cup chopped snow or snap peas (blanched 3 minutes, then cooled)
2 tablespoons dry white wine, such as Chenin Blanc
Salt and freshly ground white pepper
¼ to ½ cup freshly shelled green peas (blanched 3 minutes, then cooled)
1 teaspoon minced mint
1 teaspoon minced chervil

Sauté the scallions and celery in butter on medium heat. Add the chicken stock and, if desired, the dried hot pepper. Reduce the liquid to 1 cup by slow simmering. Remove the saucepan from the heat and add the cream and the snow or snap peas. Purée in a blender or food processor. Strain, then return the mixture to the saucepan and add the wine. Taste and add salt and white pepper as needed. Heat until hot, but do not allow to boil. Serve garnished with the shelled peas, mint, and chervil.

## Black-Eyed and Other Southern Peas

This group of legumes (*Vigna unguiculata* and *V. unguiculata unguiculata*) goes by a variety of names: Southern peas, cowpeas, field peas, crowder peas, and black-eyed peas. All need warmth and will bear in sixty to seventy days in areas where both days and nights are warm during the growing season. They are, therefore, quintessentially Southern. Black-eyed peas should be planted when the soil temperature is above 65°F. Don't worry about irrigation until flowers appear; then give them an inch of water a week. Hold off on the fertilizer, too; extra nitrogen prevents black-eyed peas from setting pods. Shelled peas can be boiled for immediate use, or canned, frozen, or dried.

## Pea Greens

The uppermost 6 inches of the stems of shelling, snow, and snap peas can be harvested and eaten in steamed or stir-fried dishes, added to salad or used on a sandwich instead of lettuce. By using the shoots, you can extend the harvest of a fall planted crop if frost damages the pods. Cook them only until they turn bright green and look wet. The leaves of Southern peas can be cooked like spinach.

# The Potato Family

The potato family (Solanaceae) is native to Central and South America and includes potatoes, tomatoes, peppers, and eggplant. Potatoes prefer cool temperatures and are grown in spring and fall, while the others (tomatoes, peppers, and eggplants) are warm-season crops.

## Eggplant

Eggplant (*Solanum melongena*) makes a tidier plant than the tomato, seldom requiring more than one stake for support, and little in the way of pruning. It is not as easy to grow as the tomato, however. Wait to plant until the weather is warm and settled. If started too early, eggplant is likely to be devastated by flea beetles. The leaves of cold-stressed plants become perforated with pinholes due to feeding by the beetles. In addition to large, purple Italian varieties, eggplant comes in pink, white, lavender, and striped types as well as elongated hot dog shapes and nearly spherical forms. Some of the best space savers are varieties intended for harvest as "baby" eggplant. These grow on compact plants.

**Culture:** Sow eggplant seeds eight to ten weeks before your preferred transplanting date, which should be at least two weeks after your last spring frost. Wait longer if possible, because eggplant is not deterred by summer heat. Most cultivars require seventy to ninety days from transplanting to begin producing. Harden seedlings off on a shelf or table more than 36 inches above ground level. This deters flea beetles from attacking. Cover the transplants with floating row cover for at least three weeks after transplanting—the longer the better. You can also protect new transplants with plastic milk jugs if you have only a few plants. Cut the bottom from a jug and place it over the seedling, leaving off the cap to provide ventilation. Leave the jugs in place as long as possible.

Eggplant adapts well to container culture. Give each plant about 5 gallons of soil. Look for smaller cultivars, such as Ichiban, Little Fingers, and Bambino for container growing.

To avoid disease, do not grow eggplant in soil that has grown peppers, potatoes, or tomatoes during the past three years.

**Harvest and Yield:** Eggplant is ready to harvest when the skin is shiny. Smaller fruits have better flavor. When the skin becomes dull colored, the fruit is probably too mature to use.

While some eggplant varieties, especially the elongated Asian types, such as Ichiban, can produce as many as a dozen fruits under good growing conditions, expect about six per plant on average.

**Storage and Preservation:** Eggplant can be stored for a few days under refrigeration but is best used as soon as harvested. Eggplant relish, or caponata (recipe follows), can be canned, but canning or freezing raw eggplant is not recommended.

**Uses:** As a rule, eggplant is sliced and salted briefly before using. This removes excess moisture and reduces bitterness in an over-the-hill specimen. Peel or leave unpeeled, depending on your recipe. Eggplant slices can be fried, baked, stir-fried, or steamed by themselves but are usually combined with other ingredients.

## Caponata

1 pound eggplant, sliced and cut into chunks
2 teaspoons pickling salt
2 tablespoons vegetable oil
1 medium onion, sliced
3 ribs celery, diced
1 pound tomatoes, peeled and chopped
½ cup wine vinegar
1 tablespoon sugar
½ cup green olives
1 tablespoon capers, rinsed
Salt and freshly ground black pepper
2 tablespoons chopped fresh parsley

Salt the pieces of eggplant. Place the eggplant in a colander, cover with a plate, add a can of beans or other weight, and allow them to drain for 45 minutes. Remove the weight and carefully blot the eggplant dry with kitchen towels.

While the eggplant drains, heat the oil in a skillet and gently cook the onions until they are translucent and soft, about 10 minutes. Add the diced celery and cook for another 10 minutes, stirring occasionally. Add the tomatoes and cook for another 5 minutes. Stir in the vinegar, sugar, olives, and capers; reduce the heat and simmer until the tomatoes have formed a sauce, about 10 minutes longer. Set this mixture aside and keep warm.

When the eggplant is ready, pour oil into another skillet to a depth of ¼ inch. Heat until the oil is almost smoking. When a piece of eggplant is dropped in, it should sizzle immediately. Carefully add the remaining eggplant. Cook, turning the pieces with a spatula, until the eggplant is golden brown on all sides. Turn off the heat, remove the eggplant with a slotted spoon, and drain it on paper towels. Stir the warm eggplant into the warm tomato sauce. Season with salt and pepper. Taste carefully and add more vinegar, sugar, salt, or pepper as needed. Finally, stir in the chopped parsley.

Allow the caponata to sit overnight at room temperature to marry the flavors, and then serve with crusty bread as a first course. Store any leftovers in the refrigerator and use within 3 days.

---

## Peppers

Growing good peppers (*Capsicum annuum*, *C. chinense*, *C. baccatum,* and interspecific hybrids) is relatively easy in soil of average fertility. Sweet bell peppers yield the largest fruits by weight and are number one in popularity, but you can also grow banana peppers, both sweet and hot; chilies of various types; and specialty peppers like the extremely hot habañero. Peppers can be used at all stages, from immature to fully ripe, and thus provide a steady crop over a long season. As a rule, they dislike cool soil, uneven moisture, and too much nitrogen.

**Culture:** Start peppers in cell trays about eight to ten weeks before the last spring frost. Soil temperature must be above 75°F for good germination. Even then, peppers are slow to germinate. Some can take a month. Cool

### ⅏ Blossom Drop

Ironically, poor production in peppers can be due to too much heat. If nighttime temperatures exceed 80°F, blossoms will drop. For this reason, in hot summer areas, bell peppers, which are less tolerant of hot, muggy weather than are chili peppers, can be grown as a late-season crop. Time plantings so fruits mature during cooler days but before nights drop below 65°F.

temperatures and excess moisture will lead to poor germination and/or death of young seedlings due to fungal infestation.

When two pairs of true leaves have formed, transplant the seedlings to 3- or 4-inch pots and *keep them warm*. Nighttime temperatures should not be below 65°F, and plants should be watered with warm water. Pot them up to larger containers if you have a late spring and can't get them into the garden. Setbacks during early growth stages will reduce the ultimate harvest. Never allow plants to wilt. When conditions are appropriate, meaning that the soil temperature is at least 65°F, you can move them to the garden. Fertilize the planting area with cottonseed and bone meals at transplant time. Sprinkle a tablespoon of each into the bottom of the planting hole, cover with a little soil, and then set the plants in place. Space them 18 inches apart. Add a sturdy stake to support the plants later when fruits set. Feed growing plants with a liquid fertilizer, such as fish emulsion, every two weeks until flower buds appear.

> Another cause of blossom drop is overfertilization. As soon as blooms appear, stop feeding. Too-low humidity can also reduce fruit set. One way to maintain appropriate humidity is to plant in blocks of four plants, allowing them to create their own microclimate.

Keep all peppers free of weeds and thin the fruits mercilessly if you want superior specimens. The small green ones can be used in the kitchen immediately. Peppers mature in anywhere from less than sixty to more than eighty days, depending on the variety.

With glossy green leaves and brilliantly colored fruits, pepper plants are highly decorative. They are thus a good choice for integrating into landscape plantings. Doing so saves space in the garden for other vegetables.

> Peppers adapt readily to container culture. Small hot peppers, such as Thai chili and habañero, will grow in a 12-inch pot. Give other chilies, bell, and banana peppers a 5-gallon container. Because container peppers need close attention to avoid dry soil, they are excellent candidates for self-watering containers.

**Harvest and Yield:** Harvest peppers as needed. Days to maturity on seed packets are indicative of the time needed to reach the green pepper stage. Ripening to red, yellow, orange, etc., will take another month. Yields per plant are similar to eggplant in the case of sweet bell types. Expect six to ten nice ones. Hot peppers may yield in great abundance under good conditions.

You can uproot pepper plants before frost kills them and store with the roots immersed in a bucket of water in a protected, lightly shaded spot. They will keep this way for about a month and will continue to ripen. Small pepper plants in containers can be overwintered in a sunny spot indoors and returned to the garden in the spring.

**Storage and Preservation:** Some cultivars store better than others at room temperature. Check seed catalogs to identify good keepers. All peppers freeze well. Simply trim, chop, and place in freezer containers.

The classic way to preserve chilies is to dry them. In warm, humid weather, they will rot before they dry thoroughly, however. In areas outside the Southwest, you will likely need a dehydrator, or you can place fruits directly on the racks of your oven. Set the heat to its lowest possible setting and leave the oven door open. Remove when the fruits are wrinkled and leathery, but not so dry that they crumble in your hands. Store home-dried peppers in a closed container in the refrigerator. Ripe peppers can also be roasted before canning. Because of their low acid content, a pressure canner is required.

**Uses:** A classic technique for keeping the flavor of fresh hot peppers for winter use involves storing them in a jar of vinegar. You can use the vinegar to season soups, bean dishes, and so forth. Use a ratio of 1 cup chopped pepper to 2 cups vinegar. Place the jar in the refrigerator and wait two weeks before you begin using the vinegar.

Pickled peppers of nursery rhyme fame are easy to make at home. Follow the recipe for dilled green tomatoes on page 249, substituting whole, perfect banana or chili peppers and omitting the dill and bay leaves. Make a small slit in each fruit with the tip of a knife before placing them in the jar to allow the pickling liquid to get inside.

## BALSAMIC BELL PEPPERS AND MUSHROOMS

2 bell or sweet banana peppers (any color)
2 tablespoons olive oil
8 ounces fresh mushrooms, cleaned and cut into two or three pieces each
2 tablespoons balsamic vinegar
Salt and freshly ground black pepper

Trim and seed the peppers and cut them into bite-size chunks. Heat the oil in a skillet and fry the mushrooms until they turn darker and begin to release their juices, then add the peppers and toss until they are tenderized, 1 to 2 minutes. Increase the temperature and boil until the pan is almost dry, then add the balsamic vinegar, salt, and a few grinds of pepper. Cook and stir until the vinegar is reduced to a glaze. Serve immediately as a side dish.

## Potatoes

The flavor of homegrown potatoes (*Solanum tuberosum* subspecies *tuberosum* and hybrids) probably accounts for their lasting popularity with home gardeners. The space demanded by potatoes, about 4 square feet per plant, may render them too greedy for inclusion in the smallest gardens, but if you can squeeze in a few hills, they are a cinch to grow. I've had plants come up and yield potatoes from peelings added to the compost. These will produce only small potatoes without proper care, though.

Potatoes originated in the New World tropics and were domesticated roughly 10,000 years ago. Consequently, the number of varieties is vast. At least 5,000 are known, deriving from about 200 natural species. As a food crop, they powered the rise of the Incan Empire. Modern crop breeding has introduced pest and disease resistance from naturally occurring species, such as *S. fendleri*, whose range reaches north to Texas. From big russets to tiny fingerlings, potatoes offer something for every palate and every gardener. Look for local favorites in your garden center, or seek out heir-loom types from mail-order suppliers. Besides the familiar white-fleshed ones, potatoes come in red, yellow, and blue, along with various shapes, skin colors, and starch levels.

Potatoes are heavy feeders and demand lots of water but can produce 2 pounds per square foot. Growers in cool summer climates will have more cultivar choices than do gardeners farther south. In the Deep South, pota-toes are often grown as a winter crop. Regardless of where you live, you can grow potatoes.

**Culture:** Potatoes require rich, slightly acidic soil with plenty of compost added. You can plant potatoes from the grocery, but doing so places you at risk of introducing viruses that may cause problems in subsequent years. Instead, purchase seed potatoes that are certified virus-free. In Tennessee, we plant potatoes on St. Patrick's Day, roughly a month before the last anticipated frost.

Cut seed potatoes into pieces about the size of an egg, with at least two eyes per piece. Allow them to dry at room temperature for a few days before planting. You can get a jump on the season by placing whole seed potatoes in a warm, sunny place, spread out on several layers of newspaper, until the eyes have produced sprouts about an inch long. The whole thing can then be carefully planted out and will emerge more quickly, giving you an earlier crop.

Bury the seed potatoes about 3 inches deep, spacing them a foot apart. Space rows 4 feet apart, or devote a raised bed to potatoes only. (You can follow them with a crop of beans, lettuce, or spinach after harvesting.) If you use a raised bed, it should be rather deep. I like to prepare a "two-story" bed, with a 1-foot-deep base frame filled with growing mix and a frame of the same size that can be stacked on top later. When the potatoes are 6 inches tall, cover them with soil until just the tips of the leaves are exposed. When they have grown another 6 inches, repeat this step. I plant in the base frame and then add the top frame when it is time to shovel on the additional soil. After the second round of burial, the top frame will be full to the brim.

The reason for burying the leaves twice is to increase the yield. All the potato tubers formed by the plants will be produced between the seed tuber and the soil surface. Hence, the larger the underground portion, the more potatoes you will harvest.

Growing Potatoes in Containers: Gardeners with limited space can grow potatoes in large containers. Drill drainage holes into the bottom of a 30-gallon plastic garbage can. Fill to within a foot of the top with growing mix and plant five or six seed potatoes evenly spaced. Add more growing mix as described as the potatoes grow. When ready to harvest, dump the whole thing and sort out the potatoes. You can even pack growing mix and chopped leaves into a plastic garbage bag with some drain holes in the bottom. Roll the top of the bag down like a sock for stability, planting potatoes in about 2 feet of growing mix. As the potatoes grow, add more mix and unroll the top of the bag to support it.

Beetle Control: Flea beetles often infest potatoes early in the season, but in my garden do not seem to reduce yields. A more serious pest is the Colorado potato beetle, a native North American species that is a problem in most areas of the country. These insects should be picked off and killed as soon as you find them. Otherwise, each female will lay numerous eggs that hatch into voracious larvae, and the infestation can quickly get out of hand. Inspect the crop daily as the weather begins to warm up. Control can be accomplished through other means also. Research shows that the farther this year's crop is planted from last year's, the fewer pests of all kinds are present. Therefore, rotate crops appropriately. Floating row covers can prevent beetles from reaching the crop in spring. Digging a trench around the potato patch and lining it with plastic sheeting has also been shown to work. The sides of the trench should be steep, at an angle greater than 45 degrees. Beetles fall in as they approach the plants and can't climb out, allowing you to carry out mass executions.

One of the simplest and best beetle controls is a 4-inch layer of wheat straw mulch. Mulch creates a suitable microenvironment for natural predators, such as ground beetles, ladybugs, and lacewings, all of which feed on potato beetle larvae. It may also prevent beetles from finding your patch, probably by masking chemical signals beetles use to locate their food. This technique alone can increase productivity by one-third, according to Cornell University experts. Another simple technique is to locate the potato patch near flower gardens. The flowers attract many kinds of insects, in turn attracting generalized predators such as ladybugs.

In northern regions, planting extra-early varieties, such as Caribe, may help in beetle control because the cooler climate slows insect reproduction rates, and the potatoes mature before the beetle population skyrockets.

Herbs and plant extracts may also be useful in controlling or repelling beetles. Catnip, sage, and citrus oils all have potential. The herbs can be planted near the potatoes, while citrus oil can be applied with a sprayer.

Biological beetle controls include both bacterial and fungal pathogens that attack the insects. A Bt (*Bacillus thuringiensis*; see page 33) strain that is specific for potato beetles has been isolated, along with a fungus, *Beauveria bassiana*. Both are available from specialty suppliers. The fungus offers the advantage that it can become established in the growing area and provide control all season. However, application of these products must be timed appropriately or the beetle's reproduction will outpace the ability of the biocontrol. Furthermore, the fungus does not like hot weather, reducing its effectiveness in the South.

If you have problems with potato beetles, use whatever combination of these techniques seems logical and appropriate for your situation. See "Integrated Pest Management" in chapter 2 for more information on insect control.

**Harvest and Yield:** Potatoes are ready to be dug when the leaves die back. If you can't bear to wait that long, after blooms appear, carefully dig down with your fingers and steal a few "new" potatoes from your plants without disturbing the remainder of the crop. Take only a couple of newbies from each of your plants. Once potatoes mature, the yield is typically 1 pound per square foot of growing area, or slightly more. This works out to about 5 to 8 pounds of potatoes from every pound planted. My own experimentation indicates that variation among different varieties grown together is about twofold; that is, some produced twice as much harvest weight as others grown under the same conditions. Try several varieties, keep careful records, and identify the best producers for your location.

**Storage and Preservation:** The Incas preserved potatoes by freezing and storing the tubers high in the Andes, but freezing is not the preferred storage method for potatoes in American kitchens. Potatoes frozen without the special treatments given to commercially frozen potato products tend to develop a mushy, unpleasant texture that the Incas apparently did not find objectionable. Pressure canning is an option, but canned potatoes can be used only in recipes calling for boiling. Many varieties of potatoes will keep for a long time under conditions of darkness, cool temperatures, and average humidity. Too much warmth or light promotes sprouting. Too much cold causes some of the starch to be converted into sugar, resulting in an unpleasantly sweet taste. A covered basket on a cold porch or in the garage gives the best results. Select potato varieties known for their keeping qualities.

**Uses:** Potatoes that have become sweet from cold storage can sometimes be remedied by moving them to a warmer spot in the dark. After a week or so, taste a sample. Soaking cut potatoes in several changes of cold water will also reduce the sugar content.

Potato dishes range from simple baked or boiled potatoes to elaborate casseroles like shepherd's pie. New potatoes are especially tasty when steamed until just tender and served with butter and parsley. Blue potato varieties usually roast well. Toss small ones or cut-up pieces of larger ones with olive oil, salt, pepper, and a generous sprinkling of chopped fresh rosemary. Roast in a shallow pan at 400°F until tender and lightly browned. Because potatoes and baby leeks are in season at the same time, they combine perfectly in this classic potato soup made easy with a food processor.

## Food Processor Vichyssoise

1 pound potatoes, peeled (I use Russian Banana)
3 baby leeks
½ cup sour cream
½ cup chicken stock (I use Swanson's low sodium)
¼ teaspoon ground white pepper
Kosher salt
¼ cup finely chopped parsley

Place the potatoes in just enough water to cover, bring to a boil, and cook for 5 minutes. Add the chopped leeks, reduce the heat, and simmer until the potatoes are tender. Remove from the heat and allow to cool. Transfer the potatoes and leeks to a food processor and purée. Add the sour cream, chicken stock, white pepper, and salt. Process to combine. Thin with a little more chicken stock if needed. Transfer to a covered container and chill for at least 2 hours. Top each serving with a sprinkling of parsley.

## Tomatoes

Nearly everyone loves tomatoes, and gardeners all over the United States can grow them. Properly staked and cared for, indeterminate tomatoes will be the most productive plants in your garden. I've grown both local heirlooms like Cherokee Purple and modern hybrids like Celebrity with excellent results. Heirloom tomato flavors are truly outstanding, but they typically are regionally adapted. You will need to do some research to find the best ones for your location, or experiment for a couple of seasons to identify them yourself. Hybrid tomatoes, which are widely available from garden centers, are easier to grow than heirlooms. Hybrids taste just fine, but the flavor of most can't compare with the best heirloom types. Home-canned tomatoes are not much work, and the result is superior to grocery products.

**Culture:** Growing good tomatoes requires an understanding of their two growth forms: determinate and indeterminate. *Determinate* tomatoes reach a mature size and then bear most of their fruit all at once. They are typically compact plants good for small spaces but do not give a harvest over a long season. Because of this reason, they are a good choice if you plan on canning. *Indeterminate* tomatoes do not stop growing. They must be supported and pruned to be maximally productive. However, they bear over a long season and include a wider range of varieties. Virtually all heirloom tomatoes are indeterminate.

All tomatoes are subject to a host of diseases and conditions that can be controlled to some degree by good culture technique and wise selection of cultivars. Different varieties have different degrees of resistance to disease. This is another reason to grow the varieties best adapted to your area. Consult the Internet, other gardeners, or the folks at the garden center for suggestions.

**Starting and Transplanting:** Start seeds in cell trays and transplant to the garden when they are about 6 inches tall or larger. Germinate seeds at about 80°F, and then transplant to 3-inch pots when two sets of true leaves are present. If you keep daytime temperatures at 80°F and nights at 60°F, you will get the best growth and earliest fruit production. Gentle air movement supplied by an oscillating fan will help produce stocky plants with sturdy stems. Water the young plants sparingly, but do not allow them to wilt. Wait until the soil temperature is 65°F before transplanting them into the garden. Harden off plants as described on page 47.

When you are ready to plant, remove all but the top third of the leaves and bury the stem almost up to the lowermost set of remaining leaves. I mix a quart or two of composted cow manure into the soil in the hole just before planting. Water daily for the first week to encourage the establishment of a strong root system, and then switch to normal irrigation.

**Watering and Mulching:** Uneven watering causes fruit to split in hot weather. Some varieties, such as Green Zebra, are crack resistant. Others, such as Black Krim, are especially prone to this problem. "Boom-and-bust" watering can also lead to blossom-end rot, a condition resulting from the plant's inability to take up calcium from the soil. The fruit tip opposite the stem begins to turn brown and watery. This progresses until the entire fruit is ruined. Any variety of tomato can be affected. Be careful with irrigation and apply a deep mulch. Mulch also helps to prevent soil from reaching the lower leaves, reducing the chances for fungal infections. I prefer natural mulch, such as straw or pine needles, but many gardeners swear by plastic sheeting. The plastic helps warm the soil, allowing a somewhat earlier planting than otherwise. Black plastic is most often used to optimize the heating effect, but red plastic has been shown to increase productivity.

**Staking and Pruning:** Determinate tomatoes should be tied to a sturdy stake or confined to a cage, although some are stocky enough to support themselves. Indeterminate varieties always need staking. Use an 8-foot stake sunk at least 18 inches into the ground. Start tying the plant to the stake when the first blooms appear. Use strips of cloth or special soft twist ties to avoid damaging the stems.

> Indeterminate and many determinate tomatoes grown in containers should be supported with a stake sunk into the ground outside the container. Otherwise, the whole thing can tip over. Surrounding the plant with a cage and then securing the cage to a ground stake makes the most sense.

Some gardeners prefer to sucker their tomatoes. Both determinate and indeterminate types can benefit from this pruning, especially where summers are relatively mild. Examine the point at which each leaf emerges from the main stalk. You should see a small side shoot, or sucker, beginning to grow from this spot. Completely remove all suckers up to the first bloom cluster. These can be rooted in a glass of water for eventual planting out as a late crop. As the plant grows, continue tying it to the stake at intervals of about 1 foot. Loop the tie around the stem just under a large leaf for maximum support. Suckers will appear at every leaf node. Remove all but the bottom pair of leaves from each sucker. Doing so prevents the sucker from taking energy that would otherwise go to fruit production, while maintaining good leaf cover that helps prevent the fruits from being damaged by hot sunshine. In the South, most growers skip suckering to prevent sunscald. Better to have fewer perfect fruits than a lot of sunburned ones!

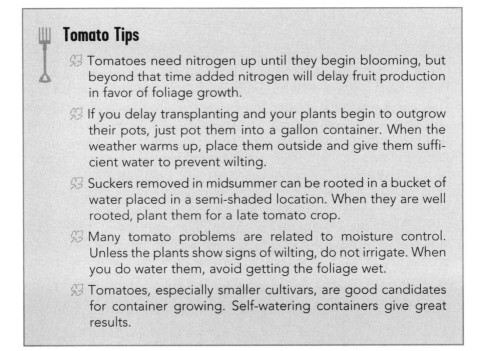

## Tomato Tips

- Tomatoes need nitrogen up until they begin blooming, but beyond that time added nitrogen will delay fruit production in favor of foliage growth.

- If you delay transplanting and your plants begin to outgrow their pots, just pot them into a gallon container. When the weather warms up, place them outside and give them sufficient water to prevent wilting.

- Suckers removed in midsummer can be rooted in a bucket of water placed in a semi-shaded location. When they are well rooted, plant them for a late tomato crop.

- Many tomato problems are related to moisture control. Unless the plants show signs of wilting, do not irrigate. When you do water them, avoid getting the foliage wet.

- Tomatoes, especially smaller cultivars, are good candidates for container growing. Self-watering containers give great results.

Instead of suckering, remove any bloom clusters that form on suckers, and allow the leaves to grow.

**Harvest and Yield:** Days to maturity found on seed packets or in catalogs indicate the time from transplant to first harvest. The best harvest usually comes about two weeks later on indeterminate tomatoes. Harvest tomatoes at varying stages of ripeness, depending on your needs. Green tomatoes as hard as baseballs are preferred for frying. For canning, red, ripe fruits that are still firm work best. For fresh eating, wait until the fruits are fully ripened and feel slightly soft when you squeeze them.

Although yield varies with growing conditions and plant genetics, you can expect 20 pounds of fruit from a well-grown indeterminate plant.

**Storage and Preservation:** Some varieties of tomatoes keep well at cool room temperature for weeks after they are picked. Firm, unblemished fruits should be wiped clean with a cloth and placed in an airy location that does not get too cold. Refrigeration below 50°F will destroy the garden-fresh flavor, so do not store raw whole tomatoes in your refrigerator.

Canning is the traditional method for preserving homegrown tomatoes. Instructions appear on page 240. Tomatoes can be frozen, too; just drop them in plastic bags and freeze. When thawed, the skins will slip off easily, and you can use the pulp in soups, stews, or spaghetti sauce.

Tomatoes with low moisture content, such as Roma, lend themselves to sauce making and can also be dried. Tomato cultivars developed specifically for drying are readily available.

Green tomatoes can be turned into delicious pickles. See the recipe on page 249.

**Uses:** Here are a couple of recipes that illustrate the vast array of dishes in which tomatoes can play a starring role.

## Uncooked Tomato Sauce for Pasta

1 pound garden-fresh tomatoes, cut into bite-sized chunks
½ pound fresh mozzarella cheese, cut into bite-sized pieces
1 handful fresh basil, torn into small pieces
1 handful fresh parsley, minced
¼ cup extra-virgin olive oil
1 tablespoon red wine vinegar or fresh lemon juice
1 clove garlic, minced
Salt and freshly ground black pepper
Freshly grated Parmigiano-Reggiano cheese
½ pound dry pasta (any variety)

Bring a large pot of water to a rolling boil. Combine all the ingredients except the pasta in a large bowl. Add the pasta to the boiling water and cook at a rapid simmer until the pasta is al dente. The exact time depends on the pasta but is usually 8 to 10 minutes. When the pasta is done, drain it in a colander. Add the drained pasta to the sauce in the bowl immediately, stirring to combine. The heat from the pasta should begin to melt the cheese. Serve immediately.

# Fried Green Tomato Napoleons with Green Sauce

For two servings

2 green tomatoes, each about the size of a baseball
Salt and freshly ground black pepper
4 tablespoons canola oil
Cornbread mix for dredging
2 ounces fresh goat cheese
2 handfuls fresh field greens, washed well and spun dry
Green Dressing (recipe follows)
Sriracha or other hot sauce (optional)

Slice the tomatoes into uniform slices about ⅜ inch thick, discarding the end pieces. You should have six slices. Spread the slices on a plate or tray and sprinkle lightly with salt and a few grinds of black pepper. Heat the oil in a large, heavy skillet until its surface ripples. Dip the tomato slices in the cornbread mix, coating them well on both sides. Shake off the excess and fry in batches in the hot oil until golden, turning once, about 4 minutes per side. Transfer the cooked tomatoes to a rack set over paper towels and keep warm.

When all of the tomatoes are cooked, assemble the dish on two plates. Place a tomato slice in the center of the plate, top with a tablespoon of goat cheese, and a second tomato slice. Repeat with the remaining cheese and tomatoes. Surround the tomato napoleons with field greens and drizzle the green dressing over all. Spice it up with Sriracha sauce if desired.

# Green Dressing

12 leaves mizuna or other mild mustard greens
2 large stalks fresh cilantro
2 large sprigs fresh parsley
1 large clove garlic, peeled
1 tablespoon extra-virgin olive oil
1 teaspoon red wine vinegar
½ teaspoon salt
Freshly ground black pepper

Bring a pot of water to a boil. Holding the mizuna, cilantro, and parsley by the stems like a bouquet of flowers, immerse the leaves in the boiling water for 30 seconds. Remove and plunge into a bowl of ice water. Drain well. Cut off the unblanched portion of the stems and discard. Squeeze the greens dry in your hand, and transfer them to a blender jar. Add the remaining ingredients and blend until you have a uniform dressing. Serve immediately.

# 4

# Vegetables: Part Two

I n chapter 3, I discussed the vegetable crops that are most likely to provide even a novice gardener with an abundant harvest over the entire growing season. In this chapter, we will look at the many other vegetables that can be included in your homestead food garden.

## Cool-Season and Warm-Season Crops

Vegetables can be classified as cool-season crops or warm-season crops. Where summers are hot and humid, cool-season crops can be grown in both spring and fall. Where winters are mild, some of them grow well during that season. Many are adapted to overwintering under cover, even in the harshest climates. Here is a list of the common cool-season families:

- **Cabbage Family:** arugula, broccoli, Brussels sprouts, cabbage, cauliflower, collards, kale, kohlrabi, mustard, radish, rutabaga, turnip, upland cress, watercress
- **Carrot Family:** celery, celery root, fennel, parsnips, and salsify
- **Daisy Family:** lettuces
- **Goosefoot Family:** beets, spinach, and Swiss chard

Garden vegetables that must be grown in warm soil comprise the warm-season crops. Most also require fertile soil, and all need plenty of water to thrive. Here is a list of the common warm-season families:

- 🌿 **Grass Family:** corn
- 🌿 **Hibiscus Family:** okra
- 🌿 **Morning Glory Family:** sweet potatoes
- 🌿 **Squash Family**: cucumbers, summer squash, winter squash

Two families with both cool-season and warm-season members are

- 🌿 **Pea Family:** peas, fava beans (cool), green beans, soybeans, lima beans and Southern peas (warm)
- 🌿 **Potato Family:** potatoes (cool), eggplant, peppers, tomatoes (warm)

> Various types of leafy greens belong to an assortment of families. Miner's lettuce, for example, is mostly a cool-season crop. A few greens are warm-season crops, such as Malabar (Basellaceae) and New Zealand (Aizoaceae) "spinach," neither of which is related to spinach.

# The Cabbage Family

Members of the cabbage family, Brassicaceae, are often referred to as "brassicas" in gardening reference books. The vegetables in this cool-season family are arugula, broccoli, Brussels sprouts, cabbage, cauliflower, Chinese cabbage, collards, kale, kohlrabi, mustards, radishes, rutabaga, turnips, upland cress, and watercress. Surprisingly few botanical species are represented by this multitude of crops, testifying to the vast genetic diversity in the family and the power of human's selective breeding over the centuries.

## Arugula

Arugula, known also as the "peanut butter plant" or roquette, needs only a few weeks from seed to harvest. Botanically *Euruca sativa*, this green crop should be sown successively, beginning as soon as the soil can be worked in spring. It also makes a fine winter crop for a cold frame. The variety Even Star Winter withstands cold down to 6°F. Sow seeds ¼ inch deep in average garden soil with plenty of organic matter. Harvest when plants are about 3 inches tall. Hot weather will result in a harsh, bitter flavor. Arugula can also be added to pesto or steamed. Arugula has been famously associated with upscale dining since President Obama campaigned in Iowa.

## Broccoli

One of the most nutritious brassicas, broccoli (*Brassica oleracea var. botrytis*) has been dubbed a "super food" because of its many beneficial effects on human health. Broccoli heads, which are actually the flowers, must mature while the weather is cool or else they may become tough and bitter. In hot summer areas it is best as a fall crop. In the Deep South, broccoli can be grown as a winter vegetable. In cool-summer areas, gardeners can produce two crops per year. Besides the familiar heading-broccoli varieties, you can grow sprouting broccoli, broccoli raab, or "broccolini," (*Brassica oleracea var. italica*), which has a slightly more bitter flavor. The flowers of this variety never form large, tight heads, however, the plants are cold tolerant (6°F) and can be overwintered for the earliest possible spring harvest.

**Culture:** Each broccoli plant requires about 4 square feet of growing space. If the plants suffer stress at any point from seed to flower, the yield and quality of the crop is likely to be severely impaired. Commercial growers therefore start their own plants from seed, to ensure they have been properly cared for. If possible, do the same, although broccoli plants are widely available in spring from garden centers.

Seeds germinate best at 75°F. For easiest handling, sow three seeds in each of several 3-inch pots, covering them with ¼ inch of potting mix. Water well and keep evenly moist throughout the development of the seedlings. Provide as much light as possible. I use a south-facing window supplemented with four 40-watt fluorescent lamps in two "shop light" fixtures. The broccoli seedlings would be happy with even more light. Do not allow seedlings to become stunted. When most of the seeds have germinated, select the best one in each pot and cut the others off at ground level with scissors. At this point, the growing temperature can be cooler, 60°F. Use a small fan to maintain good air circulation and to promote stocky stem growth.

Transplant to the garden about sixty days before you expect to harvest, when the seedlings have several sets of leaves. Space plants on 12-inch centers in raised beds or in rows 18 inches apart. Side dress with cottonseed meal when the plants are a foot tall. Apply a deep mulch of compost or other organic material to protect the shallow roots from heat and to conserve moisture. Irrigate as needed to keep the soil evenly moist but not soggy. Fall crops should be started about three months before the first hard freeze. Broccoli will grow at 40°F, but really cold temperatures during development may produce undersized heads. Again, for best results, timing is everything.

Infestation by the cabbage butterfly, although controllable with Bt, if overlooked will render the crop unusable. Other problems may include aphids, which can be controlled with regular sprayings of insecticidal soap, flea beetles, slugs, and cutworms. Use neem oil or pyrethrum for flea beetles, trap slugs or install a copper barrier, and shield the lower 2 inches of the stem of new transplants with a strip of paper or aluminum foil to thwart cutworms.

**Harvest and Yield:** Cut the main head while it remains tight, dark green, and without a trace of yellow. If you wait too long to harvest, the plants will be bitter. Many varieties of broccoli produce side shoots after the main head is removed, increasing the yield. Expect well-grown plants to give you 2 to 4 pounds of broccoli.

**Storage and Preservation:** Freshly harvested broccoli will keep about a week under refrigeration in a plastic bag. To freeze, cut the heads into pieces that suit your needs and wash well in salted water to remove any small insects that might be hiding. Drop the pieces into rapidly boiling water and blanch. Three minutes is an appropriate time if the broccoli has been separated into florets. Larger pieces should be blanched for 4 minutes. Start timing when the water returns to a boil. Drain well, plunge into a sink full of cold water, and drain thoroughly before packing into freezer bags or containers.

**Uses:** Broccoli can be steamed, boiled, fried, roasted, or baked, and it works well on its own as a side dish or as a secondary player in casseroles, pasta, and stir-fries. Thaw frozen broccoli before proceeding with a recipe, if substituting for fresh, and reduce the cooking time by half. Here are two recipes where broccoli is the main ingredient. The Jade Green stir-fry dish was the first Asian-style dish I ever made, and I continue to enjoy it whenever fresh local broccoli is available.

## Broccoli Steamed with Bay Leaves

For two servings

1 pound trimmed broccoli stalks with florets
3 large bay leaves
3 tablespoons butter
½ teaspoon salt
Freshly ground black pepper

Bring water to a boil in a saucepan that will hold the broccoli in one layer. Add all ingredients, reduce the heat and simmer slowly, covered, for 10 minutes, turning the broccoli once. Remove the broccoli from the pan with tongs, place on a plate, and keep warm. Discard the bay leaves. Raise the temperature and reduce the pan liquid to 3 tablespoons. Serve the broccoli drizzled with the pan sauce.

## Jade Green Broccoli

For two servings

1 teaspoon sugar
1 tablespoon cornstarch
1½ tablespoons soy sauce
2 tablespoons vegetable oil
1 pinch salt
1 clove garlic, minced
1 pound fresh broccoli, in bite size pieces
2 tablespoons dry sherry

Combine the sugar, cornstarch, soy sauce, and ½ cup water in a small bowl and set aside. Heat a wok or skillet until it is hot and add the oil and salt. Reduce the heat, add the garlic, then the broccoli, and stir-fry for 2 minutes. Add the sherry and cover the pan. Cook an additional 2 minutes. Uncover, add the sauce ingredients, and stir until the sauce thickens. Serve immediately over rice or noodles.

---

## Brussels Sprouts

A cool-season crop that allows multiple pickings seems ideal for the back-yard homesteader, and Brussels sprouts (*Brassica oleracea var. gemmifera*) fit the bill. Warm weather when the sprouts are maturing makes them bitter. Plants are hardy to 0°F and frost improves their flavor. Therefore, grow Brussels sprouts as a fall or winter crop. Some varieties have been selected for overwintering, for the longest possible harvest period.

**Culture:** For fall planting, sow seeds about 120 days before the first hard freeze is expected. Follow the cultural instructions for broccoli.

**Harvest and Yield:** Brussels sprouts can be forced to yield all of their crop at once by topping the plants when the lowermost sprouts reach ¾ inch in diameter. This is a good idea when you want to freeze most of your product. For a longer harvest, remove the leaf at the base when each sprout reaches ½ inch in diameter. Harvest sprouts when they are an inch in diameter.

**Storage and Preservation:** Brussels sprouts removed from the plant will keep about a week in a plastic bag in the refrigerator. Pull plants from the garden by the roots, remove all but the top three or four leaves, and set them upright in a bucket or box in an unheated garage or root cellar. They will keep this way about a month. To freeze, wash and trim the sprouts and sort them by size. Those that are ¾ inch or less should be blanched for 3 minutes, while 1-inch specimens will require four minutes. After blanching, plunge into cold water and drain well before packing into freezer containers.

**Uses:** Brussels sprouts are particularly good with cream sauces, but they lend themselves to a variety of preparation techniques. Try them steamed, then tossed with olive oil, fresh thyme leaves, and halved green seedless grapes, lightly seasoned with salt and pepper.

## Cabbage

From sauerkraut to coleslaw, people all over the world eat *Brassica oleracea var. capitata.* Heat-tolerant cultivars exist, but generally speaking cabbage is a cool-weather plant. Compared with its relatives, broccoli and cauliflower, cabbage is easy to grow. It needs protection from slugs, cabbage butterflies, and drought. Red leaf varieties and Savoy cabbage, in which the leaves are strongly crinkled, both grow like regular cabbage.

**Culture:** Like other brassicas, cabbage requires fertile, moist, and well-drained soil. Raised beds work best. Each plant should be allocated 4 square feet, achieved by spacing them 12 inches in each direction. Follow the cultural instructions given for broccoli. Early-maturing cabbage, best for spring production, usually needs about sixty-five days from transplanting. Late cabbage, requiring ninety or more days, is best for fall planting where summers are hot. Prevent cabbage from bolting by keeping the soil cool with a deep organic mulch. Maintain adequate moisture. Uneven watering may cause heads to split.

**Harvest and Yield:** Harvest when the head has reached a size appropriate for the variety. This can vary from 2 pounds for compact, early varieties to over 10 pounds for larger, late-maturing types.

**Storage and Preservation:** As a rule, late-maturing cabbages are the best keepers. Freshly harvested cabbage will keep at least a month under root cellar conditions. Cabbage can also be frozen as wedges or shreds. Blanch wedges three minutes and shreds half that time. Plunge into cold water and drain thoroughly before packing into freezer containers. See chapter 8, which discusses fermented foods, for instructions for making sauerkraut, a classic way to preserve fresh cabbage all winter.

**Uses:** Undoubtedly the most popular raw cabbage dish is coleslaw. Shredded cabbage can also be added to Asian stir-fry dishes. It is a major component of *mu shu* recipes, for example. One of the best ways to preserve cabbage is to can it as chow-chow relish.

## Chow Chow

Makes about 6 pints

7 cups chopped cabbage
2 cups chopped green tomatoes
2 cups chopped onions
2 cups chopped green bell peppers
1 cup chopped red bell pepper
3 tablespoons pickling salt
2½ cups cider vinegar
1½ cups sugar
2 teaspoons celery seed
2 teaspoons dry mustard
1 teaspoon whole yellow mustard seed
1 teaspoon ground turmeric
½ teaspoon ground ginger

Combine the vegetables with the pickling salt in a large bowl. Refrigerate for 12 hours. Transfer the mixture to a colander and allow to drain in the refrigerator for 8 hours. In a large stockpot, combine the vinegar, sugar, and seasonings. Bring to a boil, reduce the heat, and simmer for 10 minutes. Add the drained vegetables, stir well, and simmer for an additional 10 minutes. Pack into pint or half-pint jars and process for 10 minutes in a boiling water bath. (See the complete instructions for canning pickles and relishes on page 247.)

## Cauliflower

Cauliflower (*Brassica oleracea var. botrytis*) often presents real challenges to gardeners outside cool summer regions. In the hot, humid South, or the arid Southwest, bringing in a decent crop of cauliflower requires both good timing and good luck. Everything previously mentioned about growing broccoli without stress applies doubly to cauliflower.

**Culture:** Follow the instructions given for broccoli. Pay attention to suppliers' recommendations for different cultivars. Some are better for spring sowing, others for a fall crop. Maturity time is the same as for broccoli, about sixty to ninety days from transplanting. Heirloom types will need to have the outer leaves tied up over the forming head to keep it white. Modern selections, described as "self-blanching" in catalogs, do not require this step.

**Harvest and Yield:** Harvest when the heads are tight and pure white. To prevent mold from forming, avoid harvesting when the heads are wet. Well-grown plants should yield a head weighing about 2 pounds.

**Storage and Preservation:** Cauliflower only keeps a few days under refrigeration. Dark spots are a sure sign it's time to use it or compost it. Freezing is the best method of preservation. Follow the instructions for freezing broccoli florets. After blanching, spread the pieces of drained, cooled cauliflower on wax paper on a baking sheet and freeze overnight. The next day, transfer the individually frozen pieces to a resealable freezer bag. You can then dump out as much as you need and keep the rest frozen.

**Uses:** Cauliflower can be steamed, baked, fried, or roasted, and can stand on its own with a light dressing or cream sauce, or be added to a mixed vegetable dish. Simple preparations seem to suit it best.

## GRATIN OF CAULIFLOWER

For two servings

1 tablespoon unsalted butter
2 cups cauliflower florets, thawed if frozen, steamed 5 minutes if fresh
½ cup chicken broth
¼ teaspoon dried thyme leaves, or ½ teaspoon fresh leaves
Salt and freshly ground black pepper
2 tablespoons fine dried breadcrumbs
2 tablespoons shredded Parmigiano-Reggiano cheese

Preheat the oven to 350°F. Butter a shallow gratin dish large enough to hold the cauliflower in one layer. Arrange the florets in the bottom of the dish. Pour the chicken broth over them and sprinkle with the thyme, salt, and pepper. Place the dish in the oven and bake for 15 minutes, or until most of the liquid has evaporated and the cauliflower is fork tender. Combine the breadcrumbs and cheese in a small bowl. Remove the dish from the oven, sprinkle the top with the crumb mixture. Turn on the broiler and broil the gratin until the top is lightly browned, about 2 minutes.

## Chinese Cabbage

The Chinese have been cultivating *Brassica campestris* since at least the fifth century. Numerous forms exist, variously called Chinese cabbage, celery cabbage, bok choy, Napa cabbage, and several less common names.

**Culture:** All the Chinese brassicas do best in fall, because the lengthening days of spring will promote bolting. In mild winter areas, production can continue all winter long. Compact varieties are suited to cultivation under cover. Conditions for growth are the same as described for broccoli. Fast maturing varieties can be direct seeded, while those that require longer growing time can be started in containers in late summer for transplanting in early fall. Space plants from 6 to 12 inches apart, depending on the mature size of the cultivar you are growing.

**Harvest and Yield:** Cut the entire plant at soil level when it reaches mature size for its type. Remove and discard the outer leaves and wash the heads well in cold water. Yields will range from a few ounces per plant in the case of miniature bok choy to 5 or 6 pounds for a large head of Napa cabbage.

**Storage and Preservation:** Drain washed heads well and store for a week or more in the refrigerator. Use a perforated plastic bag for best results. Some cultivars, in particular Napa types, will keep a long time under root cellar conditions.

**Uses:** The classic method of preserving Napa cabbage produces *kimchee*, a fermented dish similar to sauerkraut. Instructions for making it are presented in the section of chapter 8 on fermented foods.

Bok choy and other types of Chinese cabbage make delicious additions to stir-fry dishes, or can substitute for cabbage or celery in Western recipes. My favorite type of Chinese cabbage is the bok choy cultivar Mei Quing. It forms perfect miniature heads about 6 by 2 inches, and grows to perfection under a plastic row cover in early winter. The recipe that follows was inspired by a recipe created by renowned chef Charlie Trotter.

## Types of Chinese Cabbage

Basically, there are two types of Chinese cabbage: heading (*B. campestris* var. *pekinensis*) and nonheading (*B. campestris* var. *chinensis*). The heading types, collectively known as *pe-tsai*, can be further subdivided into *chihili* and *che foo* groups. Members of the chihili group are identified as Chinese cabbage in grocery stores, while the che foo group goes under the name "Napa cabbage." The nonheading forms produce loose, upright stalks with smaller leaves. They are usually dubbed "bok choy" in the market.

## BABY BOK CHOY IN VEGETABLE HERB BROTH

For two servings

1 cup vegetable stock
4 freshly picked baby bok choy, trimmed
Approximately 2 tablespoons minced fresh cool season herbs, such as chervil, cilantro, oregano, parsley, thyme or a combination, plus more for the garnish
Salt and freshly ground black pepper

Bring the stock to a simmer and add the bok choy and 1 tablespoon of the herbs. Sprinkle with salt and a little pepper. Steam until a fork can be easily inserted into the base of the bok choy, about 10 minutes. Taste and add the remaining the seasonings if necessary. Serve the bok choy in bowls, ladling the broth over. Garnish with the herbs if desired.

---

## Collards

A staple of Southern gardens for generations, collards (*Brassica oleracea var. acephala*) differs from its relatives in that it tolerates heat. Nevertheless, its best flavor develops in cooler weather, so collards are well suited for fall and winter production, just like other brassicas.

**Culture:** In general, follow the growing instructions given for broccoli. Direct seed about ninety days before the first fall frost, or start transplants in late winter for spring production. Cool weather improves the flavor and quality, while hot weather has the opposite effect.

**Harvest and Yield:** Harvest individual leaves as you need them. Flavor and quality are best when the leaves are under a foot in length.

**Storage and Preservation:** Freshly picked collards should be rinsed in cold water and drained thoroughly, and will keep under refrigeration for about a week. To freeze them for cooked greens, tie a bundle of stems together with cotton kitchen string and immerse them, stems up, in a kettle of boiling water for two minutes. Remove, rinse under cold water, and drain well. Cut off the uncooked portion and discard. Pack the cooked leaves in freezer containers.

**Uses:** Freshly picked tender, young collard greens can be added to salads. Mature leaves are best cooked.

## Southern Style Collard Greens

For two servings

3 strips thick-cut bacon
1 big bunch collard greens, woody stems removed and the leaves cut into ribbons
1 cup water or light stock
Salt and freshly ground black pepper
Cider vinegar for serving

Cook the bacon slowly in a saucepan until most of the fat has been rendered and the bacon is crisp. Remove with a slotted spoon to a plate lined with paper towels and reserve. Heat the bacon fat until it is almost smoking, add the collards, and sauté. Adjust the heat as needed to prevent burning. When the collards are wilted, add the stock and salt and pepper to taste. Cover the saucepan and cook until the collards are very tender, about 45 minutes. Uncover and allow the liquid to evaporate somewhat. Serve the collards slightly drained. Pass cider vinegar so diners can add as much as they like.

This dish is traditionally served with cornbread to soak up the delicious juices, or "pot liquor."

---

## Kale

Like collards, kale, which is the same species and variety, is best eaten cooked. The leaves are generally too tough, even when young, for use in salad. A closely related species, *Brassica napus*, or Russian kale, is notable for its colorful foliage.

**Culture:** Culture of kale is similar to the other members of the cabbage family. Direct seed or transplant for early spring or fall and winter harvest. Read catalog descriptions and choose the variety bred for the season you intend to grow it, as there are spring, fall, and overwintering cultivars.

**Harvest and Yield:** Kale can be harvested at any time after the plants have enough leaves to withstand cutting. Like collards, cold improves its flavor, and some varieties can be harvested from underneath snow cover.

**Storage and Preservation:** Freshly harvested kale should be washed, thoroughly drained, and stored under refrigeration, where it will keep a week or more. It can be frozen as described for collards.

**Uses:** Kale can substitute for collards in the Southern-style greens dish described earlier, but it is also delicious when fried in olive oil with garlic and tossed with pasta and cheese. One of my favorite ways to use it is in this hearty stew originally from the Iberian peninsula.

## Caldo Verde

For two servings

¼ pound fresh kale
¼ cup Spanish olive oil, or any good olive oil
2 ounces garlic-seasoned smoked pork sausage, such as Spanish chorizo, andouille, or kielbasa
2 medium-size potatoes
1 teaspoon salt
Freshly ground black pepper

Wash, trim, and finely shred the kale and set aside in a saucepan containing the olive oil. Slice the sausage into rounds about ¼ inch thick. Film a skillet with a little oil and fry the sausage pieces until lightly browned. With a slotted spoon, transfer the sausages to paper towels to drain. Reserve.

Peel the potatoes and cut them into chunks. In a large saucepan, combine 3 cups water, salt, and potatoes. Bring to a boil and simmer until the potatoes are very tender, about 15 minutes. Remove the potatoes with a slotted spoon, reserving the liquid in the pan. Transfer the potatoes to a bowl and mash with a fork, leaving a few chunks.

Move the potatoes to the saucepan containing the kale and olive oil; add a few grinds of pepper. Bring to a boil and simmer for 3 minutes. Thin, if necessary, with some of the reserved potato cooking liquid. Add the reserved sausage and continue to cook just until heated through. Serve the *caldo verde* with a crusty country-style bread.

---

## Kohlrabi

Also known as cabbage turnip, kohlrabi (*Brassica oleracea var. gongy-lodes*) forms a bulbous stem at the base of its rosette of leaves. While the leaves can be harvested and eaten like cabbage, it's the swollen, sweet basal bulb you're after.

**Culture:** Both early and late varieties of kohlrabi are available, with maturity dates from direct seeding ranging from sixty days to more than twice that long. Sow ¼ inch deep and thin to stand 6 to 12 inches apart each way, depending on the mature size expected. Culture is the same as for broccoli.

**Harvest and Yield:** Long-maturing forms can be planted in late summer and left in the ground for harvest all winter, especially if grown in a solar greenhouse or large cold frame. Early varieties are better suited to spring planting. Purple forms mature more slowly than their pale green counterparts. Harvest at the size you desire.

**Storage and Preservation:** Kohlrabi stores well under root cellar conditions. It can also be chopped, blanched, and frozen as described for cauliflower.

**Uses:** Kohlrabi has a savory, nutlike flavor. Try substituting it for cauliflower in the gratin recipe given earlier. Shredded, it makes great coleslaw.


## Mustards

Several varieties of *Brassica rapa* are cultivated for their spicy greens. Culture requirements are the same as for cabbage, although mustards are generally direct seeded. Cover seeds with ¼ inch of fine soil, and keep well watered. Thin to stand 6 to 8 inches apart. Harvest when small for salads, or allow to mature for cooked greens. The flavor of this group of plants varies from mild to pungent, depending on the variety and degree of maturation. Read catalog descriptions carefully. Most cultivars mature in around forty days, and are ideal for either spring or fall growing. Many are hardy enough to be overwintered under plastic. Warmer weather will result in harsh flavors and toughness.

**Bekana:** This species, *Brassica juncea*, is mild enough for salads even when mature.

**Mizuna** (*Brassica rapa japonica*) is an Asian mustard green that offers the distinct advantage of multiple harvests from a single planting. The tartly flavored, ragged leaves can be cut three or more times. It grows in any reasonable garden soil during cool weather, and will be ready a mere three to four weeks from sowing. Flea beetles can be a problem when the weather is too warm and dry. Grow under a floating row cover and keep well-irrigated to foil the tiny pests.

**Mustard:** These greens (*Brassica rapa*) often have brilliant red coloration. Sow seeds ¼ inch deep in early spring or late summer. Thin to 8 inches apart and keep well watered. Some varieties may be too strongly flavored to eat raw, but steaming renders them milder. Cold-tolerant types can be overwintered under cover.

**Tatsoi** (*Brassica rapa narinosa*) produces rosettes of dark green, spoon-shaped leaves. Tolerant of cold and shading, it should be grown as described for mizuna. It adds a mustardy tartness to salad mixes, and can also be stir-fried or steamed.

## Radish

The radish (*Raphanus sativus*) is one of the easiest spring vegetables to grow, and matures a crop in about a month from sowing. Besides the round, red varieties commonly seen, there are elongated forms and colors ranging from white to purple. Certain radish cultivars are intended for fall growing for winter storage only, while others grow well in both spring and fall. The Japanese daikon (*R. sativus var. longipinnatus*) grows over a foot long, but most radishes are harvested at a much smaller size.

**Culture:** An ideal choice for growing in limited space, radishes can be succession planted for multiple crops throughout the cool parts of the season. They demand only loose, well-drained soil of average fertility for their expanding roots. Elongated forms must have deep, loose soil similar to that required by carrots.

**Harvest and Yield:** Pull whole plants when the roots reach ¾ inch in diameter, if you are growing round types. Elongated forms are best when about 4 inches long. Daikon and other winter storage radishes should be harvested when they reach the anticipated size for the variety.

**Storage and Preservation:** Fresh red radishes can be kept in the refrigerator for at least a week. Wash well, remove the tops and roots, and store them in plastic bags. Winter storage types should be harvested before a hard frost, and stored under root cellar conditions. Radishes of all types can be pickled.

**Uses:** Try French Breakfast, which produces a pink and white, watermelon-shaped root about an inch and a half in length. Slice the roots thinly and place on buttered bread with a little salt. Try roasting whole radishes with other root vegetables.

## Turnips

Turnips (*Brassica rapa var. rapifera*) grow like radishes but need more space to develop their tennis-ball-size roots. Some turnip cultivars have purple shoulders on the roots, while others produce a pure white crop. Plants removed by thinning can be used for cooked greens, and some cultivars, such as Seven Top, are intended for the production of tops alone. Baby turnips can be pulled when the roots are the size of a golf ball.

---

### ⊔ Rutabaga

Also known as Swedish turnip, the rutabaga (*Brassica napus var. napobrassica*) is not as widely appreciated as it should be. It is grown as a fall crop just like turnips. Thin the seedlings before they are thirty days old. Harvest the roots when they are about 4 inches across. Rutabagas require ninety days to mature, and should be dug before the first hard freeze. Rutabagas can be boiled and mashed like turnips or potatoes, and are often added to winter stews that feature beef or game. Trim, peel, and cut into chunks before cooking.

---

**Culture:** Turnips may be planted in spring or late summer. In warmer climate areas, choose a fast maturing variety for spring planting. Warm weather and long days impair the flavor and texture of turnips. Cultivate turnips in well-drained soil that is loose and crumbly. Sow seeds about ¼ inch deep, water well, and thin seedlings to stand 4 inches apart each way. To control flea beetles, keep the bed covered with a floating row cover.

**Harvest and Yield:** Turnip thinnings can be added to salads, and the tops are excellent as cooked greens. Harvest the roots when they are the size you desire, but don't let them get much larger than 2 inches in diameter or the flavor will not be as good.

**Storage and Preservation:** Wash freshly harvested turnips, cut off the tops to within an inch of the shoulder and keep under root cellar conditions. They will keep for weeks. Turnips may be pickled using the same recipes as for pickled radishes. (See the section in chapter 8 on pickling.)

**Uses:** Turnip greens are cooked as described earlier for collard greens. The roots can be boiled, roasted, or baked. Freshly sliced raw turnips make delicious crudités.

## Upland Cress

This terrestrial form of watercress, discussed below, grows in cool weather and with much less moisture than watercress, although it must not be allowed to dry out. In early spring, hydroponically produced clumps of the glossy, bright green leaves appear in my local market. Grow upland cress if you do not want to provide for watercress's moisture needs. It has the same requirements otherwise.

# Watercress

This peppery green has been consumed since ancient times, and is naturalized in many parts of North America. Watercress (*Nasturtium officinale*) should not be confused with the nasturtium flower, which belongs to another botanical family.

**Culture:** Contrary to popular belief, watercress does not require running water to grow. It is normally found growing in streams, but adapts to container culture so long as its needs are met. Hardy to Zone 4, it can be started from seeds or cuttings. Sometimes you will find watercress in the grocery store with small roots still attached. Place these in a glass of water in a sunny spot, and change the water daily until the roots are 2 inches or more in length. Then transplant to a permanent location.

If you have a garden pond with a recirculating pump, you can plant watercress in pots placed at the water's edge, submerged up to the crowns of the plants. Watercress needs clean, slightly alkaline water, and will not thrive if planted in acidic conditions or in water that is stagnant, rich in nutrients, and choked with algae. Use a potting mix composed of sand, gravel, and a small amount of compost, about one fourth of the total volume. Avoid peat- and pine-based components. Thoroughly saturate the mix before planting. Mulch the plants with pea gravel to keep the compost from floating out of the pot.

If you do not have a pond, you can submerge the pots in buckets or tubs. Change the water at least once a week. You can even grow the plants without submerging their roots, but in warm weather, the pots may need watering several times daily. Grown in this fashion, the plants will need regular fertilization due to the frequent flushing of the pots. Commercially produced watercress is often grown hydroponically, which is what the method just described amounts to. When the plants are grown with their roots continuously submerged, they need far less fertilizer, because the water reservoir traps and holds nutrients. Regardless of the method you select, grow watercress in full sun, with afternoon shade in the South.

**Harvest and Yield:** Watercress grows vigorously and should be ready to harvest about two months after sowing seeds, sooner if started from cuttings. Each plant will yield multiple harvests of several stems. In mild winter areas, watercress is evergreen. Despite subfreezing winter weather, watercress thrives in a polluted ditch along my route to work, green leaves emerging from beneath a cover of snow.

## Transplanting Wild Watercress

I have seen cautionary notes urging gardeners to avoid the temptation to transplant watercress found in roadside ditches or otherwise in the wild. So long as you have permission to remove plants from private property, this method of obtaining a start offers more advantages than disadvantages. We were once told that watercress from the roadside would absorb lead and other harmful compounds from automobiles, or that it would be contaminated with bacteria such as *E. coli*. While these are valid reasons not to *harvest* wild watercress for immediate consumption, taking a few plants to start a colony back home poses few risks. Contaminants, if any, will only be present in the small pieces you bring home. New growth will absorb its nutrients from your pristine pond or culture bucket, and will therefore be uncontaminated. As for bacteria, rinse the plants thoroughly in chlorinated tap water before transplanting. Any harmful bacteria will not survive the sunshine and unpolluted environment in your garden.

One benefit of bringing home cuttings from a nearby wild clone is that the plants will already be adapted to climatic conditions prevailing in your area. And of course, if you can secure a few slips from a clear, clean stream by all means do so.

**Storage and Preservation:** Freshly cut watercress keeps just fine sitting in a glass of water on the kitchen counter. It may even root there. As with other greens, however, it is best when eaten fresh from the garden. Compound butter can be made with watercress and frozen, but otherwise the plant is not usually preserved.

**Uses:** Watercress is delicious by itself or in salads, on bread spread with cream cheese, and in soups.

# The Goosefoot Family

This group (Chenopodiaceae) includes two closely related species: spinach and beets. The other member is Swiss chard, a beet grown for its foliage rather than roots.

# Beets

Like other root crops, beets (*Beta vulgaris*) need only modest amounts of nitrogen, and perform best in soil rich in phosphorus. The soil pH is important for beet production. If it is too acid (less than 6.0), adjust by adding limestone in the fall, or add wood ashes to the planting row. Individual beet "seeds" are actually fruits containing four seeds. Thinning, therefore, is always a must. Incorporate the leaves of the removed seedlings into salad mixes, where they will contribute both flavor and color. Besides the traditional red varieties, such as Early Wonder and Detroit Dark Red, you can find yellow beets (Golden, Touchstone Gold Hybrid) and an interesting red-and-white one, Chioggia. When sliced crosswise, Chioggia resembles a target. Like the turnip, some beet varieties are grown just for their greens.

**Culture:** Sow seeds ½ inch deep in a well-prepared bed. Beets do not transplant well and should be sown directly into the garden. Keep the bed well irrigated throughout the growing period. Time your planting so the roots will be ready to harvest before the season heats up. Start about a month before your first frost date, and allow two months for each planting to mature.

**Harvest and Yield:** Baby beets about the size of a golf ball are suitable for use in salad dishes, and more mature ones, tennis ball size, for classic dishes such as borscht and red flannel hash. Harvest beets when they have colored up properly and have reached the size you want. Overgrown specimens are woody and worthless, so it is best to err on the side of early harvest. Beet tops can also be cooked and eaten. In raised beds, thin to space plants 4 inches each way, or nine plants per square foot. Each plant, of course, produces one beet.

**Storage and Preservation:** Beets store well under root cellar conditions, and can be canned or pickled for winter use. Cultivars selected for winter storage are available.

**Uses:** Beets can be eaten raw in salads, boiled, steamed, or roasted. Roasting beets minimizes bleeding and results in the most intense flavor. The tops can be boiled alone or with other greens, added to stir-fries and casseroles, or, if small and tender, to salads. The flavor of beets pairs well with acidic foods such as sour cream and citrus.

## Roasted Beets

Select the number of beets you desire for your recipe. Wash them well, removing any wilted tops and trimming the remaining tops to 1 inch above the crown. Use the tops, if fresh and wholesome looking, in another recipe. Trim off the root tip. Place the prepared beets on a large sheet of aluminum foil and drizzle them with oil, using about 2 teaspoons per beet. Gather the foil up around the beets to completely enclose them and seal tightly. Do not compress the foil around the beets, but rather leave some air space inside the packet. Place the packet directly on the rack of a preheated 400°F oven. Roast for 45 minutes.

Carefully remove the packet from the oven and set aside to cool, undisturbed, for 15 minutes. Open the packet away from your face, in case residual steam remains inside. Using a kitchen towel, rub off the skin from the beets. Trim off the ends with a paring knife. The roasted beets will keep, covered and refrigerated, for a week. They can be sliced and added to a salad plate, pickled for long-term storage, or made into borscht.

---

## Borscht I

It is said that every Russian household has its own recipe for borscht. Here is my own take on this delicious beet soup.

1 medium beet, roasted and diced
1 medium onion, diced
1 carrot, diced
1 medium russet potato, peeled and diced
2 cups vegetable stock
Salt and freshly ground black pepper
½ cup coarsely grated stale bread

Combine the vegetables and stock in a saucepan and bring slowly to a boil. Simmer, partially covered, until the potato is very tender. Taste and season with salt and pepper. Stir in the bread and continue to cook until the soup is thickened. If the soup becomes too thick for your liking, add additional vegetable stock or water. Serve at once or use as the base for the variation that follows.

---

# Borscht II

1 recipe Borscht (see previous recipe)
Salt and freshly ground black pepper
Sour cream
Dill or other fresh herb, finely minced

Cool the soup from the previous recipe to room temperature or refrigerate overnight. Transfer to the jar of a blender and add 1 cup water. Blend until smooth. Cover and chill until very cold. Taste and add salt and pepper as needed.

Serve cold in chilled bowls, topped with a dollop of sour cream and a sprinkling of fresh herbs. Dill goes especially well, but parsley, cilantro, chives, or basil will be fine.

---

## Swiss Chard

Swiss chard is a variety of beets (*Beta vulgaris var. cicla*) selected for foliage and stem production. The plants are highly productive and tolerate frost. They are thus well-suited to backyard production in spring and fall. Varieties have pure white stalks, or may be red, orange, purple, or a combination of colors. The plants provide enough decorative interest to be included in front yard landscaping.

**Culture:** Culture is identical to beets, but the plants should be thinned to stand 6 or more inches apart each way. Swiss chard may also be started in pots and transplanted to the garden when about 3 inches tall. This will produce the earliest harvest. You will harvest over a long season, so the plants need room to keep producing. If grown under plastic, you can harvest all winter long. Keep fertilized with compost or manure tea to provide nitrogen for leaf production.

**Harvest and Yield:** Clip the individual leaves at the base of the plant as you need them. You should be able to harvest several pounds from each plant.

**Storage and Preservation:** Swiss chard may be blanched and frozen. The stems can be pickled like beets. Fresh storage for a few days in the refrigerator is possible, but it is better to harvest as needed.

**Uses:** Add chard to stir-fry dishes, boil with other greens, or incorporate into a casserole. Cooked Swiss chard stems are a classic addition to frittata.

## Swiss Chard Frittata

1 large onion, peeled, halved lengthwise, and sliced into half moons
Salt
¼ cup olive oil
2 cups chopped Swiss chard stems and leaf bases
2 tablespoons unsalted butter
5 eggs
¼ cup grated Parmigiano-Reggiano cheese
Freshly ground black pepper

Put the onion, a big pinch of salt, and olive oil into a 10-inch cast iron skillet and place over low heat. Cover and cook until the onions have wilted and are translucent. Uncover and continue cooking until the onions are golden brown. Add the Swiss chard, stir, and continue cooking until the edges of the chard pieces begin to color. Remove the vegetables with a slotted spoon and transfer them to paper towels to drain and cool. Pour off any oil from the skillet and wipe with a paper towel.

Preheat the broiler. Melt the butter over the lowest possible heat in the skillet. In a large bowl, combine the cooked vegetables, eggs, cheese, and a few grinds of pepper. Mix well, then pour into the skillet. Cook until the bottom is set and the top is runny. Put the skillet under the broiler until the top is set but not browned. Remove from the oven and let sit a few minutes before serving.

## Spinach

Spinach (*Spinacea oleracea*) is an ancient green that likes cool weather. Because it can be used both fresh and cooked, this plant offers plenty of options for spring and fall cropping.

**Culture:** Soil conditions should be the same as for beets and Swiss chard, but with added nitrogen. Sprinkle a half cup of cottonseed meal over every 8 square feet of growing space. Seeds will germinate in cold soil. Beginning as soon as the ground is workable in spring, sow spinach in succession every two weeks. Direct seed, or start indoors and transplant. Keep the bed well watered and apply mulch around the plants to retain moisture and keep the soil cool. As the weather warms up and the days lengthen, spinach will bolt. It is an excellent fall crop. In many areas, it will overwinter, withstanding temperatures down to zero, and produce the earliest possible spring crop.

**Harvest and Yield:** Harvest the largest leaves from each plant as you need them. Each crop should produce several pickings. When the time comes to pull the entire plant, you can freeze any excess. Eight or 10 square feet should produce about a pound of frozen spinach.

**Storage and Preservation:** Spinach freezes well, and this is the preferred method of preservation. Wash, trim, and blanch the leaves for 1 minute. Plunge into cold water, drain well, and pack into freezer containers.

**Uses:** Spinach can be eaten on its own as a salad vegetable or cooked green. It is incorporated into numerous dishes, often with the word *Florentine* somewhere in the name of the recipe. Creamed spinach is eaten alone or used in any number of luxurious dishes, including this old-fashioned brunch dish.

### Eggs Florentine

1 clove garlic, peeled and left whole
1 cup heavy cream
1 cup cooked spinach, chopped
Salt and freshly ground white pepper
A tiny grating of nutmeg
2 English muffins, split and toasted
4 eggs, poached and held in cold water

Place the garlic and the cream in a saucepan and bring to a simmer over low heat. Cook until slightly thickened, 3 to 5 minutes. Remove from heat and allow to cool slightly. Remove and discard the garlic. Add the spinach, a pinch of salt, and a few grinds of white pepper. Taste and adjust the salt if needed. (Spinach itself is variably salty, so tasting is important.) Add the nutmeg. Return the mixture to the stove and heat until hot. Place two English muffin halves on each of two plates. Ladle the creamed spinach over them, dividing it equally. Top each plate with two poached eggs and serve immediately.

## Miscellaneous Greens

Among the easiest and most productive cool-season crops are the numerous varieties of less familiar greens, such as corn salad and purslane. They provide both visual and taste variety to your salads. Because many kinds do well in containers, salad crops can provide fresh food for gardeners with limited space.

Long popular in Europe, these salad greens have found their way onto American plates over the past two decades. Dandelion, endives, purslane, and sorrel all can be grown alongside lettuce. Miner's lettuce prefers shade, where few other vegetables will grow. All perform best during cool weather.

## Dandelion

Bane of suburban lawns, the dandelion was originally used as a salad green or potherb, and made its way to America as seeds packed in the luggage of European colonists. Escaped from cultivation *Taraxacum officinale* has become a weed. However, the leaves of cultivated dandelions make a delicious addition to salads, and it poses no threat to the rest of your garden because for top quality it should be harvested long before flowers are produced. Tea made from the dried leaves has long been recommended as a diuretic, and decoctions of the roots have been used to treat liver problems. As one might expect, it is easy to grow and not fussy about soil conditions.

## Endives

Belgian endive and radicchio are botanically the same plant, chicory (*Chicorium intybus*). Both are grown for winter forcing to produce the edible shoots. During the growing season, all effort is directed toward developing plants with the healthiest roots possible. In the case of Belgian endive, the roots are dug and stored in fall for forcing during the winter. In the case of radicchio, the plants produce heads in the fall. Belgian endive roots can be brought out of storage and forced as needed, making it the more logical choice for a small food garden.

Another chicory species, *C. endivia*, gives us the salad crops known as curly endive or friseè and escarole or Batavian lettuce.

**Culture:** Belgian endive requires 110 to 130 days of growth to produce mature roots. Since it is desirable for the plants to experience a couple of light frosts before they are dug, count backward beginning a week after your normal frost date to determine the best time for planting in your area. Sow seeds ¼ inch deep in well-prepared soil amended with compost. Sprinkle a little bone meal and cottonseed meal on the planting site and work it into the top 2 inches of soil prior to sowing. Sow seeds in rows about a foot apart, spacing them every 3 inches. When seedlings have true leaves, thin them to stand 6 inches apart. Keep the plants well watered. You should have plenty of nice top growth by harvest time.

Curly endive and escarole require about ninety days to mature, and are grown like lettuce. Cool weather is necessary for best quality, so they should be grown as a fall crop in hot summer areas.

**Harvest and Yield:** After the mature endives have experienced two or three light frosts, carefully dig them with a garden fork. Be sure not to damage the taproot. Trim off the leaves an inch above the crown, and trim the roots to a uniform length of 6 to 9 inches. Store the trimmed roots in peat moss in the refrigerator until you are ready to force them for eating.

Curly endive and escarole heads are harvested as needed, and will keep about a week under refrigeration.

**Storage and Preservation:** As long as the roots of Belgian endive are kept under refrigeration, they won't sprout. To force a crop of sprouts, fill a 5-gallon plastic bucket half full with potting mix. The bucket should have a few holes drilled in the bottom to permit drainage. Place several roots upright on the potting mix. The roots can be crowded together, if you wish. Cover the roots with 6 to 8 inches of sand or sawdust, move to a location at 50 to 60°F and keep well watered. After about three weeks, you should be able to see the tips of the sprouts protruding above the surface of the sand or sawdust. At this time, they are ready to harvest. If you carefully remove the sand, cut the endive leaves just above the crown and then replace the sand, you should have a second crop in three more weeks' time.

Radicchio cultivation is identical, except that the plants are left in the ground, and require only about ninety days to mature a crop. In areas where summers are brutal, radicchio will do best with afternoon shade. Otherwise, grow them as just described for Belgian endive. After the first frost, remove the outer leaves, leaving the central head. As the weather cools down, the heads will become darker red and more delicious. Harvest them as needed.

In the case of curly endive and escarole, harvest the heads as needed. Some varieties do best if when blanched, you tie the tips of the outer leaves together to enclose the rest of the head. This reduces bitterness and makes a crisper head.

**Uses:** Radicchio and Belgian endive can be added to salads, but they are great in dishes where they star. Try cutting a whole head in half, grilling it until the leaves are browned on the edges, and serving drizzled with a vinaigrette dressing. Individual leaves of Belgian endive make great appetizers, topped with a dab of crab salad or pimento cheese.

Escarole and curly endive add a delicious, slightly bitter note to salads or can be chopped and stir-fried in a little olive oil with garlic and/or onions and served as a side dish.

## Mache

Also known as corn salad and lamb's lettuce, *Valerianella locusta* is not only one of the nuttiest flavored salad greens but it is also among the hardiest, surviving even at 5°F. In many parts of the country, it is best as a fall and winter crop. Two cultivated forms exist, large-seeded and small-seeded. The former are more heat tolerant, and therefore suited to early spring planting for harvest before summer heats up. They produce a rosette of leaves similar to a small butterhead lettuce. Small-seeded varieties do best in fall, and are more difficult to harvest because the leaves are smaller. However, they are considered to be superior in flavor. Sow seeds thinly in rows about 6 inches apart, covering them with ¼ inch of fine soil. Thin the large-leaved types to stand about 6 inches apart. They transplant easily, so you can use the thinnings to expand the size of the patch. Don't bother thinning small leaved varieties. For these, about six weeks after sowing you should have a small harvest. Thin selectively and leave the remainder of the plants to overwinter in place. They will provide an abundant and early harvest in February. Mache bolts rapidly once the temperature reaches 80°F.

## Miner's Lettuce

Native to North America, miner's lettuce (*Claytonia perfoliata*) acquired its name during the California gold rush. It produces spinachlike greens and an edible rootstock said to resemble chestnuts in flavor. The plant grows in any well-drained soil of average fertility. Unlike other green crops, it prefers dappled shade, and will even grow in the deep shade of evergreen trees. Plant seeds in early spring. A related species, *C. virginiana*, is known as "spring beauty." It is found in the mountains of the eastern United States, and its small, potatolike tubers were a staple of Native Americans.

## Orach

This cool-season green crop, *Atriplex hortensis*, brings a slightly spicy flavor to salads, but its brilliant dark red coloration makes it a standout. Sow in early spring or late summer, thinning seedlings to stand 8 inches apart. Add the thinned plants to salad.

## Purslane

Purslane (*Portulaca oleracea*) is unusual among salad greens because of its succulent leaves. It also contains significant amounts of omega-3 fatty acids. With news reports on the value of omega-3s in promoting circulatory

## ⚒ Sprouts and Microgreens

Sprouts made their American debut during the 1960s when many people began embracing vegetarianism along with other alternative lifestyle choices. That they now appear on the shelves of most supermarkets is a testament to their enduring popularity. And why not? Sprouts, and their close relatives, microgreens, taste great, look beautiful on the plate, and are loaded with beneficial phytochemicals. It is asserted, for example, that broccoli sprouts contain a higher percentage of these compounds than does mature broccoli. Sprouts are grown using nothing more than healthy seeds and water, while microgreens typically grow in soil. Often, the same seeds can be used for either one, but each type of seed gives best results with one of two methods: sprouting in a simple jar or bag, or sprouting on a wet substrate. The former method produces a random mass of sprouts, while the latter produces tall, vertical sprouts or microgreens.

Beginners should start with the jar method. All you need is a pint jar, a rubber band, and some cheesecloth. Place 2 teaspoons of the seed in the jar. Fill with water. Place the cheesecloth over the top and secure with the rubber band. Allow to sit overnight. Drain and rinse well. Set the jar on its side, allowing excess water to drain onto a plate or towel. Twice daily, rinse the seeds again under cold running water and drain thoroughly. Keep the jar in indirect light. When the sprouts are large enough to eat, it is time to harvest.

To grow microgreens, use a finely sifted seed-starting mix. Save one of those clear plastic clamshell containers from the grocery and poke a few holes in one side (the shallower side, if it is asymmetrical) for drainage. Fill with growing mix and water thoroughly. Add seeds, covering them if they are large. Water well again. Close the top and keep in indirect light. When the seedlings touch the roof of their mini-greenhouse, open the lid. Keep watered until the sprouts are ready to harvest. Harvest by cutting them just above the soil line with scissors.

Among the many seeds you can sprout: alfalfa, broccoli, lentils, mung beans, and radish. Good choices for microgreens are alfalfa, beets, broccoli, sunflower, and wheat.

system health, look for purslane to enjoy increasing demand. Considered a weed by many, purslane is extremely easy to grow. Scatter seeds where you want the plants to grow or start in flats and transplant to the garden in early spring. It is a member of the purslane family, Portulacaceae.

## Sorrel

Sorrel (*Rumex acetosa*) provides another example of a plant widely considered a weed but esteemed by gourmet cooks. Why its marvelously acidic flavor has not captured the attention of more American palates remains a mystery to me. Unlike other greens, it is perennial, but in warm summer areas it suffers miserably if water is not abundantly supplied. Establish the plant in rich, moist, well-drained soil. Even where summers are warm, if properly tended it will bear harvests for several years without replanting. Sorrel adds its lemony flavor to soups as well as salad mixes. Look for a variety with beautiful red veining in the leaves.

# The Carrot Family

The carrot family (Umbelliferaceae) provides us with some of our most savory and useful vegetables and herbs. These Old World biennials have been cultivated since the tenth century A.D. Besides carrots, this group includes celery, celery root, fennel, parsnips, and salsify.

## Carrots

Good carrots will grow in comparatively little space with minimally fertile soil. Full-size, foot-long carrots will be difficult to achieve if you don't have really deep soil. Instead, choose varieties that produce short, fat roots, such as Thumbelina.

**Culture:** Carrots require loose, deep, moisture-retentive soil that is free of pebbles. The growing bed should be cultivated to a depth 6 inches deeper than the anticipated length of the mature carrots. They appreciate phosphorus which is best added as rock phosphate powder several months before the growing season. Do not add nitrogen to the growing area. Too much nitrogen results in hairy, forked roots.

## ⑪ Baby Carrots

Grow cultivars that yield true baby carrots, which have good color and taste when only 2 or 3 inches long and ½ inch in diameter. Supermarkets seldom offer genuine baby carrots. Rather, they sell pieces of larger carrots whittled down by machine. Cultivars such as Little Finger and Bambino produce perfect baby carrots with luxuriant tops, even under trying circumstances.

As soon as the ground can be worked in the spring, or earlier in a cold frame, sow the tiny seeds ¼ inch deep. It is always necessary to thin carrots, because crowding can reduce the yield by as much as half. Aim for a spacing that maintains 2 inches between each plant and its neighbors if growing in a raised bed. Seeds are slow to germinate. Keep the bed moist and have patience. Once the plants are 4 inches tall, mulch well. Even soil moisture content is important to avoid cracked roots.

Carrots have two major pests. Wireworms can do serious damage and are more likely if the garden has previously been covered with grass. Don't plant carrots in a bed newly reclaimed from a lawn. Adding wood ashes to the growing area can also deter these pests. The carrot rust fly can be repelled by interplanting carrots with scallions. If you have a problem with this insect, do not plant carrots in the spring of the following year. To prevent diseases, do not plant any member of the carrot family in the same spot again until two years have passed.

**Harvest and Yield:** Pull carrots when they have colored up and are the size you want. Commonly available cultivars mature on average in about seventy days; the larger the carrot, the longer they take. Eight feet of row will produce at least two dozen large carrots, and twice that many of a miniature variety. Cut the tops off but do not wash the roots.

**Storage and Preservation:** Carrots keep well under root cellar conditions, cool and slightly moist. They can also be left in the ground over winter, provided the soil does not freeze. Insulating them with a deep layer of straw will allow you to harvest as needed all winter. Or grow your winter crop under a plastic row cover or in a cold frame.

Carrots can be canned or frozen, but they keep so well fresh you may not want to bother with preserving them. They also make delicious pickles.

**Uses:** Carrots are an essential component of *mirepoix*, the mix of equal parts onions, carrots, and celery that forms the flavor foundation of numerous European savory dishes. They can star in every course, from carrot soup to carrot cake. Time your plantings so you have both baby carrots and snap peas in the garden, and you can make this easy and delicious spring treat.

## Baby Carrots and Snap Peas

For two servings

8–10 baby carrots, trimmed
2 tablespoons dry white wine
A few sprigs lemon thyme
Salt and freshly ground black pepper
8–10 fresh sugar snap peas, trimmed
2 tablespoons unsalted butter, cut into small pieces

Place 2 tablespoons water, the carrots, wine, lemon thyme, and salt and pepper in a saucepan. Bring to a simmer and steam until the carrots are barely tender when pierced with the tip of a paring knife. Add the sugar snap peas and continue steaming for 1 minute. Remove the vegetables with a slotted spoon and keep warm. Discard the thyme sprigs. Increase the heat and boil down the liquid in the pan until you have about 2 tablespoons remaining. Remove from the heat, swirl in the butter, a piece at a time, to produce a smooth sauce. Serve the sauce over the vegetables.

## Celery and Celery Root

Both of these savory plants naturally occur in bog conditions, and both need a long, cool growing season. Celery (*Apium graveolens var. dulce*) matures in about three months. It is grown primarily for the succulent stems and their leaves. A variety known as "cutting celery" is grown for leaves only, which have an intense celery flavor. Celery root, or celeriac, (*A. graveolens var. rapaceum*) requires about a month longer to develop its swollen, savory roots.

**Culture:** Sow seeds in flats at 70°F. Germination may take three weeks, so the starting mix should be sterilized to minimize the danger of fungal disease in the seedlings. The easiest way to sterilize a small amount is to fill the cell tray and pour boiling water over the starting mix. Wait until it cools before sowing. Move plants to their permanent location when they have several sets of true leaves. Abundant water is an absolute requirement for success. Celery may therefore be easier to grow in containers than directly in the garden, while celery root is best grown in the ground. Neither celery nor celery root likes hot, fierce sunshine, so partial shading may improve your chances of success. Container-grown plants can simply be moved around as the season requires. Regular fertilization with manure tea, fish emulsion, or seaweed extract will keep the plants growing rapidly. If plants are exposed to conditions cooler than 55°F, they will bolt.

**Harvest and Yield:** Harvest celery stalks as you need them from the outside of the plant, and leave the rest to continue growing. If hot weather is approaching, harvest the whole plant by cutting it at ground level. Celery root should be pulled when the roots are about the size of a baseball.

**Storage and Preservation:** Rinse celery, remove any damaged parts, and store in plastic bags in the refrigerator. Rinse celery root, remove all but a tuft of fresh green leaves at the top, and store under root cellar conditions, where they will keep several months.

**Uses:** Most recipes require only a small amount of celery, which means you can get a lot of mileage out of a single, container-grown plant. It is an essential component of *mirepoix* (equal amounts of onions, carrots, and celery) used widely in European cooking. Celery teams up with onions and bell peppers in many Cajun and Creole dishes, also.

Celery root should be peeled, cut into pieces as required by the dish. It can star on its own in salads or a gratin, or be substituted for celery in any dish.

## Fennel

This vegetable is often regarded as an herb. Leaves, seeds, and the swollen, bulbous base of *Foeniculum vulgare* all have culinary uses.

**Culture:** Fennel does not get along well with other vegetables, so choose a spot to the side of the garden to install a few plants in well-drained soil. Direct sow in full sun after all danger of frost. In warm summer areas, fennel is best as a fall crop, allowing about 90 days for the plants to mature before the first frost. Cover the seeds with ¼ inch of fine soil and expect germination in about ten days. Thin to stand about a foot apart. Don't bother with fertilizing, as fennel does fine without it.

**Harvest and Yield:** Pick fronds as you need them. Harvest fennel bulbs when they are about 3 inches in diameter. Cut the entire plant off at soil level. Avoid wetting the fronds if you plan to use them.

**Storage and Preservation:** Fennel keeps well under root cellar conditions. Trim most of the fronds before storing.

**Uses:** Fennel pairs well with fish and pork, and can be added to pasta and vegetable dishes. Small, young bulbs can be very thinly sliced and added to salad. Italians maintain that rounder bulbs are more flavorful. Here's a classic cooked fennel side dish:

## Braised Fennel with Butter and Parmesan

Two to four servings

1 fennel bulb
¼ cup unsalted butter
Salt
3 tablespoons freshly grated Parmigiano-Reggiano cheese

Slice the fennel bulb vertically into ½-inch slices. Place the butter in a large saucepan, arrange the fennel slices in the bottom of the pot in a single layer, and add water to barely cover. Bring to a simmer and cook slowly until the fennel is fork tender and the water has been absorbed. Sprinkle with a pinch of salt, toss gently with the cheese, and serve at once.

## Parsnip

Not often considered by home gardeners, parsnip (*Pastinaca sativa*) takes much longer to produce a crop than does the carrot. However, its keeping qualities and cold hardiness recommend it.

**Culture:** Sow seeds ¼ to ½ inch deep in loose, well-drained soil that has been deeply cultivated. Do not allow the soil to dry out during the germination period, which may be as long as three weeks. When the plants are well established, thin to 4 inches apart each way if growing in a raised bed. Parsnips do not require high soil fertility, but they do need a cool growing period of about four months. They are, therefore, best as a fall crop.

## Salsify

Also known as the oyster plant, salsify (*Tragopogon porrifolius*) produces carrotlike roots that taste like shellfish. Culture of salsify is identical to that for parsnips. Fall planting is the best approach. The plants are smaller and can be spaced 2 to 4 inches each way. Frost improves flavor. Dig before the ground is frozen. Roots are about an inch in diameter and 6 inches long.

Store under root cellar conditions—that is, cool and slightly damp. Roasted or baked, this vegetable performs well in gratins and ragouts where its seafood flavor is appropriate.

**Harvest and Yield:** Most varieties produce roots 2 to 3 inches in diameter at the crown and about 10 inches long. You can harvest anytime after they have reached a usable size, but best flavor development occurs after a good frost. This, and their low demands for fertility, makes them a good crop to follow potatoes, which are typically out of the garden by the Fourth of July.

**Storage and Preservation:** Leaving parsnips in the ground during winter is the simplest approach, provided your climate is mild enough that the soil does not freeze solid for an extended period. Freezing won't hurt your parsnips, but makes harvesting them a chore. Northern growers solved this problem by storing them in small batches in boxes of soil. When you want parsnips, you bring a box inside to thaw.

**Uses:** Parsnips can stand in for carrots, or be combined with them, in any recipe. Seldom eaten raw, as they are somewhat tough, they can be roasted, fried, or boiled. Mashed, boiled parsnips can stand in for potatoes, or be combined with them in various proportions, using whatever recipe you prefer for mashed potatoes.

# The Squash Family

These warm-season vegetables (Cucurbitaceae) typically need more room than green crops. Growing them on a trellis is the best way to accommodate them where space is at a premium. Bush varieties of summer squash and cucumbers can also be grown in minimal space, even in containers.

## Cucumber

Unfortunately the target of several pests and diseases, the cucumber (*Cucumis sativus*) nevertheless is among the most productive members of the squash family. Two types are commonly available to home gardeners. Pickling, or Kirby, cucumbers mature at less than 6 inches in length, are slightly curved, and often have prickly spines. They are typically ready for harvest about two months after sowing. Slicing cucumbers, the other type, take a couple of weeks longer. They grow straight, are often quite long, and typically lack spines. Pickling cucumbers can be eaten raw in salads, but the slicing types don't usually make good pickles. Therefore, if you only have room for one or two plants, grow a pickling type.

**Culture:** Cucumber seeds can be started in peat pots and transplanted, but they are also easy to direct seed. Wait until the weather is stable and the soil temperature is above 65°F. Best germination is at about 80°F. Fill pots, or build up a mound of soil, or hill, about 10 inches in diameter. Sow three seeds per hill or pot. Add a quart of good compost to the bottom of the planting hole. If starting indoors, keep warm, above 75°F. When the seedlings have a pair of true leaves, cut the two weakest off at soil level. Feed with a soluble food, such as manure tea. Pot-grown seedlings must be hardened off carefully before moving to the garden. Take great care not to disturb their roots when transplanting. Provide a trellis of string, wire, or thin branches for the tendrils to grasp. Young seedlings need plenty of water until they are big enough to begin climbing, at which time the plants are more drought tolerant. Mulch to maintain even moisture. Fertilize the plants a week after transplanting, and again when blooms appear. Male blooms will appear first, followed by female blooms, which can be distinguished by the tiny cucumber below the petals. At this stage, the plants need regular irrigation to prevent misshapen fruits.

If cucumber beetles are a problem in your area, the simplest approach is to cover the growing area with floating row cover until the female flowers appear. Crop rotation, planting resistant varieties, and attention to proper culture technique can help to avoid common diseases. Crowded, stressed plants are much more likely to have problems than plants with plenty of room, food, and water.

**Harvest and Yield:** Pick cucumbers daily to keep plants producing. Select fruits that are fully developed and of the characteristic size for the variety you are growing. Yellowish fruits are overly mature and likely to be bitter. You can expect 10 pounds of cucumbers from each plant, often more.

**Storage and Preservation:** Wipe freshly picked cucumbers with a cloth. Do not wash them or you will encourage molding. Store unwrapped in the crisper drawer of the refrigerator and use within three days. By far the best way to preserve cucumbers is pickling. Chapter 8 on food preservation includes recipes for cucumber pickles.

**Uses:** Fresh cucumbers are delicious in salads. Combined with yogurt, they become Greek *tsatsiki* or Indian *raita*. They can be cooked, too, in stir-fries or as cream of cucumber soup. My favorite cucumber dish, however, is gazpacho.

## GAZPACHO

For six to eight servings:

2 medium tomatoes, chopped
1 large cucumber, peeled, seeded, and chopped
1 small green bell pepper, seeded, and chopped
1 small red onion, chopped
3 tablespoons fine, dry breadcrumbs
1 clove garlic, minced
Juice of 1 lemon
3 tablespoons extra-virgin olive oil
A handful of fresh herbs (parsley, basil, chives, tarragon, chervil) minced
1 teaspoon salt
½ teaspoon sweet Hungarian paprika
3 cups water, tomato juice, chicken stock, or vegetable stock
Sour cream
¼ cup minced red or yellow bell peppers, for garnish
Chopped scallions, for garnish

You can use a food processor to chop the vegetables, but the texture will not be as good as if they are chopped by hand. All of the vegetables should be chopped into pieces about the same size. Combine the chopped vegetables, breadcrumbs, garlic, lemon juice, olive oil, herbs, salt, and paprika in a large bowl. Cover the mixture and place in the refrigerator to chill. Separately chill the 3 cups of liquid. These components can be held in the refrigerator overnight, if desired.

When ready to serve, combine the vegetable mix with the chilled liquid. Stir well and serve topped with sour cream. Garnish with the peppers and scallions, if you'd like. If you wish, add heat by substituting a hot pepper for some of the bell pepper.

## Melons

Succulent, sweet melons are considered fruits by some people, but they are annuals traditionally included in the vegetable patch. The most commonly grown varieties are muskmelons (*Cucumis melo var. reticulatus*). Cantaloupes (*C. melo var. cantalupensis*) are similar, but with smooth skins rather than netted skins like muskmelons. Watermelon (*Citrullus lanatus*) should be considered only if you can provide at least 40 square feet per plant, and that is for a dwarf variety.

**Culture:** Culture of melons is more demanding than that of cucumbers, but the methods are the same. Follow growing instructions for cucumbers, making sure the plants go into loose, fertile, well-drained soil at neutral pH. Soil that is excessively acid or alkaline will greatly reduce yield. Provide a trellis to save garden space. As fruits develop, support them with slings made of scrap cloth tied to the trellis. Note the anticipated mature size of fruits. Small fruits can be just as tasty as large ones, and are better suited to trellis culture.

**Harvest and Yield:** Harvest melons when the fruit slips easily from the stem. Pay attention to maturity dates to help determine harvest time. The fruits will develop a pleasant sweet smell when they are ready. Each fruit can weigh several pounds. The overall harvest will depend strongly on growing conditions, and even the same variety will not perform as well in some years as in others.

### Avoiding Damping Off

The large seeds of cucurbits are particularly susceptible to damping off when started indoors. This condition, produced by fungi naturally present in the soil, causes young seedlings to rot at ground level and fall over. Soil that is cool and damp promotes damping off. Therefore, follow recommendations with regard to proper germination temperature. Seed starting mix should be ideally be sterile, but you can achieve good results by pasteurization of your homemade mix. Dampen the starting mix as though you were going to sow in it. Place the damp mix in a large ovenproof container, such as a cheap aluminum roasting pan, and pop it into a preheated 350°F oven. Bake, stirring now and then with a large wooden spoon, until an oven thermometer inserted into the center of the mass reads 180°F. Turn off the oven and remove the pan when it is cool enough to handle.

**Storage and Preservation:** Melons will keep a few days under refrigeration, but for finest quality eat soon after harvesting. Melons can be frozen, but will be mushy if thawed completely, and therefore are best used in smoothies. Melon pickles are a possibility, too.

**Uses:** Melons are generally eaten fresh, whether in chunks wrapped with prosciutto, as a component of a chilled fruit soup or in a salad.

## Squashes

Two types of squashes, winter and summer, actually include four species of plants. Winter squashes are good keepers and include *Cucurbita argyrosperma*, *C. maxima*, *C. moschata*, and *C. pepo*. They have thick, hard skins, yellow or orange flesh, and often grow quite large. This group includes acorn and butternut types, cushaws, spaghetti squash, and pumpkins. Summer squashes, *C. pepo*, include zucchini, pattypan types, and yellow crookneck and straight neck varieties. One interesting summer squash, Tromboncino, is a form of *C. moschata*. Pumpkins are either *C. maxima*, *C. moschata*, or *C. pepo*. Small-space gardeners should consider only compact, small-fruited "pie" pumpkin varieties.

**Culture:** Follow the culture instructions given for cucumbers. Summer squashes generally produce a large, bushlike growth form. Each needs at least a square yard of growing room. Space-saving varieties have been developed. One exception is Tromboncino, which like winter squashes produces an extensive vine that should be supported by a trellis. Winter squashes need either a trellis and support for the developing fruits, or a space of 40 to 50 square feet to spread out. One exception is a bush variety of *C. moschata* that produces 5-foot vines called Baby Butternut.

Squashes fall victim to a collection of maladies. Insect pests include the squash bug, vine borers, and cucumber beetles. Keeping plants under row cover until blooms appear can thwart these bugs. Trap squash bugs by laying pieces of flat cardboard on the ground at the base of the plants. In the morning, lift the cardboard and knock the bugs that have gathered underneath into a bucket of soapy water. This pest lays clusters of orange eggs on the underside of leaves, and will also attack tomatoes and peppers. Inspect leaves for eggs and destroy them. Either mash with your fingers, or use a flowerpot label to scrape the egg cluster into soapy water. The vine borer is harder to deal with, in my experience. The adult, a night-flying moth, lays eggs at the base of the plant. The larvae burrow into the stem and eat their way toward the leaf end. You can slit the stem with a knife, cutting parallel to its length, and remove the larva. Various suggestions for inhibiting the females from depositing eggs, such as dusting young plants with rotenone or adding ashes or charcoal to the planting hill, produce mixed results. One strategy is to grow Tromboncino. The borers avoid this species. Among winter squash, butternut types are *C. moschata* and are thus your best bet for avoiding borers.

Avoid squash diseases by good cultural practice, but I have had good results in controlling mildew attacks with neem spray. Squash bugs spread bacterial wilt, so controlling them controls the disease, too.

**Harvest and Yield:** Harvest summer squash at the size you deem best. Female summer squash flowers with the baby fruit still attached are a delicacy. Winter squash should be checked for ripeness when the skin becomes dull in appearance. If you cannot dent the skin with your fingernail, mark the calendar and harvest your winter squash about two weeks later. Cut off the fruit, leaving an inch of stem attached to it. Individual winter squash can weigh 2 pounds or more. One zucchini can produce 20 pounds of fruit under good conditions. It is usually not necessary to grow many plants to enjoy all the squash you may want. Harvest baby zucchini as soon as the bloom opens.

**Storage and Preservation:** For summer squash, wipe with a cloth and store under refrigeration for up to a week. Do not wash until you are ready to prepare them. Winter squash keep best at a temperature of 45 to 50°F. An unheated

## ⊔⊔ Pollination Problems in Squashes!

North America is currently experiencing problems with honey-bee colonies. The result is that there are fewer pollinators around, leading to problems for growers of squashes, melons, and cucumbers, all of which require insect pollination. Parthenocarpic varieties that can produce fruit without an insect pollinator are available for zucchini and cucumbers. Developed with the needs of commercial growers in mind, they are still worth trying in the home garden if you have had trouble getting fruit to set.

garage or root cellar works well, and the fruits should remain in good condition all winter. Summer squash can be canned, pickled, frozen, or dried. Squash blossoms keep a maximum of three days under refrigeration. Line a plastic storage container with paper towels and carefully arrange freshly picked squash blossoms in a single layer. Cover and place in the refrigerator.

**Uses:** Summer squash is delicious raw in salads, or can be stir-fried, steamed, or baked. Hollow out the fruits and steam until tender, then fill them with a savory stuffing and bake. Summer squash casserole is a staple in the South. Winter squash lends itself to sweet dishes and warm spices, and can be used in recipes that call for pumpkin or sweet potatoes.

## ZUCCHINI AGRODOLCE

For two servings

1 medium zucchini or 2 small ones, washed and trimmed
2 tablespoons olive oil
Salt and freshly ground black pepper
2 tablespoons sugar
2 tablespoons cider or red wine vinegar
1 tablespoon water
¼ teaspoon Kosher salt

Slice the zucchini into rounds about ¼ inch thick. Heat the oil in a skillet. When the surface ripples, add a pinch of salt, a few grinds of pepper, and the zucchini. Spread the zucchini in one layer, adjust the heat, and cook 3 minutes, or until the slices are beginning to brown. Meanwhile, combine the other ingredients in a metal bowl large enough to hold all the squash and dressing. Stir to dissolve the sugar. Turn the zucchini slices with a spatula and continue cooking until the bottom side begins to brown. Remove from the heat and allow to cool somewhat. Carefully scrape the warm squash and the cooking oil into the bowl with the dressing. Toss to coat.

Leave at room temperature if serving within two hours, or refrigerate overnight. Bring to room temperature before serving as part of an antipasto platter.

# The Grass Family

Grasses feed more humans and animals than any other plant. Imagine vast herds of grazing animals across the plains of Asia, Africa, and North America, all foraging on native grasses. All the major grains, wheat, rice, barley, rye, and corn are members of this family. In some parts of the world, a person's daily ration of bread or rice consumes a third of his or her income. Grain production is possible on a homestead scale, but the most commonly homegrown member of this family is corn.

## Corn

Nothing announces the arrival of summer in all its glory like sweet corn fresh from the garden. The quintessential American crop, corn has devotees everywhere. Home gardeners sometimes shy away from planting a corn crop because it needs room. Nevertheless, with a little ingenuity you can squeeze in enough corn to make the project worthwhile.

Modern plant breeding has produced numerous hybrid corn varieties, including "enhanced sugar" and "super sweet" hybrids whose kernels contain much more sugar than older, heirloom types. Super sweet corn was developed to meet demand for corn syrup, and when sold for fresh consumption is able to withstand days between harvest and purchase at your local supermarket. When an ear is removed from the stalk, enzymes begin to convert the sugars into starch, so the longer the time since the ear was picked, the less sweet it is. This phenomenon is the source of the oft-repeated advice to start boiling the water before heading out to the garden if you want truly sweet corn on the cob. That kind of care becomes unnecessary with super sweet hybrids, but then, they lack the "corny" taste of their nonhybrid ancestors. Some people even find them too sweet when freshly picked. Home gardeners, therefore, can experience the special flavors of sweet corn by growing traditional, open-pollinated types, or older "normal sugar" hybrids. Cultivars such as Country Gentleman and Golden Bantam have been around for years. Among the "normal sugar" hybrids, Iowa Chief and Silver Queen are old standbys.

In addition to sweet corn grown for eating fresh, you may also want to try some dent corn. Traditionally, young dent corn was picked for roasting ears, but its primary use is for making cornmeal and hominy. The most popular variety in my part of the country is Hickory King. It grows tall and majestically, taking about four months to mature a crop for cornmeal. Young ears are ready a month earlier. A red variety originating in Italy, Floriani Red Flint, has been mentioned favorably in recent years.

> In limited space, you can make the corn patch do double duty. Grow a tall, late-maturing variety of corn and plant pole beans at the base of the stalks after they are a foot tall. This traditional companion planting works because the beans provide extra nitrogen for the corn. Choose a bean cultivar that won't overwhelm the corn. Early Cornfield and White Half Runner beans are popular ones.

Gardeners with space and an experimental bent can expand their corn horizons to include popcorn and even Asian "baby" corn. Either grows like sweet corn. Baby corn is highly productive, and will form new ears after being picked.

Seed corn is often treated with chemicals to prevent soil fungi from attacking the germinating seedlings. To prevent the treated corn from being fed to animals or used for human food, a dye is added to the seeds, usually hot pink in color. You can avoid the need for these added fungicides by following proper culture techniques.

**Culture:** Corn requires plenty of nitrogen, water, and sunshine. It also needs warmth. Do not rush to plant early in the season, or you run the risk of seeds rotting in the ground. Wait until the soil temperature is 65°F or warmer. Old-timers in the Tennessee Valley prefer to wait at least until "the leaves on the oak trees are as big as a squirrel's ear."

Choose a garden spot about 15 feet square and amend the soil with compost, cottonseed meal, and a sprinkling of lime if your soil is acidic. Corn prefers a neutral pH. A site that has previously grown legumes can be expected to grow good corn. Sow an inch deep in hills of two or three seeds. Space the hills about 18 inches apart each way, more if you are growing a tall, late-maturing variety. Block planting ensures good wind pollination. Don't plant in long rows or you will have many "gap-toothed" ears. If you plan on saving your own seed, grow only one variety and plan on saving seeds from at least 10 percent of your plants. Maintaining vigor and purity in corn seed requires isolation of varieties by a half mile or more, not practical for the backyard gardener.

Water the corn patch well, and keep the soil moist with a mulch of straw, which will also help reduce competition from weeds. Cultivate care-fully to eliminate any that do spring up. Side dress the plants with a balanced organic fertilizer when they are about a foot tall, and again when tassels appear. Fish emulsion is one good fertilizer option, and mimics the practice of Native Americans who buried a fish in each hill of corn seeds.

**Harvest and Yield:** Most corn cultivars only produce one or two ears per plant. To extend the harvest, you can plant varieties that mature at different times. As a rule, the shorter the time to maturity, the shorter the stalks, so early maturing cultivars take up less room. Limited space gardens can sometimes accommodate two early varieties planted in succession. Average maturity time is around seventy-five days for yellow cultivars, and ninety to a hundred days for white ones. Do not accept catalog maturity dates as gospel, however, because corn's development is really a function of *days of warmth*. Therefore, expect variation in maturity time depending on your location and the weather.

Harvest when the silks turn brown and look dry. Peel back the husk on an ear and crush one of the kernels with your thumbnail. If sweet, milky juice appears, the corn is ready. If not, carefully replace the husk and check again in a couple of days.

**Storage and Preservation:** Nonhybrid corn should be eaten or processed within twenty-four hours (at most) of picking. Corn freezes well, on or off the cob. Blanch cut kernels for three minutes in boiling water, plunge into cold water, and drain well before packing in freezer containers. Trim cobs, cut or break to a uniform length, and blanch for ten minutes. Then treat as for cut corn. Some people find that home-frozen corn on the cob develops an off-flavor, and prefer to freeze only cut kernels. In any case, kernels take up less freezer space. Popcorn should be stored on the cob in a cool, dry place. Dent corn is generally made into cornmeal prior to storage, or can be stored warm and dry and ground as needed, provided you have a grain mill.

**Uses:** Some would undoubtedly argue that the best way to enjoy garden fresh corn is boiled or roasted on the cob. While I tend to agree, plenty of other options exist. Cut freshly harvested corn from the cob safely by trimming off the pointed end with a knife, cutting perpendicular to the length of the cob. Stand the cob on this flattened end and cut the kernels off, beginning at the stalk end. Blanch the kernels as just described for freezing and use them in stir-fries, salads, and casseroles.

The following recipe draws rave reviews when I serve it on a summer buffet or take it on a picnic. All the fresh ingredients will be in season in late summer. The recipe is easily doubled to feed a crowd.

## Corn and Black Bean Salad

For four to six servings

2 cups corn kernels, cut fresh from the cob
2 cups cooked black beans, rinsed well and thoroughly drained
4 scallions, white and green parts, trimmed and cut into ½-inch pieces
1 medium ripe red tomato, cored, seeded, and diced
1 green bell pepper, trimmed, seeded, and diced
1 jalapeño pepper, seeded and minced
Juice of 2 limes
¼ cup extra virgin olive oil
1 handful fresh cilantro leaves and small stems, chopped
Salt and freshly ground black pepper

Combine all ingredients in a large bowl and refrigerate, covered, for at least an hour before serving, and preferably overnight.

For more heat, leave the seeds in the jalapeño or add hot sauce. Substitute green beans, cut into ½-inch pieces and steamed until tender, for the black beans to create a dish wholly from the garden.

# The Hibiscus Family

Only one hibiscus family member, okra, makes it into the vegetable garden, although cotton and various ornamental varieties represent this family elsewhere. Hibiscus flowers, provided the plants have not been sprayed, are edible. They can be used as festive serving cups for cold foods, or shredded and added to salad. Dried hibiscus flowers are used to make tea.

## Okra

Okra (*Abelmoschus esculentus*) arrived in the United States by way of the slave trade during colonial times. The word *okra* and its other name, *gumbo*, are both anglicized versions of African words for this vegetable. Undoubtedly, it has been eaten by humans since prehistoric times.

**Culture:** Sow directly where the plants will grow when the soil temperature is at least 65°F, or start indoors for transplanting three weeks after germination. Grow okra where you have previously grown a nitrogen-hungry crop, such as corn or spinach. Too much soil nitrogen will reduce the yield of pods and favor leaf production. Nevertheless, okra must have good soil with plenty of organic matter. It does poorly on heavy clay soils with poor drainage. Sow seeds about an inch deep. Soaking them overnight before planting will speed germination. Thin plants to stand at least a foot apart each way for compact cultivars, and twice this distance for the larger varieties. Rows must be separated by at least five feet to facilitate picking, so where space is limited, raised beds are the way to go.

**Harvest and Yield:** You should have pods ready to harvest about six weeks from transplanting. The best quality pods are about 3 inches in length, although some cultivars can be allowed to grow longer without becoming too tough. Okra must be harvested daily, removing every pod. Leaving stray pods on the plant reduces the overall yield, and the pods themselves become woody and inedible. Wait until the dew is off the plants to pick, and do not wash the harvest. Okra plants are covered with short bristles that will irritate your skin. Wear long sleeves and gloves when you harvest. Okra will yield more than a pound of pods per square foot.

**Storage and Preservation:** Store the pods in a perforated vegetable container under refrigeration for a maximum of three days. If the pods begin to turn dark, use them immediately. Freezing okra could not be simpler. Wipe pods clean with a dry towel. Cut crosswise into pieces about ½ inch in length. Place in freezer containers and store in the freezer. Blanching is not necessary. Small whole pods may also be frozen, or they can be split lengthwise. Whole okra pods are often added to curries, both African and Asian. Select perfect, tender pods and pickle them whole, following the instructions for pickled green tomatoes on page 247. Pickled okra needs only to be rinsed before using it like fresh okra in soups and stews.

**Uses:** Although my favorite way to eat okra involves coating it with corn-meal and deep-frying, the quintessential Southern okra dish is gumbo. Made with any type of meat or seafood, and often with a combination of both, this stew has as many recipes as there are Southern cooks. My version is for carnivores, but you can substitute beans and mushrooms for the meats and create a vegetarian gumbo. Not only does this recipe feature the best vegetables and herbs of high summer but all of the other ingredients are at your favorite grocery store.

## John's One Pot Creole-Style Gumbo

For four servings

3 tablespoons vegetable oil
3 tablespoons all purpose flour
¼ cup each finely chopped onions, celery, and green bell pepper
2 tablespoons minced garlic
1 teaspoon Creole seasoning (see page 235)
¼ cup peeled, seeded, and diced fresh tomato
Freshly ground black pepper
3 cups chicken stock
3 bay leaves
2 to 3 dashes hot sauce
½ teaspoon Worcestershire sauce
¼ teaspoon dry thyme, or a sprig of fresh thyme
2 ounces andouille or other garlic-flavored smoked pork sausage, diced
¾ cup sliced fresh okra
½ pound shrimp, peeled and deveined
1 teaspoon chopped fresh oregano
1 tablespoon torn fresh basil leaves
Steamed white rice
Chopped scallions
Hard-boiled eggs (optional)

In a large saucepan or Dutch oven, heat 3 tablespoons oil until it ripples on the surface. With a wire whisk, whisk in the flour. Reduce the heat and cook, stirring constantly, until the mixture is the color of milk chocolate. Take care not to let this roux burn or you'll need to begin anew. Also, do not allow the roux to splatter on your skin as it can cause severe burns. Remove from the heat and stir in the chopped onions, celery and pepper, stirring constantly until the roux stops sizzling and becoming darker in color.

Add the garlic, Creole seasoning, tomato, and a few grinds of pepper. Continue cooking for 2 to 3 minutes. Add the stock, bay leaves, hot sauce, Worcestershire sauce, and thyme. Bring to a simmer, cook 8 to 10 minutes. Stir in the sausage and okra. Simmer 20 minutes. Add the shrimp and fresh herbs. Simmer until the shrimp are pink, about 3 minutes. Serve over rice garnished with green onions and chopped hard-boiled egg. Pass additional hot sauce.

# The Morning Glory Family

The nutritious swollen roots of the sweet potato are produced on plants with insignificant flowers, unlike other members of the family such the common morning glory with its late summer show or moon vine, whose 6-inch flowers open at night to release a perfume reminiscent of gardenias.

## Sweet Potatoes

Sweet potatoes (*Ipomea batata*) are not started from seed, but rather from small plants, or "slips," sprouted from stored roots. If you have a warm, brightly illuminated spot, you can start your own, but most people prefer to purchase slips from a commercial grower.

**Culture:** Sweet potato slips should be planted after the ground has warmed to 65°F. They require a loose, sandy loam with plenty of organic matter. High nitrogen soils will result in much leafy growth and few roots. The traditional method is to mound up the soil into a hill, to improve drainage, but this is not necessary if using raised beds. Space individual plants at least 12 inches apart each way. Rows, if used, must be 3 feet apart, and the planting area about 2 feet wide. The vines or standard varieties like Beauregard or Southern White will run all over the place, although there are compact varieties that remain in bounds, including Vardaman and Porto Rico.

The hotter the weather, the faster they will grow. Provide an inch of water a week. Mulch to control weeds and maintain even moisture at the roots. In cooler climates, many gardeners swear by black plastic sheeting as a mulch. Applied several weeks before planting time, it absorbs solar heat and warms the soil, permitting earlier than normal transplanting of sweet potatoes (and other warm-season crops, too).

**Harvest and Yield:** After about four months of growth, sweet potatoes should be ready to harvest. Each slip should produce two or three nice potatoes, or up to 5 pounds if the season has been favorable. Harvest as needed until frost threatens, and be sure to dig them all before frost kills the vines or their keeping quality will be seriously impaired.

**Storage and Preservation:** Spread freshly dug potatoes in a shady spot to cure for a day or two (provided frost is not predicted) after harvest. Carefully rub off most of the soil and store them in baskets or boxes in a cool, dry place. They should keep about three months.

**Uses:** Baked, steamed, or fried, sweet potatoes are good on their own enhanced with butter, maple, and similar flavors. They can substitute for winter squash in any dish, too. Sweet potato pie is a traditional Southern dish that mimics pumpkin pie. It is sometimes served in a pastry crust, but more often is served without a crust, topped with marshmallows.

# Warm Season Greens

When summer heats up, spinach goes to seed and lettuce develops burnt tips and attracts aphids. That is when these two spinach substitutes can fill in.

## Malabar Spinach

Malabar spinach (*Basella rubra*) is an Asian plant whose leaves are high in vitamins A and C. It grows as a sturdy vine that requires a trellis, and is a good crop to follow peas. The succulent stems and leaves can be stir-fried, added to salads and in general can substitute for spinach. Seed germinates best at 80°F, and requires a long time to show. Start indoors in pots about a month before transplanting, and move into the garden when the weather is warm and settled. Space plants a foot apart. You can begin harvesting in about two months from transplant time, and continue up until frost.

## New Zealand Spinach

This plant, *Tetragonia expansa*, originates in New Zealand and has been grown in America since colonial times. Grow exactly like spinach. Soak the seeds overnight in water before planting to soften the hard seed coat and speed germination. Space plants 12 inches apart in fertile, well-drained soil. In about two months, you should be ready to harvest the tasty greens. New Zealand spinach tolerates drought better than conventional spinach.

# Perennial Vegetables

Perennials return each year larger and more vigorous, and therefore typically provide a better yield as they increase in size. Not all of them thrive in all gardens, however. If you can accommodate their needs, include them in your vegetable crop plan.

## Globe Artichoke

Unfortunately, this giant thistle (*Cynara scolymus*) with delicious flower buds does not grow well in many parts of the country. Most of the artichokes sold in the United States are grown near Castroville, California, where they luxuriate in Pacific fogs and moderate temperatures. A recent introduction, Imperial Star, matures a crop in only one year and is therefore considered an annual. It may offer hope to growers unable to bring the standard varieties through winter.

Artichokes take up a lot of space, at least a square yard per plant. I have tried repeatedly to bring in a crop because I love to eat artichokes. So far, I've had no success, probably due to the punishingly hot and humid summers my region experiences. If your climate is moderate during the summer months and experiences only light frosts in winter, you can give artichokes a try with a reasonable expectation of success.

**Culture:** Seeds should be started two months before the last expected frost, in cell trays maintained at about 75°F. Sow them ¼ inch deep and keep them well watered. When the seedlings have two true leaves, transplant to 4-inch pots. Keep them in bright light at around 65°F during the day, with a 10°F temperature drop at night. When the plants are sixty days old, they are ready to be transplanted to their permanent location. Enrich the soil with plenty of compost, sprinkle ¼ cup of cottonseed meal in the hole to supply nitrogen for rapid growth, and give each transplant a circle of growing space 3 feet in diameter. Mulch to conserve moisture, and make sure the plants receive ample water if the weather is dry. The fast-maturing Imperial Star requires about three months from transplant to harvest. Other varieties won't bloom until the following spring.

**Harvest and Yield:** Each plant produces a primary flower bud. When this is removed, additional buds form on side shoots, although none will be as large as the first bud. Harvest when the bud is tight, with no sign of opening, cutting the stem about 4 inches below the base of the bud.

**Storage and Preservation:** Set the cut end in a glass of water (like any other cut flower) and refrigerate. Use promptly, within a week or less. Freezing and pickling are the best preservation methods. Trim the buds and cut into quarters, rubbing the cut surfaces as you go with a cut lemon to keep them from discoloring. Cut out the hairy "choke" and the innermost leaves. Drop the prepared buds into boiling water and cook until barely tender, about ten minutes. Test by inserting a fork into the thickest part of a piece. If you feel little or no resistance, they're done. Drain in a colander and plunge into ice water to stop the cooking.

From this point, they can be patted dry, packed into containers, and frozen, or placed into half-pint jars with garlic and herbs, covered with basic pickling solution (see page 248), and processed for ten minutes in a boiling water bath.

**Uses:** You can boil artichokes (see instructions below). Artichoke pickles make a fine addition to an antipasto tray or Greek-style salad. Frozen quartered artichokes can be used like many other vegetables in stir-fry dishes, soups, and appetizers.

## BOILED ARTICHOKES

Select a pot large enough to accommodate the artichokes and water to cover. Bring the water to a boil while you prepare the artichokes. Trim off the stem end so the bud will sit on a plate. Rub the cut surface with half a lemon. Turn the artichoke on its side and, with a large knife, trim off the upper third of the leaf tips. Rub with lemon. With scissors, snip off all the remaining leaf tips, removing the sharp spine and about ½ to ⅓ of the leaf. Again, rub with lemon.

When all the buds are trimmed and the water is at a rolling boil, drop in the artichokes, add a tablespoon of salt, and squeeze in all the juice remaining from the cut lemon. When the water returns to a boil, reduce the heat and simmer, uncovered, until an inner leaf can easily be pulled off. (Grasp the leaf with tongs to avoid burning your fingers!) The time required will vary, but start testing after 15 to 20 minutes. When they are done, remove from the heat and set stem side up in a colander to drain. Serve warm, accompanied by melted butter or seasoned olive oil, or at room temperature with your favorite salad dressing.

To eat, set the bud stem side up on a plate. Pluck off a leaf with your fingers, dip in the accompanying condiment, and use your teeth to scrape off the thickened base. Discard the remainder. When you have eaten most of the leaves, you can scrape out the central choke with a spoon, revealing the succulent flower base.

## Jerusalem Artichoke

This member of the sunflower family (Asteraceae), botanically *Helianthus tuberosus,* is neither an artichoke nor from Jerusalem. Rather, it is native to North America and may be found growing along roadsides. The tubers, produced abundantly, have a nutty flavor and a potatolike texture.

Plant the tubers in spring in well-drained garden soil. Because this is a native plant, it needs little care. It is capable of overwhelming slower-growing species and should be given a small plot of its own.

Harvest Jerusalem artichokes before blooms appear in late summer. Try to remove as many of the tubers as possible, as those which remain in the ground over winter may become weedy.

Store the tubers like potatoes. They neither can nor freeze well.

## Asparagus

Asparagus *(Asparagus officinalis)* has been enjoyed since ancient times. It is a member of the lily family (Liliaceae) and, like other members of that clan, prefers rich soil with no competition from weeds. It takes at least two years to get an asparagus patch producing, but once established, the same bed can yield a crop every spring for decades.

**Culture:** Purchase plants rather than starting from seed. This saves a year of waiting and avoids the hassle of dealing with delicate seedlings. Select a variety that produces only male plants; all-male varieties outperform females three to one because the plant's energy is directed into spear formation rather than seed production. Seedlings can also become weeds when they drop from the parent plant.

Asparagus is particular about its soil pH and the amount of phosphorus available. Test the soil and adjust the pH to neutral with lime or aluminum sulfate as required. This is best done in fall. Recheck the pH in spring after the additive has had time to work. Order your asparagus plants to arrive in early spring. Store them in a cool, dry place until planting time. To avoid root rot, wait until the soil temperature has reached 50°F before planting.

Dig shallow furrows 4 to 6 inches deep and as long as you require (see "Harvest and Yield" on page 141 to calculate yield). Space multiple rows 5 feet apart to enable you to walk between them when the tall, fernlike asparagus foliage matures in late summer. Apply 1 pound of bone meal per 10 feet of row. (This recommendation applies to bone meal containing 12 percent phosphorus. For other phosphate sources, adjust the application accordingly.) Set the plants down the middle of the furrow and cover to the original soil line with soil and compost. Do not compact the soil tightly over the roots, or you will inhibit emergence of the shoots.

Mulch the bed with whatever you have available, and promptly remove any weeds that come up through the mulch. The best asparagus grows in a weed-free environment.

**Harvest and Yield:** Avoid harvesting any shoots the first season after transplanting, and take only a few during the second season. Thereafter, you should get a decent crop each spring. After harvest, side dress the plants with plenty of compost and keep them irrigated during dry spells.

Each crown should produce half a pound of asparagus per season once established. Crowns should be spaced about 18 inches apart in the row. To allow for room on each end, therefore, a row with only two crowns should be about 4½ feet long. For each additional crown, add 18 inches. Thus, 10 feet of row is necessary to produce half a dozen crowns, yielding 3 pounds of spears per season.

**Storage and Preservation:** Asparagus is best eaten fresh but can be frozen or pickled. In either case, trim the stalks, peel them or leave them unpeeled as you prefer, and drop them into rapidly boiling water for one minute. Drain, transfer to ice water to stop the cooking, and drain again thoroughly. Pat dry with paper towels and freeze immediately. Alternately, place them upright in pint jars. (You may have to trim the spears to achieve a uniform length. If so, use the trimmings in soup or a stir-fry, or freeze for later use.) Add a sprig of tarragon to each jar and cover with basic pickling liquid (see page 248). Process according to the usual instructions for vegetable pickles (see page 239).

**Uses:** Asparagus can be boiled, steamed, grilled, or quickly fried, baked in quiches and casseroles, and enjoyed raw or pickled in a salad.

## Horseradish

Another perennial, horseradish is a member of the Brassicaceae. It looks like a huge, white carrot, with foliage resembling turnip tops. Chopped or grated, it adds a special form of heat to many types of dishes. It is especially good with potatoes, added to mayonnaise as a sandwich dressing or with cold roast meats. Growing it is a cinch. Simply take a piece of healthy-looking root with a little of the green top attached (you can find this at the grocery store, or perhaps a friend will share) and plant it in a corner of the garden in full sun. It will soon sprout and establish itself. Leave it unharvested for the first year, then dig the following spring, replant a portion and use the rest. Legendary for its tenacity, a horseradish plant will grow in that spot forever afterward. Do not allow plants to flower and produce seeds, or you risk having a weedy pest popping up here and there.

## Rhubarb

Rhubarb is grown from root cuttings and, like asparagus, requires establishment in rich, fertile, well-drained soil for a couple of seasons before you can harvest the juicy stems. High oxalic acid content renders the leaves inedible and if consumed in sufficient quantity, they can actually be poisonous. Rhubarb has its fans, and the plants are quite decorative in summer, but the harvest period is rather brief and the plants take up a lot of room. Most dishes pair it with fruit such as strawberries and require added sugar to counteract some of its tartness.

# 5

# Herbs for Flavor and Health

Herbs constitute a group of plants the boundaries of which constantly shift, depending on whom you ask. Herbal remedy lists may include plants that are not herbaceous in the botanical sense—that is, shrubs and trees. Some compilers even extend the definition to include any useful plant, whether it is employed for food, medicine, or other purposes.

On the new American homestead, herbs are an integral part of the garden. In the kitchen, the flavor of freshly picked herbs cannot be duplicated, and in the grocery, fresh herbs are among the most expensive produce items. These facts, coupled with their generally compact growth forms, make herbs the ideal choice for food gardening in containers. Even the smallest balcony can accommodate a few pots of herbs. Gardeners with more room can add herbs to vegetable beds and flower borders, allowing for plenty of plants to preserve for winter. Potted herbs can be grown successfully indoors during the winter. Some varieties are hardy enough to be left outdoors for year round harvest.

## Choosing What to Grow

Herbs are annuals, biennials, or perennials. The biennial herbs, such as parsley, are typically grown as annuals. Most people select perennial herbs first, because they provide a harvest with the least amount of effort. Purchase small plants in pots and transplant them to a larger container. With good care, you can harvest a few sprigs after a couple of weeks. In general, annual herbs are grown as vegetables, planted in patches in raised beds or rows, and harvested as needed. At the end of the season, they're finished and must be preserved for winter use.

If you will be growing herbs in containers only, decide how many 12-inch pots you can accommodate for the winter in the brightest light you have available indoors. Imagine each of those pots with an individual herb plant. Which herbs would you like? Select the ones you most prefer using in the kitchen, prioritizing your choices until you have filled your winter pots (on paper, at least). These varieties would constitute your basic herb garden. If you have the room, you can add more choices to the basic list.

# Herb Gardening Strategy

Having fresh herbs when you want them requires a bit of strategic planning. If you pick an individual plant too frequently, its vigor declines and its cooking qualities suffer. Therefore, if you use a lot of a particular herb, you may want multiple plants. Parsley provides a good example. Picking too many leaves from a single plant will cause it to bolt prematurely, becoming harsh and unpleasant tasting. I find I need an 8-foot row to provide all the parsley I can use. Fortunately, our climate is sufficiently mild that parsley can be picked all winter except during the bitterest cold spells. We try to have new plants ready to replace the winter parsley by February.

In the case of shrubby herbs like thyme, too much pruning will result in scraggly, mostly woody clumps. Instead of using the same plant all year, in June select some choice stems and root them as cuttings, rather than using them in the kitchen. When they are well rooted, transplant to pots of fresh soil and care for them for the remainder of the season. When frost threatens, these are the plants you can bring inside, ready to be clipped during the winter months.

## General Advice on Growing Herbs

Herbs as a group present few problems, even to a novice gardener. They seldom attract insects, with the notable exception of the parsley worm, and disease rarely strikes. Growing herbs among vegetables often confers some protection to the latter from insect damage. I prefer to grow annual herbs as part of my vegetable beds and to keep perennial herbs in large pots.

**Obtaining Plants:** Annual herbs grow from seeds. They generally germinate easily and can be started indoors under lights or directly seeded with no special treatment. Perennial herbs are best started from cuttings. Seed-grown specimens may vary considerably in flavor and other qualities from their parents. If the only source you have for a particular variety is seeds, grow several plants and choose those that taste and perform best for you, discarding the others.

You can buy herbs in small pots at garden centers. If they are propagated as cuttings from named cultivars, you should get good results and the flavor you anticipate. Beware of "generic" plants. These are probably seedlings and will be subject to variations.

An easy way to acquire herb plants is to root cuttings from the produce market. I obtained my French thyme and Greek oregano plants this way. Simply purchase a healthy looking bunch. Try to shop when the herbs have just arrived. Most grocers will be happy to let you know when to expect them. From the bunch, select five or six of the best-looking stems. Use the rest, of course, in the kitchen. Strip the leaves from the bottom few inches of stem, dip in rooting powder, and transfer to a small pot. They should root in three weeks or so. You can also root the cuttings in a glass of water near the kitchen window, but this is less reliable. Besides thyme and oregano, rosemary, sage, mint, and basil will all root using either method.

Besides the commonly available herbs, hundreds more can be found in catalogs and online. If you are lucky enough to have an herb farm in your area, this may be your best source for locally adapted varieties, growing suggestions, and advice on preserving and using herbs.

**Sun, Soil, and Moisture Requirements:** Grow herbs in full sun. The majority of herbs are not fussy about the soil they grow in, as long as it is well drained. Some will develop harsh flavors if grown in soil that is too rich. Herbs should grow well anywhere you would plant perennial flowers. As a rule of thumb, annual herbs need soil with more organic matter than do the perennial herbs. Even moisture throughout the growing season ensures the annuals will grow quickly, producing lush, tender leaves. The descriptions in this chapter point out where specific herbs deviate from these preferences.

# Annual Culinary Herbs

## Basil

Although technically perennial, basil (*Ocimum basilicum*) must be grown as an annual in most of the country because of its complete lack of cold tolerance. A few nights in the 30°F range and the leaves develop black spots and begin to drop. Start basil from seed and transplant to its permanent location after all danger of frost has passed and the ground is well warmed. It will bear continuously all season. Soil of good fertility, as is appropriate for tomatoes, will yield the best crop. After a heavy harvest, side dress the plants with compost or a balanced organic fertilizer. Pinch flowers as they form to keep the plant producing. Picking leaves encourages new growth to develop from axial buds, so regular harvesting is recommended.

Immerse cut stems in a vase of water almost up to the lowermost leaves. Do not refrigerate. Instead, leave them on the counter in indirect sun, if possible. They will keep this way for several days, and may even root. During the growing season, you will probably have such an abundance of basil that storage will not be necessary. To have a regular supply all summer and additional plant to move indoors, start a dozen basil plants.

Basil cuttings root quickly. Take them from your early crop and root in water. Transplant the cuttings into the garden (or 12-inch pots) when the roots are about 2 inches long and keep them well watered until the plants resume growth.

Numerous basil varieties are available. For general culinary purposes, choose a large-leafed green type, such as Genovese. Mammoth bears huge leaves big enough to use for wrapping pieces of food for steaming. For limited space gardens and small containers, try Boxwood, a small-leaf variety that forms a plant about the size of a soccer ball. Lemon (*O. citriodora*) and lime (*O. americanum*) basils grow just like the standard variety and can add a new dimension to pesto or salad dressing. Basils with colorful foliage, such as Purple Ruffles and Red Rubin, not only taste "brighter" than green basil, but they add a decorative note wherever you place them.

## Chervil

Chervil (*Anthriscus cerefolium*) peps up food with a licorice note not unlike that of tarragon, but subtler. It grows easily, preferring light shade and cool, moist conditions. Grow it in spring or fall if summers are hot where you live. Culture is similar to that for parsley, discussed later. I have been growing Brussels Winter chervil for two years now. It overwinters easily in my plastic covered cold frame.

## Cilantro

Cilantro (*Coriandrum sativum*) grows best when the weather is cool but will tolerate considerable warmth. It does well throughout the season in my Zone 6 garden. Summer plantings should receive afternoon shade. For quickest germination, soak seeds in water overnight before broadcasting where the plants will grow. Make successive small plantings a week apart to have a continuous supply. Harvest by pulling plants up by the roots.

Wash off the soil, but try not to wet the foliage, as this reduces its keeping qualities. Remove immature or damaged plants from the bunch, and refrigerate on a layer of damp paper towels in a tightly closed container.

## Dill

Another cool weather annual herb, dill (*Anethum graveolens*) is welcomed near the end of the season when it is traditionally used in making pickles. Spring sown dill will have foliage ready to clip about the time you dig the first new potatoes. Dill flowers attract beneficial insects. Grow it alongside okra, as the two have similar requirements, or intersperse a few dill plants with your onions to deter onion fly. Some dill varieties produce both usable foliage and seeds. Bouquet is a popular selection for seed production. Dukat and Fernleaf have been bred to produce mostly foliage with few seeds. Both are compact and suitable for container growing.

## Parsley

Parsley (*Petroselinum crispum*) will overwinter in mild areas, providing both late and early crops from the same fall planted patch. With careful succession planting, you can have parsley available any time. Italian, or flat leaf, parsley has the most intense flavor. Curly varieties, like Krausa are valued not only for garnishing platters; they also tolerate cold better than the flat leaf types. Parsley grows like carrots but needs more nitrogen to keep the leaves dark green and the plant productive. Cutting too frequently or too early may cause parsley to go to seed. Grow multiple plants and rotate your harvest among them. Parsley transplants more easily than most members of the carrot family. Soak seeds for four days, changing the water each day, before planting three or four seeds in a 4-inch pot. When several true leaves have developed, remove all but the strongest plant in each pot. Transplant to the garden around the frost-free date. Keep well watered and side dress regularly, especially if you harvest heavily. Mulch to keep the soil cool and retain moisture. Summer plantings in the South will benefit from afternoon shade.

## Tarragon, Mexican

In areas that are too hot and humid for French tarragon, this member of the marigold clan provides an adequate substitute. Botanically *Tagetes lucida*, it thrives in full sun on lean, well-drained soil. The bright yellow flowers look good in bouquets and taste like tarragon, too. In protected areas, this plant may return from the roots after being cut down by winter cold.

# Perennial Culinary Herbs

These plants return every year, although some may need protection in cold winter zones. A few may become woody and worn out from frequent harvesting, but can be rejuvenated by rooting new cuttings.

## Bay

A bay tree (*Laurus nobilis*) represents something of an investment. Cuttings root with difficulty. The plant needs to be several years old to withstand regular pruning. North of Zone 8, the roots will need protection or the plant must be brought indoors for winter. On the plus side, however, the dark evergreen foliage looks great in the landscape, the tree adapts easily to a large container and fresh bay leaves taste better than dried ones.

Bay grown in a container can be maintained at reasonable size by careful pruning. The plants make excellent topiary subjects. Spring is the best time to prune, but wait until your plant is at least two years old before you prune out any but dead or diseased branches. Spring is also the best time to fertilize and to repot, if needed. Feed the tree a second time around the Fourth of July. Rich, well-drained, slightly acid soil in full sun will give the best results. Do not allow plants to dry out completely during the growing season.

The best time to take cuttings is in autumn. Cuttings should be about 6 inches long, chosen from an upright growing branch. Try starting three or four, with the assumption that only one will root successfully. Dip in rooting hormone and stick in a sterile mixture of equal parts sand and vermiculite, moistened well, in a 4-inch pot. Keep in a humid chamber until roots have grown out the bottom, then move out into bright light. Keep well watered. Transplant to a 12-inch container the following spring.

Wintering a bay tree indoors will work best if you can provide good light from a south-facing window and/or bright artificial light.

## Chives

A member of the onion clan, chives (*Allium schoenoprasum*) grows easily in any well-drained garden soil in full sun to partial shade. It produces tubular, onion-flavored leaves about a foot tall all season long. The plant flowers best if grown in full sun. Not merely decorative, the purple-pink pom-pom shaped flowers taste good in salads and stir-fries, too. Chives also adapt well to container cultivation and will produce its tasty leaves all winter in a sunny window. Grow from seeds, following the instructions for growing green onions (see page 59), or purchase started plants. Clumps can easily be divided annually to increase your supply. Simply dig, separate into several smaller clumps, and replant.

## Chives, Chinese

Also called "garlic chives," *Allium tuberosum* produces larger, flatter leaves than regular chives. The flavor is more reminiscent of garlic than of onions. This plant grows so easily from seeds as to become a pest, but its prolific nature can be tamed simply by removing the flowers before the seeds turn dark. Newly opened flowers, produced in late summer, have a long vase life and their sturdy long stems make them welcome in arrangements. Grow this herb in any well-drained soil, which need not be particularly fertile. Like regular chives, it is easily divided.

## Lemon Verbena

Among the lemon-flavored herbs, *Aloysia triphylla* has the most intriguing flavor, lemon with floral undertones. It is not reliably hardy north of Zone 9 but can be overwintered indoors if you have a warm, sunny spot for it. It also roots easily from cuttings, so you can produce small plants in late summer for overwintering, and then move them outdoors again when the temperature will reliably remain above 40°F. They will grow to about 3 feet in diameter, yielding abundant leaves for flavoring teas and fruit dishes. Lemon verbena wilts almost as soon as it is harvested, so it is seldom used as a decorative garnish. However, the thin leaves are easy to dry. Just place on parchment paper on a baking sheet and dry for two to three hours in your oven, set to the lowest possible setting. Leave the oven door open. Home dried leaves will keep their flavor for months.

### Yellow Chives

Asian markets sometimes offer yellow chives. These are merely garlic chives that have been blanched. To achieve this effect, surround newly emerging foliage with a newspaper tube to shield out the sun. The resulting leafy growth will be yellow-green, tender, and mild flavored.

## Lovage

This relative of celery has a flavor similar to celery, but more complex. A cool weather crop, *Levisticum officinale*, grows as tall as 5 feet. It needs rich, moist, well-drained soil in full sun to partial shade. Where summers are hot, full afternoon shade is beneficial. Severe winter weather will kill the roots, but in mild climates lovage will return in the spring. Add lovage leaves and tender stems to any dish where celery is appropriate.

## Marjoram

Sweet marjoram (*Origanum hortensis*) tastes much like its relative, oregano, but has sweeter overtones reminiscent of cedar. It is perennial in Zone 10, but adapts very well to container cultivation and can be brought inside for the winter. It requires well-drained soil in full sun and not too much watering. Fertilization can lead to a harsh flavor.

## Mints

The flavors of mints, *Mentha* species, go well with many dishes both sweet and savory. The majority of this group of plant species and hybrids do not come true from seed; therefore, the best way to obtain plants is to purchase cuttings struck from known cultivars.

> Always taste mint plants before you buy, to make sure you get the flavor you want. Mint is child's play to root, so you can purchase a bunch at the grocery store and produce plants that way. Just strip the leaves from the bottom of the stem, recut the lower end of the stem at a 45-degree angle and set in a glass of water in a sunny window. Roots will form in a couple of weeks. Transplant to the garden when the plants are well rooted.

Mints are hardy to Zone 5, and grow best in constantly moist to wet soil in partial shade. Try growing them in a mixture of sand and compost kept constantly moist. Soil that is too rich will produce rampant, straggly growth, small leaves, and an unpleasant flavor. In good growing conditions, mint can become an invasive pest. For this reason, most gardeners keep it confined to a large container. Besides peppermint and spearmint, look for apple- and citrus-flavored mint cultivars.

Mint varieties easily cross with each other, and the flowers are highly attractive to pollinators. As a result, seedlings will display a range of flavors if you grow different varieties near each other and allow them to self-sow.

## Oregano

Look for genuine Greek oregano, a selection of *Origanum* species, with fine culinary qualities. The best place to obtain plants may be the grocery store. Seedlings frequently lack good flavor. Start cuttings and then transplant to 4-inch pots. When they are about 6 inches tall, move to the garden or to a large container. Oregano plants hug the ground and spread vigorously. They are hardy only to Zone 5, but adapt so easily to containers that you have no excuse for not bringing a pot indoors for the winter. As for marjoram, provide lean, well-drained soil and hold off on the moisture. Keep the plants in full sun. If your plants bloom, delay the harvest, as the flavor will be impaired. Enjoy the blooms, which can be used as a garnish or in a vase. Then cut the plants to the ground to allow them to regenerate. Out of bloom, keep them clipped back and they'll keep producing leaves all season long. Greek oregano retains its flavor well when dried.

## Rosemary

Said to improve memory function, *Rosmarinus officinalis* enhances the flavor of roasted meats with its pinelike fragrance. The soil for growing rosemary should be slightly alkaline. Mix ground limestone with your regular potting mix and grow the plants in full sun with average moisture. Do not allow plants to dry out completely. Rosemary is one of the best herbs for container cultivation and takes so well to pruning that rosemary topiary has become commonplace in garden centers. For culinary purposes, look for named selections.

Start cuttings from the grocery store as previously described, or purchase plants at a garden center. Rosemary seed germinates poorly and the seedlings need a lot of coddling to bring them to maturity. Among the hardiest cultivars is Arp. Barbecue produces long, straight stems that can be used as skewers, partially stripped of their leaves. Prostrate forms can cascade over the side of a pot or at the edge of an in-ground bed. Rosemary dries easily and retains flavor well.

## Sage

Common garden sage, *Salvia officinalis*, is hardy to Zone 4. It is highly decorative, often used as the centerpiece of an herb planting. Culinary sage has crinkled, blue-green leaves about 1 by 3 inches. Variegated forms are available, but they are more decorative than flavorful. Some are even downright unpleasant tasting. The best sage variety I have grown is Berggarten, which forms a rounded mound about 2 feet in diameter. A dwarf form appears from time to time in garden centers, and is well worth growing if you can find it. Give sage the same conditions recommended previously for oregano.

## Tarragon

Genuine French tarragon, *Artemesia dracunculus*, cannot be produced from seeds, because its seeds are sterile. Seed purported to be for tarragon will most likely yield *A. dracunculus var. sativa*, or Russian tarragon, bitter flavored and unsuitable for cooking. Purchase rooted cuttings or start your own from 6- to 8-inch stems from the grocery store, as described above for other herbs. Where summers are warm and moist, tarragon can be difficult to grow, yet it will tolerate only the lightest touch of frost. In many parts of the country, container cultivation is the only option. Provide lean, well-drained soil that is slightly alkaline. Avoid peat and pine products in the growing mix. Select a container holding about a cubic foot of growing medium. Mulch with gravel, and avoid overwatering. Tarragon is subject to numerous fungal diseases that thrive on excessive moisture. If you are successful in meeting its needs, a well-grown plant may be easily divided every two years. If you cannot seem to keep tarragon alive, grow the annual Mexican tarragon, described previously.

## Thyme

Surely among the most useful of culinary herbs, thyme (*Thymus vulgaris*) grows under conditions similar to those favored by its Mediterranean compatriots, oregano and marjoram. Lean soil, moist but well drained, and plenty of sunshine will give the best results. Cuttings from the grocery store are easy to root as described for oregano. Look for French thyme, which produces long, straight stems from which the leaves are easy to strip. Not only is its growth habit convenient, this form of thyme can be harvested all winter, as it remains evergreen in Zone 6. Various other thymes, representing several species and hybrids, are also available. Of these, the most useful in the kitchen are lemon- and lime-flavored forms, *T. vulgaris var. citrosa*. Other thymes are more useful for their decorative, rather than culinary, value.

## A Basic Culinary Herb Garden

Traditionally, herbs were grown in the dooryard, a space just out-side the kitchen door. Typically, about 4 feet square, the garden provides all the fresh herbs the cook can use, and some to preserve for later. Look at what you can grow in 16 square feet in full sun.

**Perennials**

- **Chives**—bordering the sides of the bed, 16 clumps total, 8 per side
- **Rosemary**—centerpiece of the bed, trimmed to conical shape, 1 plant
- **Oregano**—in front of the rosemary, 2 plants on either side
- **Thyme**—bordering the front of the bed, 6 plants

**Annuals**

- **Basil**—to follow early season annuals, behind rosemary, 3 plants
- **Dill**—plant in clumps in spring or fall, behind rosemary
- **Chervil**—plant in clumps in early spring or late fall, behind rosemary
- **Cilantro**—plant in clumps in spring or fall, behind rosemary
- **Parsley**—use to fill in as desired, or substitute for cilantro and chervil
- **Violets**—for color and interest, intersperse 6 viola plants with the thyme along the front of the bed

# Other Especially Useful Plants

Numerous other plants that often grown alongside traditional herbs may have uses other than purely culinary. Many, for example, can be made into teas with medicinal properties. Others, such as edible flowers, bring color and interest to the plate along with their unique flavors.

**Anise Hyssop:** A decorative perennial admired for its flowers and flavorful leaves, anise hyssop (*Agastache foeniculum*) attracts pollinators to the gar-den as well. It tolerates a little shade, and prefers afternoon shade where summers are hot. Direct seed in the garden after the frost date. This plant does well in average soil and moisture conditions. Grow with other herbs, or in a perennial flower border. It reaches about a foot in height.

**Bergamot:** Actually several species of *Monarda*, these plants are native to North America and attract pollinators and hummingbirds. Lemon bergamot (*M. citriodora*) produces flower heads in pale violet shades. Leaves have a citrus flavor that is retained when dried. Seedling flower color and flavor may vary considerably from the parent. Unless you have room to grow many seedlings and select the best for your garden, purchase vegetatively propagated plants with known characteristics. Red bergamot (*M. didyma*) is another native of the eastern United States. Its bright red flowers attract hummingbirds and can be used in salads. Colonial Americans used the dried leaves, leading to the common name of "Oswego tea." Both species of bergamot are perennial to Zone 4, and with protection can survive farther north. They grow best in partial shade, ideally afternoon shade, and rich, moist soil with plenty of organic matter. Dry conditions will lead to powdery mildew and harsh flavors. Both these members of the mint family spread by runners. Dig them periodically and replant the new outer growth, discarding the old center of the plant.

**Catnip:** Not only a feline favorite, this herb (*Nepeta cataria*) produces a sedative that has been traditionally used to relieve cold and flu symptoms. Tea infused from the dried leaves has a soothing effect and promotes drowsiness. A member of the mint family, catnip grows best in full sun in moist, well-drained soil high in organic matter. It forms a mound about 2 feet in diameter. Pale lavender flowers on taller spikes appear in summer. Plants are hardy to Zone 4. Not all cats will be attracted to catnip. Those who are may lie in the center of your plants, eat the leaves, or otherwise despoil them. Fortunately, you can cut the stems back after such an episode and new growth will replace them.

**Chamomile:** A member of the aster family, chamomile (*Matricaria recutita*) grows in full sun in lean, well-drained soil. An annual, its self-sown seedlings will pop up all over the garden but are easily removed where you do not want them. The fragrant flowers, small white daisies with yellow centers, are dried and used to make apple-scented tea that has long been used medicinally. Note: people with allergies to ragweed pollen should not consume the pollen of this or any other member of the aster family.

**Daylily:** An Asian native that has been naturalized along roadsides throughout much of the eastern United States, *Hemerocallis* species and hybrids have a devoted following. Hundreds of cultivars exist, in nearly every color but true blue. Plants of this group tolerate heavy clay soils, drought, and neglect, and seldom are bothered by pests. The unopened buds may be steamed and eaten like green beans, or dipped in batter and deep fried. Opened flowers, which only last for a day anyway, can be chopped and added to soups, salads, and stir-fries. The plants are easily divided any time of the year, even when in bloom. Culinary quality varies greatly among the many cultivars. Fragrant varieties, some with a distinct lemon scent, are also the best tasting. When in doubt, sample before you purchase a plant. One of the best all-around cultivars is Mauna Loa, a fragrant, yellow-orange with good flavor that blooms twice during the summer.

**Echinacea:** Studies indicate this genus of plants (*Echinacea purpurea, E. angustifolia,* and others) produces phytochemicals that stimulate the immune system. A member of the aster family, coneflowers are native prairie plants. Drought tolerant once established, they grow best in full sun in well-drained soil of average fertility. Most plants remain under 3 feet tall. The various species freely hybridize, and you will get self-sown seed-lings that show a range of variation. Plant breeders have used this trait to create some bizarre-looking cultivars, but the wild-type, 3-inch, pink-pur-ple flowers with their yellow-orange centers look best to me in a mixed border or herb bed.

Seeds require a cold period to germinate, so plant in fall to overwinter outdoors. Mark the spot and transplant the seedlings in spring when they have two sets of true leaves. Alternatively, seeds can be sown in flats that are refrigerated after enclosing in a plastic bag to keep them moist. Brought out into the warmth in early spring, the flats will be full of seedlings by the end of April.

All parts of the plant show pharmacological activity, but the dried roots are most often recommended. For this purpose, choose *E. angustifolia. E. purpurea* is easier to grow, but does not produce a thick rootstock. Instead, it is grown for leaf production. Several other species of Echinacea can be found in seed catalogs. All are worth including in the garden for their deco-rative value alone. They also attract butterflies and goldfinches.

**Geraniums:** Scented geraniums, relatives of the familiar red window box vari-eties, are derived from several species of *Pelargonium.* Their fragrant leaves (flowers are often insignificant) can be dried for teas and potpourri. With more than 50 cultivars of rose-scented geraniums alone, this group has something for everyone. A partial list of fragrances includes apricot, cinnamon, coconut, nutmeg, and pineapple. Seedlings do not resemble their parents, as a rule, so obtain plants vegetatively propagated from a known cultivar. From Zone 7 south, geraniums will survive winter if cut back and mulched well after the first frost kills the leaves. Otherwise, lift plants and bring them indoors for winter. They can be stored bare root in a frost-free place and brought out of dormancy in spring. Geraniums are not particular about soil and are drought tolerant, although container-grown specimens should not be allowed to dry out thoroughly. Feed regularly with a liquid organic fertilizer, such as fish emulsion.

**Ginger:** This tropical perennial (*Zingiber officinale*) grows from the fleshy rhizome sold in grocery markets as ginger root. Choose a plump, healthy looking specimen with numerous "eyes" like potatoes. The best time to plant is in the spring, but you can grow ginger any time if you can protect it from frost. Purchase the rhizomes in quantity when they are on sale and store them dry and cool until you need them. Soak the rhizome in a bowl of lukewarm water overnight before planting if it has become shriveled.

Select a container at least four times larger than the piece of rhizome you are planting. A 12- to 14-inch azalea pot works well. This will allow for the development of an extensive root system. Fill the container three-quarters full with a good, well-drained potting mix containing plenty of compost. Place the soaked rhizome on top of the mix with the eyes pointing upward. Cover with more potting mix and water well. Place the container in a plastic bag in indirect light until green shoots appear. (This can take a month.) Then remove the bag and water well. Keep the plant in bright, indirect light and never allow the soil to dry out. Growing plants need protection from wind and should be brought indoors any time the temperature is headed below 50°F. The ideal growing temperature is 75°F to 85°F.

It can take as long as a year for a container-grown ginger plant to reach its mature height of 2 to 4 feet. Plants started indoors in February will nevertheless produce a harvestable crop by the following September. You can achieve more robust growth by transplanting a container-grown specimen to the garden when nighttime temperatures are reliably above 50°F. Select a spot with good drainage, partial sun, and rich soil. Dig in plenty of compost and sand if your soil is heavy clay. After transplanting, feed the plants every three weeks with a soluble organic fertilizer, such as fish emulsion or liquefied seaweed. Ginger thrives on hot, humid weather and thus adapts quite well to muggy southern summers. If you are the impatient type, you can carefully harvest a few tender shoots from the outside edge of the clump for use during the summer months. This "baby" ginger is not as pungent as the later mature crop will become.

When the leaves begin to turn yellow late in the season, it is time to harvest. Dig up the rhizomes, and immediately replant the ones you want to grow next season. If you keep the containers cool and dry, they probably will not sprout again until mid-winter. Alternatively, after a month's rest, you can start watering and feeding again to get a jump on next season. The longer the plants grow, the larger the harvest will be. Ginger freezes well. Just peel, chop, and place in suitable containers. You can also store chunks or slices of fresh ginger in a jar, covered with brandy. Dried ginger root keeps well but loses some of its bite. Ginger can also be candied like citrus peel.

**Lavender:** Two types, English and French lavender, provide us with a host of cultivars. The one usually identified as the most fragrant is English lavender Munstead, *Lavandula vera*. Lavender tea has traditionally been used to relieve headaches, and the flowers and branches can be placed in drawers to repel insects. English lavender will suffer where summers are hot and muggy. A better choice for such climates is French lavender, *L. dentata*. While the fragrance is not as powerful as that of its English cousin, it is far more tolerant of hot weather.

As you might guess from the botanical name, the leaves of French lavender are toothed, or "dentate." English lavender, on the other hand, produces leaves with smooth margins. Both species are hardy as far north as Zone 5. Either adapts well to container cultivation and can be brought indoors for winter. The plants require a freely draining, slightly alkaline soil and must have full sun. Too much water or poor air circulation will lead to disease. Keep the flowers cut to encourage the plant to produce more. Avoid peat and pine products in the growing mix, and mulch with gravel rather than organic materials.

**Lemon Balm:** Lemon balm (*Mentha officinalis*) forms a neat, rounded mound about 2 feet in diameter and 18 inches tall. Its intensely green, toothed leaves have prominent veins and a bright citrus flavor. Seedlings, which may self-sow abundantly in good conditions, vary from their parents and should be weeded out. Cuttings root easily any time during the season. Grow in full sun except in the South, where afternoon shade is best. Soil conditions are not important, as long as drainage is good. Keep plants well watered and avoid overcrowding to lessen the chance of plants developing powdery mildew. Leaves can be used anywhere a lemon flavor is desired, and dry well for use in teas. The flower spikes are long lasting in a vase, and individual blooms can be added to salad or used as a garnish.

**Lemongrass:** Essential to Thai, Vietnamese, and other Asian cuisines, and a good source of lemon flavor, lemongrass (*Cymbopogon citratus*) is a tropical perennial that must be wintered indoors or started anew each season. Because it needs a large container for its prodigious root system, starting over each year is the best technique. It is not sufficiently ornamental to warrant the trouble of growing it indoors and in any case will need supplemental lighting during the short days of winter. Instead, visit the grocery store in early spring to buy new starts. Lemongrass is sold in bunches of several stems with most of the foliage removed. Each stem has a bulbous base. You may see tiny roots or root buds sticking out from the base. When planted, the basal portion quickly roots and grows into a clump a yard or more in height and about as wide. Insert the stem about an inch into a small pot of damp soil mix, and roots will quickly form. When new roots protrude from the drain hole in the pot, you are ready to transplant outside, but wait until all danger of frost has passed and the weather is warm.

If sited in full sun and rich, moist soil, lemongrass grows with amazing rapidity. Plants should be fertilized regularly. Add compost to the bottom of the planting hole, and side dress monthly with additional compost, fish emulsion, or seaweed extract. The ideal growing temperature is 75°F during the day and 60°F at night.

The leaves of lemongrass have sharp, serrated edges that can deliver a nasty cut. Wear heavy gloves and a long-sleeved shirt when working with them. To harvest, select stems whose base is about half an inch in diameter. Remove foliage with clippers, and trim to 8 or 19 inches in length. Stems will keep well under refrigeration for a week or two, or you can chop and freeze them. Lemongrass can also be dried and used to season herbal teas. When grown outdoors, the leaves often take on a reddish cast, enhancing the herb's decorative value in the landscape. You could even use it as a protective, although temporary, hedge.

**Nasturtium:** An old-fashioned cottage garden plant, nasturtium (*Tropaeolum majus*) is a warm-season annual that thrives best in poor but well-drained soils. Soak the large seeds overnight in water before planting them directly in the garden. The fragrant flowers, which are borne abundantly all season, are delicious in salads or soups and make superb flavored vinegar. Both flowers and leaves have a taste reminiscent of cauliflower, but with a slight peppery bite. Numerous cultivars are available. Some have a vining habit and can be trained on a trellis, while others produce upright, mounding plants. Compact forms look good in containers. Nasturtium is a good companion for the Mediterranean herbs, such as thyme and oregano, because the plants prefer similar conditions. The cultivar, Jewel, produces red, yellow, orange, and pink flowers, with some double and some bicolored blooms. Whirlybird bears a similar mix of colors on tall stems held above the foliage for easy picking. Empress of India produces compact plants with dark red coloration in the foliage and velvety red flowers. Alaska is similar to Jewel, but with pale green foliage variegated in white.

**Poppy:** The bread seed poppy (*Papaver somniferum*) is a cool season annual. Broadcast seeds where you want plants to grow in fall or winter. They will germinate in early spring. For best seed production, thin seedlings to stand about a foot apart, and stake the plants when they are a foot tall. Plants will reach 2 to 3 feet in height and bear huge, pale bluish or pinkish flowers followed by the seed heads. After being emptied of their seeds, the pods can be used in dried arrangements.

**Saffron:** Nothing is quite like the unique, indescribable flavor of saffron. The dried stigmas of an autumn crocus (*Crocus sativus*), saffron is seldom considered a choice for the home herb garden. Nevertheless, saffron crocus is as easy to grow as its spring-blooming cousins and will repay your efforts many times. A few pinches of dried saffron can set you back ten dollars in the grocery store.

Saffron grows well in zones 6 through 9 and prefers good, well-drained soil in full sun. A patch of 10 square feet, enough to accommodate about fifty bulbs, will provide an increasing abundance of spice as the plants mature and multiply. Set them out in summer, while they are dormant, 6 inches apart and 3 inches deep. You can overplant, if you wish, with annual flowers or summer herbs such as basil. Pull up the annuals when the weather turns cold, or when you see the new green shoots of saffron poking through the soil in autumn. When the lovely lavender-blue flowers open a few weeks later, harvest by picking the bright red stigmas by hand. You can use them immediately in such Mediterranean dishes as paella, bouillabaisse, and risotto, or dry them for a few days before storing in an airtight container for later use.

**Violets:** Numerous species of violets (*Viola*) have been cultivated over the centuries. One, *V. tricolor*, or Johnny-jump-up, appears in garden centers abundantly every spring and fall. Fall planted violas will bloom all winter in mild climates, or bloom in early spring after overwintering farther north. Their blooms taste like cabbage and look beautiful as a garnish or in salads. The color range is vast. Start violas from seed or purchase plants. Numerous native violets occur across North America. They range from easy to challenging to cultivate, and many are rare. Make sure any plants you get come from nursery propagation and not wild populations.

# Mushrooms

Mushrooms, of course, are not herbs. In fact, they are not even plants, but fungi. I include them here because many mushrooms have long been consumed for their medicinal qualities as much as for their culinary value. With the exception of shiitake, mushrooms pose special challenges for the would-be grower. Shiitake, which grow on dead logs, are so easy to grow that you can buy a preinoculated log and raise them under the kitchen sink. Other cultivated mushrooms grow on straw, special compost mixtures, or outside in the ground. Specialty societies, devoted not only to the cultivation of mushrooms at home but also to their identification and harvest from the wild, can be found throughout the country. Several companies sell mushroom growing supplies and starters. You can find them on the Internet.

# Preserving and Using Herbs

The most common method for preserving herbs is to dry them. Not all varieties retain their flavor after drying, however. Other methods to capture and save herbal flavors include freezing and the preparation of herbal vinegars, oils, and tinctures.

## Drying

The easiest way to dry a few sprigs of any herb is to arrange them on parchment paper on a baking sheet and place in your oven with the door open. Set the oven to its lowest setting, and check after a few hours. When the leaves are brittle and crumbly, but long before they begin to brown or burn, remove from the oven and let cool. Crumble the leaves and store in small jars or bottles labeled with the variety and date.

Where late summer and autumn weather trends warm and dry, you can secure bunches of herbs with a rubber band and hang them to dry in an airy location out of the sun. After a week or so, they should be brittle enough to store. Don't leave them hanging, or the flavor will soon become washed-out.

You can also purchase a dehydrator for herbs and other garden products. Follow the manufacturer's directions for drying herbs if you go this route.

Store dry herbs in a cool, dark, dry location and use within one year. To substitute dry for fresh herbs, use one third the amount called for in the recipe.

## Freezing

The following herbs do not dry well and can be preserved best by freezing: basil, chervil, chives, cilantro, and parsley. Freeze by one of two methods. Chop the herbs finely and place by teaspoons in the cells of an ice cube tray. Fill the tray with water and freeze. Pop out the cubes and store in a plastic bag in the freezer. Alternatively, combine the minced herbs with softened butter, using about two tablespoons of herbs per stick of butter. Form the compound butter into a log, wrap in plastic wrap, wrap again in foil and freeze. Use to season vegetable and meat dishes.

## Vinegars, Oils, Essences, and Extracts

One of the best ways to preserve seasonal flavors for later use is to isolate the flavor component from the food and store it in concentrated form. With many types of foods as raw material and a variety of methods for isolating flavors, you can create a vast array of seasonings to have ready in the pantry.

Soaking herbs and other flavoring agents in vinegar creates flavor combinations that can be used in a variety of ways. Different types of vinegar may be used, including distilled white, cider, rice, and wine vinegars. Flavoring agents can include fresh or dried herbs, spices, fruit, citrus peel, and even edible flowers.

### Red Basil Vinegar

2 quarts (in all) packed fresh red basil leaves
1 quart white wine or rice vinegar

Start with 1 quart of leaves in a clean glass jar. Cover them with the vinegar and tamp down gently with the handle of a wooden spoon, bruising the leaves slightly and ensuring they are completely immersed. Cover and place in the refrigerator for 2 weeks. Strain off the vinegar, discard the basil, and wash the jar. Add another packed quart of leaves and return the vinegar to the jar. Allow to steep in the refrigerator for 2 more weeks. Drain, transfer to sterile bottles, cap, and store in the refrigerator for up to 4 months.

## Nasturtium Vinegar

Nasturtium flowers, freshly picked
A few white peppercorns
2 cups white wine vinegar

Wash and sanitize a bottle holding about a pint. As you harvest the nasturtium flowers, drop them into the bottle until it is loosely filled to the shoulder. Drop in the white peppercorns. Add the wine vinegar and cap the bottle. Wait a month for flavor to develop before using.

---

## Berry or Cherry Vinegar

1 pound fresh raspberries, blackberries, strawberries, or pitted cherries
2⅓ cups red or white wine vinegar, or a combination

Place the fruit in a canning jar. In a small saucepan, heat the vinegar until it is almost too hot to touch. Pour the vinegar over the fruit, cap the jar, allow to cool, and refrigerate for 2 weeks.

Strain the vinegar through a cheesecloth-lined sieve, pressing down on the solids with the back of a wooden spoon to extract as much flavor as possible. Store in sterilized bottles in a cool dark place and use within 6 months.

---

Fruit vinegar can be used in salad dressing, drizzled directly on cooked vegetables, or added to juice drinks. The recipe for one of my favorites follows.

## John's Antioxidant Cocktail

1 cup tomato juice
¼ cup cherry juice
2 tablespoons blackberry vinegar

Combine all of the ingredients and chill, covered, in the refrigerator. Serve with or without added alcohol.

---

Oil can also be used to isolate flavor from foods, including many of the same ingredients used in vinegar making. For most herbs, a cup of fresh leaves will flavor a cup of oil. Experiment with your own combinations to achieve the taste your family most enjoys.

## Rosemary Oil

1 cup extra-virgin olive oil
1 cup fresh rosemary leaves

Place the oil in a double boiler and set over, not in, simmering water. Add the rosemary leaves and allow to steep 10 minutes over the heat. Remove the pan from the water and cool to room temperature. Transfer to a blender and blend for 10 seconds. Store in the refrigerator overnight.

Place a coffee filter in a funnel set over a suitable container for the finished oil. Moisten the funnel with a drop or two of cooking oil, such as canola. This is done to keep the coffee filter from absorbing too much of your finished product. Allow the oil to come to room temperature, then pour it into the funnel. It will take several hours for all of the oil to drip through. Have patience and do not disturb the process. If the oil stops dripping altogether, set up another funnel with a fresh filter and carefully spoon as much of the oil as possible into the new filter. Store, covered, in the refrigerator.

---

Rosemary oil is delicious when combined with salt, pepper, and a little grated Parmigiano-Reggiano cheese as a dip for fresh bread.

Leafy herbs such as basil, cilantro, and mint require a slightly different technique.

## Cilantro Oil

1 large bunch of freshly harvested cilantro
1 cup extra virgin olive oil or grapeseed oil

Holding the cilantro bunch by the stems, immerse the top portion into rapidly boiling water for 10 seconds. Immediately plunge the cilantro into a bowl of ice water to set the color and stop the cooking process. Drain and pat dry with kitchen towels.

Heat the oil in a double boiler as described for Rosemary Oil (see recipe on page 163). Coarsely chop the cilantro and add it to the oil. Steep for 10 minutes.

Finish the oil as described for Rosemary Oil.

Extracts and essences are essentially just concentrated tea made from flavoring ingredients and water or alcohol. Extracts made with alcohol are often called *tinctures.* When an extract is reduced in volume by the application of heat, it becomes an *essence.* The simplest essence is roasted garlic (see recipe on page 61).

The flavor of mushrooms can also be captured in an essence. For example, the water used for soaking any type of dried mushroom can be saved, reduced over gentle heat, and used to flavor soup or sauce. You can also roast fresh mushrooms, tossed with a little oil, until they are browned, then puree them in a food processor with enough water to make a creamy liquid. Strain the liquid through a fine sieve into a saucepan, then reduce over low heat until it is as rich as you prefer. Taste very carefully as the essence cooks. A similar technique can be applied to other foods and the essence can be more complex, with added herbs, citrus peel, or other ingredients. If you make a large quantity of an essence, it can be pressure-canned, but generally you will prepare small amounts that are best kept covered and refrigerated and used within a week.

Extracts can be used to add flavor to beverages, soups, sauces, and salad dressings, just to name a few. Saffron is commonly mixed with a small amount of boiling water and allowed to steep before the whole thing is added to the pot. This is a simple example of using an extract. A more complex example follows.

## White Wine Extract

1 bottle good, drinkable white wine without oak, such as Pinot Grigio
1 medium onion, diced
2 large leeks, white parts only, chopped
2 stalks celery, chopped
6 white peppercorns

Combine the ingredients in a saucepan and bring to a simmer. Cook over low heat until the volume is reduced to one third of the original amount. Strain through a sieve, pressing on the solids with the back of a wooden spoon to extract as much of their flavor as possible. You should have about 2 cups of liquid. If you end up with a lot more, return the liquid to the heat and simmer gently until reduced to 2 cups.

Wine extracts can be used as is over roasted meats or vegetables or can be added as a component of more complex sauces or braising liquids. Red wine can be combined with bold ingredients, such as tomatoes, to create extracts that stand up to rich foods like beef or game. White wine extracts lend themselves to vegetables, fish, and poultry.

Tinctures are extracts made by soaking the flavoring ingredient in pure grain alcohol. You can purchase pure grain alcohol in liquor stores in most states. It is 190 proof, or 95 percent ethanol. If you cannot find it, substitute the highest proof vodka the store stocks. The most commonly used tincture is probably pure vanilla extract, which can be made by soaking a vanilla bean overnight in enough pure grain alcohol to cover it. This must be done in a tightly sealed bottle or jar, to prevent excessive evaporation of the alcohol. You could, for example, place the bean lengthwise in a bottle and fill the bottle with alcohol. It will be ready to use after twenty-four hours.

Medicinal herbs are sometimes made into a tincture for ease of dosing. The dried roots of echinacea, mayapple, and other medicinal herbs are first extracted with alcohol before adding them to tea. As a rule of thumb, first dilute the alcohol by half with distilled water. One cup of this solution will extract 1 ounce of dried herb. Allow to stand in a covered jar overnight, then strain and bottle. Take care not to expose the tincture to the air too much, or you will lose some of the product to evaporation. Tinctures can also be prepared from nonedible berries and leaves to create dyes. As with any plant product, always research possible toxicity and be absolutely certain of your identification before ingesting a tincture or extract.

## Using Sugar as a Preservative

Sugar can also act as a preservative, as it does when we make jams and jellies. For example, layering dry sugar with a fresh herb product, such as lavender flowers, in a closed jar for a couple of weeks will produce lavender sugar, which is heavenly on blueberries. Sift the dried flowers out of the sugar before using it. For a fancy presentation, tint the sugar with a few drops of food coloring before sprinkling it on the fruit. Other herbs appropriate for sweet dishes, such as basil, lemon verbena, or other lemon flavors will release their essences into sugar. Chop before mixing with the sugar to ensure even drying.

Sugar syrup makes an excellent preservative, too. Combine equal parts sugar and water for a heavy syrup or one part sugar and two parts water for a light syrup. Heat these ingredients, stirring until the sugar dissolves, bring to a boil and simmer for one minute, uncovered. Remove from the heat and add chopped fresh herbs, citrus peel, ginger, or a combination. Allow to steep until the syrup is cooled to room temperature, then strain and store in the refrigerator. Drizzle over fruit or baked goods, or add to a recipe.

Candying is the process of cooking food in sugar syrup until all of the liquid evaporates. This technique is often used to preserve citrus peel and ginger. Citrus peel must first be treated to remove its bitter components. This is accomplished by blanching the peel in boiling water for five minutes, draining, rinsing, then repeating the process for a total of five blanchings. The blanched peel is then combined with an equal portion of heavy sugar syrup (one part sugar to one part water) and the mixture cooked slowly over low heat, stirring occasionally, until almost all of the syrup has evaporated and the peel has a translucent appearance. Off the heat, remove the peel with tongs and roll it in granulated sugar. Transfer to waxed paper to dry, then store in an airtight container in the refrigerator. Ginger can be candied in the same manner, omitting the blanching steps. Simply peel, slice, and cook the ginger with the syrup as described.

Flowers, especially violets, are often candied by a different method. Separate an egg, placing the white in a small bowl and reserving the yolk for another use. Beat the white thoroughly but gently with a fork, introducing as little air as possible. With a small artist's brush, coat the flower petals with the egg white, place on a plate, and dust with granulated sugar to coat the blossom. Using a pair of tweezers, transfer the flowers to waxed paper to dry overnight. Store in an airtight container in the refrigerator. Color the sugar with food coloring before you begin, if you wish. Simply stir a drop or two of coloring into a bowl of sugar until you have the tint you desire. Candied flowers, typically made by people with lots of patience, look sensational adorning baked goods.

## Using Herbs

Herbs can be used alone or in combinations with one another and additional flavoring agents such as citrus peel to create a wealth of condiments you will enjoy long after summer is over.

Uses for herbs can be found all over the house, not just in the kitchen. Herb bouquets can lend their fragrance wherever you desire it. Herb-infused oils can soothe chapped hands or lips. Centuries of experimentation have led humans to all kinds of great ways to use herbs. Woody rosemary stems make great skewers for grilling bits of meat or vegetables. Herbs and their flowers make ideal garnishes for dishes in which their flavor stars. Start with some of the ideas in the table that follows, and then use your imagination to create your own unique herbal products for your family to enjoy or to give as gifts.

### Culinary and Other Uses of Herbs in This Chapter

| Herb | Culinary Uses | Other Uses* | Preserve Via |
|------|--------------|-------------|--------------|
| Anise Hyssop | Licorice-flavored tea | Respiratory ailments, flowers attract pollinators | Drying |
| Basil | Goes well with tomatoes, summer vegetables, and fish; Italian and Asian dishes; acidic fruits | Gas relief, upset stomach relief | Freeze, butter, vinegar, oil, drying |

*(continued)*

## Culinary and Other Uses of Herbs in This Chapter (continued)

| Herb | Culinary Uses | Other Uses* | Preserve Via |
|---|---|---|---|
| Bay | Italian, Creole, and other savory dishes, especially with seafood and/or tomatoes | Keeps mice and ants out of pantry; diuretic tea; poison ivy relief | Drying |
| Bergamot | Citrus-flavored tea, fish or chicken dishes | Upset stomach relief, flowers attract pollinators | Drying |
| Catnip | Tea, feline fun | Sedative, flowers attract pollinators | Drying |
| Chamomile | Apple-flavored tea | Upset stomach relief, flowers attract pollinators | Drying |
| Chervil | Mild licorice flavor for fish, asparagus, and other vegetable dishes | Fever reduction | Freeze, butter, oil |
| Chives | Onion flavoring for many types of dishes, especially potato and creamed dishes | Antimicrobial phytochemicals | Freeze, butter, oil |
| Chives, Chinese | Garlic flavor for many dishes | Antimicrobial phytochemicals | Freeze, butter, oil |
| Cilantro | Latino and Asian cuisines use leaves and seeds to flavor various dishes | Fever reduction | Freeze, butter, oil |
| Daylily | Use unopened buds like green beans, flower petals in salads and soups | Diuretic and laxative properties, especially the tubers; attracts pollinators | Drying |
| Dill | Flavoring for pickles, salad dressings, soup, and many other dishes, especially fish | Gas relief, upset stomach relief; flowers attract beneficial insects | Drying, butter, oil |
| Echinacea | Flower petals can be chopped and added to soup or salad | Immune system stimulant; flowers attract beneficial insects and birds | Drying, tincture |

| | | | |
|---|---|---|---|
| Geraniums | Small amounts can be added to soups or salads where the flavor is appropriate | Aromatherapy, mosquito repellents | Drying, tincture |
| Ginger | Essential in Asian cuisine, also used in Western desserts and baked goods | Numerous health benefits attributed | Freeze, drying, candy |
| Lavender | Can substitute for rosemary in meat dishes | Headaches, anxiety, and stress relief | Drying, sugar |
| Lemon Balm | Teas, salad dressings, etc., where the lemon flavor is appropriate | Sedative, antiviral activity; flowers attract beneficial insects | Drying, sugar |
| Lemongrass | Asian teas, soups, and curries; not usually eaten but allowed to infuse flavor | Numerous health benefits attributed | Freeze, drying, oil |
| Lemon Verbena | Lemon flavor with floral notes for teas, salad dressings, and fruit dishes | Antimicrobial phytochemicals | Freeze, drying, syrup, sugar |
| Lovage | Celery flavor for meat or vegetable dishes, tea | Diuretic, gas relief | Drying, oil |
| Marjoram | Italian and Eastern European vegetable dishes and sauces | Antimicrobial phytochemicals | Drying |
| Mints | Tea, jelly, fruit desserts, and vegetable dishes | Sore throat relief, expectorant; flowers attract pollinators | Drying, tincture |
| Nasturtium | Flowers and leaves can be added to salads or soups, or used to flavor vinegar | Anticongestant; flowers attract beneficial insects | Vinegar |
| Oregano | Mediterranean dishes, especially those with tomatoes and/or cheese | Antioxidants | Drying |

*(continued)*

## Culinary and Other Uses of Herbs in This Chapter (continued)

| Herb | Culinary Uses | Other Uses* | Preserve Via |
|---|---|---|---|
| Parsley | As a garnish for almost any savory dish | High in vitamins A and C; attracts black swallowtail butterfly | Freeze, butter, drying |
| Poppy | Poppyseed for baked goods | Sedative | Drying |
| Rosemary | Vegetable and meat dishes, especially when grilled or roasted | Antioxidants, memory improvement | Drying, butter, oil |
| Saffron | Flavor and color for curries, rice, fish, and chicken dishes | Antioxidant phytochemicals | Drying |
| Sage | Meats and dressings, winter squash, and sweet potato dishes | Improves digestion, antimicrobial | Drying, oil |
| Tarragon | Chicken, asparagus, fish, and many other savory dishes; vinegar | Deters garden pests when companion planted | Drying, vinegar, butter, oil |
| Tarragon, Mexican | Substitute for tarragon where summers are too hot and humid | Antimicrobial phytochemicals; flowers attract beneficial insects | Best used fresh, drying okay |
| Thyme | Improves most savory dishes, especially those containing beef, tomatoes or beans | Upper respiratory distress relief | Drying, oil |
| Violets | Flowers added to salads or soups, or candied to decorate baked goods | Flowers or leaves used for respiratory ailments, headache and digestive problems; attracts fritillary butterflies | Candy, vinegar |

*The information reported in this column has been compiled from many sources and is intended as a guide for garden design only. Nothing presented here is intended as a medical claim, a prescription for self-medication. or a substitute for the advice of a qualified health-care professional. Do not use herbal treatments without consulting a health-care professional.

# 6

# Fruits

Technically, many of the vegetables we eat are "fruits" in the botanical sense of a fleshy structure enclosing seeds and derived from the ovary of the flower. In this chapter, however, I am defining fruits by their culinary qualities. As opposed to vegetables, fruits are sweet rather than savory. Besides flavor and sweetness, fruits contribute numerous antioxidants and other beneficial phytochemicals to the diet.

Not all small fruit cultivars are suitable for all areas of the country; indeed, different cultivars have been developed to thrive under the specifics of regional climates. You therefore should always consult your state's agriculture extension service for information on the best choices for your region.

Creating a berry patch or orchard requires more planning and effort than growing a vegetable garden. Typically, one to five years must pass from the time fruits are transplanted until the first harvest arrives. Counterbalancing this drawback, established fruit plantings do not need the constant attention required by vegetables. In fruit cultivation, seasonal chores involve pruning, mulching, weeding, and fertilizing. Each of these is best done at the appropriate season, and none is especially strenuous.

## Choosing Fruits

Your first consideration in planning for fruit production should be your family's preferences. If no one likes blackberries, it makes little sense to grow them. Also consider the quantities you will use. If the goal is production, say for jam making, you will want to grow fruit with high yields per square foot of growing space. For the smaller garden, that is likely to be strawberries, which grow well even in containers. Fruits are often categorized by the mature size of the plant, and I have followed that practice here. Strawberries are smallest, followed by brambles, shrubs, vines, and trees. Each type has different needs and places different demands on the grower.

All fruit plants grow best in well-drained, loamy soils with plenty of organic matter. All need full sun for best fruit production. Bramble and vine fruits will require trellising, the design of which depends on the fruit being grown. Of primary consideration are the climatic requirements of particular fruits. Your best bet for sorting out the many varieties into a short list of those best suited to your region is to make use of the resources of your local agricultural extension office.

## Strawberries

The strawberries we enjoy today result from a long history of selection and hybridization among several of the fifty-odd natural species. Hundreds of strawberry (*Fragaria* × *ananassa*) cultivars exist, but they can all be classified as one of three varieties:

- **June-bearing strawberries** produce a single crop in early summer.

- **Everbearing (or day-neutral) strawberries** produce a bumper crop in early summer, another smaller crop in late summer, and a few berries here and there throughout the season in between.

- **Alpine strawberries**, the third type, bear small numbers of fruits more or less continuously. The individual berries of Alpines are much smaller than those of the other types. They taste less sweet but are more flavorful than many of the commercial cultivars.

All strawberries adapt well to container culture, or may be grown more conventionally in beds. June-bearing cultivars are available that adapt well to all parts of the country. Everbearing types offer fewer cultivar choices, but one or more will probably grow where you live.

> As one might guess from the name, alpine strawberries may struggle in hot, humid regions of the country. Container-grown plants, however, have the advantage of being mobile. When the weather heats up, you can relocate them to afternoon shade.

## Strawberry Culture Considerations

Regardless of which varieties you choose, plan on moving the strawberry patch every five years, or—if they are growing in containers—repot them in fresh, sterilized mix annually. Doing so avoids a plethora of problems. The plants are subject to viral disease and pests that can reduce yields significantly. Many of these problems persist in old, dead foliage or in the soil. Regular renewal of the plants and their growing medium offers the best natural defense against these problems. In terms of standard crop rotation, strawberries also should be separated by five years from soil that has previously grown any member of the potato family. This is because several important crop diseases are common to the two groups of plants.

If late spring frosts are typical where you live, you will need to grow a mid- to late-season berry cultivar or else plan to protect the blooms from frost damage with a row cover.

## Planting in Beds

Your strawberry patch needs full sun and well-drained sandy soil of slightly acidic pH, about 6.0–6.5. Rainfall or irrigation should provide an inch or two of water per week during the growing season. Prepare the bed by amending the soil with a 2-inch layer of compost over the entire area, well worked in. Proper culture of strawberries should result in yields of about 1½ pounds per square foot.

Purchase certified disease-free plants. They should go into the ground in late winter or early spring, before they break dormancy. Depending on whether you are growing everbearing or June-bearing strawberries, you will follow one of two planting patterns:

- Everbearing cultivars produce few runners, so they are typically grown in hills spaced about a foot apart. Pathways between the hills should be at least 2 feet wide to allow easy access without creating soil compaction and damaging the shallow root system.

- June-bearing strawberries produce abundant runners. They should be planted in wide rows. To maximize yield, space mother plants (the initial transplants you purchase) 18 inches apart in rows with 2-foot wide pathways in between. A maximum of two runners per mother plant are allowed to root. Cut the others free with a spade and remove them. Choose surviving runners so as to keep all plants spaced a minimum of 4 inches apart.

Alpine strawberries are smaller and more compact than their cousins, but they also produce runners and are grown in the same way as everbearing strawberries. They need only 6 inches between mother plants, however. Some gardeners like to use Alpine strawberries for a border, planting them about 4 inches apart and removing all runners as they form.

After the berries are picked, renovate the bed by side dressing with compost and removing stray runners. You can simply mow off the strawberry bed after frost kills the above-ground plants. After mowing, rake up the debris to reduce the likelihood of disease, then mulch with 2 or 3 inches of pine needles. The following spring, check for new growth emerging, and remove the mulch from the expanding crowns. Properly maintained beds may produce for five years, although the first year will always be the best one.

> June-bearing berries that warm up too soon are subject to flower loss if you have a late cold snap. Therefore, don't be too hasty about removing the mulch, which keeps the soil cold and the plants dormant.

## Planting in Containers

Individual plants can also be grown in large containers. Use at least a 12-inch diameter pot for each plant. Remove runners from container plants as they form. Allow the occasional runner to root in a small pot before detaching it, if you want to increase your stock of plants. Just set the crown of the runner on the soil. When it roots itself sufficiently to resist a gentle tug, cut it free. Any good commercial potting mix will work for strawberries, or you can make your own by mixing equal parts of sifted compost, horticultural peat, and sand. You want a medium that drains rapidly but retains moisture evenly.

> I try to avoid the traditional strawberry jar (typically an urn with openings in the sides for planting) because it seldom holds enough soil to accommodate the roots of all the berry plants tucked into them. I also avoid hanging baskets, although they seem to be very popular. I find they dry out too quickly and thus demand too much attention during the hot summer months.

A container-grown plant may produce less, about 1 pound per plant per season. June-bearing cultivars may be grown in containers as described for everbearing types.

## Characteristics of Selected Strawberry Varieties

| Variety | Type | Harvest Time | Comments |
| --- | --- | --- | --- |
| Allstar | June-bearing | Late season | Large fruits, adaptable |
| Earliglow | June-bearing | Early season | Tasty, but fruit size decreases after first year |
| Ozark Beauty | Everbearing | Everbearing | A widely adapted choice |
| Surecrop | June-bearing | Midseason | Reliable and adaptable to various locations |
| Tristan | Everbearing | Everbearing | Good for containers, decorative foliage, and flowers; delicious fruit |
| Tristar | Day neutral | Everbearing | Best for cooler climates |

After frost kills the tops, bring the container-grown strawberries indoors to a frost-free location, such as an unheated garage. When the soil in the container is dry to the depth of an inch, remove the strawberry plants, shake off the potting mix, trim the roots, and store the plants in a plastic bag, surrounded by horticultural peat or vermiculite to absorb excess moisture. Place the bag in the refrigerator or in a cold, but frost-free spot.

## Feeding Strawberries

Side dress June-bearing cultivars with compost after harvest. Feed everbearing cultivars after the late harvest. Do not overdo the nitrogen or you will encourage the growth of foliage at the expense of flowers. For container-grown plants, more regular fertilization will be needed, due to the flushing of the container with water. Watering with compost tea or a similar soluble fertilizer every other week will keep plants productive.

## Using the Harvest

Strawberries can be frozen or made into jam or preserves. Rich in vitamin C and phytochemicals, fresh strawberries can be added to salad or turned into a cold fruit soup. They also star, of course, in desserts like strawberry shortcake.

## Strawberry Soup

For four servings

1 pint fresh strawberries, stemmed
2 cups apple or white grape juice
Juice of 1 small lemon
10 large, fresh mint leaves, plus small leaves for garnish
Salt (if desired)
Sugar (if desired)
Sour cream or yogurt to serve (if desired)

Reserve 4 perfect strawberries for garnishing the dish. Roughly chop the remaining strawberries and process in a food processor or blender, in batches if necessary, with the juices, the mint leaves, and a pinch of salt, until you have a smooth puree. Chill until very cold. Taste and adjust the seasonings as necessary. Slice the reserved strawberries lengthwise, beginning at the pointed end, stopping before you completely cut through the stem end. Ladle the soup into chilled bowls. Place a dollop of sour cream or yogurt, if using, in the center. Fan out the berries gently and float one on each bowl of soup. Garnish with small mint leaves and serve.

Bear in mind that cultivar recommendations for strawberries are always tentative. One that thrives for you may struggle and perish in a friend's garden on the other side of town. Start with recommendations from your county extension office, and stick with the varieties that prove to be the best in your particular circumstances. Find an extensive, cross-referenced list of strawberry cultivars, along with everything else you might need to know about them at strawberryplants.org.

# Bramble Fruits

Bramble fruits grow as multistemmed small shrubs. Individual stems, called *canes*, are often studded with thorns, although thornless cultivars have been developed for some species. Bramble fruits include blackberries (*Rubus* sp.) and raspberries (also *Rubus* sp.) along with the less familiar boysenberries, dewberries, and loganberries. Some species grow wild in

## Characteristics of Selected Bramble Fruit Varieties

| Variety | Type | Harvest Time | Comments |
|---|---|---|---|
| Blackberry, Arapaho | Thornless | Late season | Hardy, erect growing, easy to train |
| Blackberry, Navaho | Thornless | Midseason | Erect, excellent flavor |
| Blackberry, Cherokee | Thorny | Early season | Erect plants with good quality fruit, some disease resistance |
| Blackberry, Darrow | Thorny | Midseason | Hardy, vigorous plants with large, excellent fruit |
| Raspberry, Canby | Red, almost thornless | Midseason | Medium to large fruit with excellent flavor |
| Raspberry, Latham | Red, nearly thornless | Midseason | Small, soft fruits have good flavor |
| Raspberry, Titan | Red, very thorny | Late season | Fall bearing canes produce huge berries |
| Raspberry, Dundee | Black, thorny | Midseason | Large fruit on tall, vigorous canes |
| Raspberry, Royalty | Purple, thorny | Late season | Vigorous, highly productive, and aphid resistant |

North America, others can be found from Europe to Australia and in South and Central America. From all of this natural genetic diversity, several modern cultivars have been developed by selection and hybridization.

## Choosing Cultivars

Like strawberries, bramble fruits are so popular that plant breeders have developed cultivars suitable for all parts of the country, as well as varieties with different maturation times to extend the season. Raspberry cultivars are the hardiest and will grow in zones 3–9. Blackberries, dewberries, and loganberries are the most heat tolerant, zones 5–10; loganberries grow best in zones 6–8. Consult your area's cooperative extension service for cultivars suitable for your location.

## Other Bramble Varieties

By crossing different species and types of blackberries and raspberries, additional varieties of brambles have been produced. The loganberry, for example, was developed by James Henry Logan in the 1880s from a cross involving two blackberry and one raspberry variety. Crossing the dewberry, a ground-hugging vine form of blackberry, with the red raspberry produces the nessberry. Famed American horticulturist Luther Burbank produced his own version of the loganberry early in the twentieth century. More recently, additional crosses have given us

- **Boysenberry** (loganberry × blackberry × raspberry)
- **Ollallieberry** (blackberry × youngberry)
- **Santiam blackberry** (loganberry × California blackberry)
- **Tayberry** (loganberry × black raspberry)
- **Youngberry** (Burbank loganberry × dewberry)

Any of these may be worth a try in your location. Check with your county extension office, as they tend to be regionally adapted.

Another bramble possibility is a Japanese raspberry species, *Rubus phoenicolasius*, commonly known as the "wineberry." Fruits are about the size of a large marble, bright red, and with a complex, sweet/tart flavor. When they appeared recently at my local farmer's market, I had the opportunity to try them and can recommend them to berry aficionados. According to the grower, they should be treated exactly like red raspberries.

> Wild bramble fruits occur throughout much of the country. I recently enjoyed the fruit from a stand of what appeared to be naturally occurring loganberries growing on a friend's farm. He did not plant them, and the fruit looks and tastes like a cross between a red raspberry and a blackberry. Wild blackberries are abundant and widespread in my area, and many people plant red raspberries, so plenty of chances for cross-pollination probably exist. The birds no doubt took care of planting the hybrid fruits on my friend's property.

## Growing Methods

All brambles typically need a season of growth before producing a crop the second year, although a few may produce a minor crop the first season. The plants are members of the rose family, and like roses they flower and produce fruit on new growth borne on 1-year-old canes. After fruiting, the canes die. They should be removed to prevent the spread of diseases. Do not compost the pruned stems; instead, burn them or place them in the trash.

Proper trellising, although not absolutely necessary, will improve productivity, reduce the likelihood of disease, and make fruit easier to pick. Brambles that are allowed to scramble over the ground will eventually become a tangled mass of old and new canes. By keeping the canes separated, old canes can be easily removed after fruiting. This allows the plant to put more energy into next year's crop, rather than maintaining the now-useless fruited canes.

All bramble fruits require full sun and a deep, well-drained soil of average fertility and high organic matter content. Lay out a patch about 3 feet wide, allowing 5 feet of length for each plant. Remove sod, work the soil to a depth of 1 foot and incorporate at least 2 inches of organic matter.

Next, install the trellis. This can be a simple wire fence, a double fence, or a T-bar arrangement about 4 to 5 feet tall. The double fence works well for many gardeners because it allows you to easily separate the canes by age, tying the new canes to one side and the old canes (which will fruit this season) to the other. This is also the purpose of the T-bar.

Purchase plants from a nursery and set them 5 feet apart. The best planting time is early spring, before the plants have broken dormancy. Container-grown plants often appear in garden centers in mid to late spring, the proper planting time for nondormant stock. They cost more than dormant, bare root plants, but you have the opportunity to judge the plant's health and vigor before you buy. In either case, set the plants a little deeper than they were growing previously. After planting dormant stock, cut the canes back to 6 inches to stimulate new growth (container-grown plants need pruning only to remove dead or damaged portions). Apply 2 inches of any organic mulch to conserve moisture. As the season progresses, scrupulously remove any weeds that come up through the mulch as soon as you notice them. Brambles need plenty of water, an inch per week from the time green leaves appear until the time fruit forms. Cease irrigation when fruit is colored. Too much water at this stage will reduce quality.

During the season, separate the canes and tie them to the trellis. When fall arrives, prune out any inferior canes to maintain a spacing of at least 6 inches between canes, and cut all the remaining canes back to a foot taller than the trellis. Side dress plants with a 2-inch layer of compost the following spring. This year, last year's canes will flower, and the plant will produce new canes.

If you use the double fence or T-bar trellis, you can tie the new canes to the side opposite the fruiting canes. Remove the old canes after you harvest. In the fall, once again thin the canes to a 6-inch spacing and head back the ones left to grow. Maintain this cycle of pruning in subsequent years. It is important not to prune too early. Wait until a few light frosts have signaled to the plants to hibernate. Early pruning may encourage new growth that will soon be killed by frost. Growing unproductive canes in this fashion saps the plant's strength. Just remember the following two-year cycle.

### Two-Year Bramble Pruning Cycle

| Year | Season | Activity |
|---|---|---|
| Year 1 | Late winter to early spring | Remove only dead or diseased canes from container-grown stock at planting time, cut back dormant stock to 6 inches. |
| Year 1 | Summer | Separate canes and tie them to one side of the trellis. |
| Year 1 | Fall | Remove any inferior canes and cut all canes 1 foot taller than the trellis. Wait to do this until after a couple of frosts. |
| Year 2 | Late spring | Last year's canes will flower, and new canes will emerge. Tie new canes to the side of the trellis opposite last year's canes. |
| Year 2 | Summer | Harvest fruit from last year's canes, allowing this year's canes to grow. |
| Year 2 | Fall, after a couple of frosts | Remove all of last year's canes, and cut this year's canes back to a foot taller than the trellis. |

## Harvesting and Using Brambles

Yields vary with the cultivar, and can range from 1 to 8 quarts per plant. Red raspberries yield about 1½ to 2 pints per plant, for example. Bramble fruits, especially raspberries, are extremely perishable and should be eaten the day they are picked. They freeze well or can be made into jams and preserves. They can also be used to flavor vinegar or can be added fresh to salads or fruit soup. Traditionally, of course, bramble fruits appear in pies, tarts, and other desserts. Here is a recipe for blackberries used in an unconventional, but delicious, way.

## Pan-roasted Pork Medallions with Blackberry Pan Sauce

1½ pounds pork tenderloin, sliced into medallions about ¾ inch thick
Salt and freshly ground black pepper
1 pint blackberries
2 tablespoons canola oil
½ cup fruity red wine, such as Beaujolais
3 bay leaves
8 large leaves fresh basil

Sprinkle the pork medallions with salt and a few grinds of pepper and set them aside. Select about half the berries to reserve for garnish and puree the remainder in a blender or food processor. Pass them through a sieve to remove seeds and reserve the puree. Heat the oil in a large, heavy skillet over medium heat. When the oil shimmers, add the pork medallions and cook, turning once, until browned, 3 to 4 minutes per side. Remove the pork to a plate and keep warm.

Pour off all but a film of the fat from the skillet, add the wine and deglaze, scraping up all the browned bits and incorporating them into the sauce. Add the bay leaves and simmer the sauce until only 2 to 3 tablespoons of liquid remain. Remove and discard the bay leaves. Add the blackberry puree and bring to a simmer.

Return the pork to the skillet, along with any accumulated juices. Simmer the sauce until the pork is well-heated and the sauce begins to coat it. Meanwhile, stack the basil leaves, roll up like a cigar, and slice very thinly crosswise to produce fine shreds or *chiffonade*. Serve the pork at once on warmed plates, garnished with the basil and reserved blackberries. This is heavenly with a side of warm polenta.

# Shrub Fruits

This group includes blueberries (*Vaccinium* sp.), currants, and gooseberries (both *Ribes* sp.). Besides producing an annual crop of delicious fruit, these plants are handsome enough to be used as hedges or specimen plantings.

## Characteristics of Selected Varieties of Currants and Gooseberries

| Species | Variety | Size (ft) | Comments |
| --- | --- | --- | --- |
| Currant, Black | Consort | 4–6 | Sweet musky flavor and disease resistance |
| Currant, Red | Red Lake | 5–7 | Vigorous; considered best variety by experts |
| Currant, White | White Imperial | 4–6 | Excellent quality, but hard to find plants |
| Gooseberry | Poorman | 4–6 | Considered the best American gooseberry |

## Choosing Cultivars

Different shrub fruits grow best in different regions of the country. Currants, for example, need cool temperatures and seldom do well south of Zone 6. Take the time to research variety recommendations for your area.

Currants and gooseberries have similar cultural requirements. They will grow in full to partial sun, the latter being better in southern zones. Moist, well-drained soils will produce the best crop, while plants will usually fail either in constantly wet soils or hot, dry locations. The plants are self-fertile. Three or four plants of any variety would yield enough for the needs of the average homestead.

Three types of blueberries are available, each adapted to different conditions. High-bush blueberries (*V. corymbosum*) can grow up to 6 feet in height but prefer cooler climates. There are numerous cultivars, which are listed in the accompanying table. Most commercial and homegrown blueberries are this type. Hybridization with warm climate blueberry species has produced plants that will thrive in the South. Thus, some cultivar of high-bush blueberry can be grown in most of the country. Low-bush blueberries (*V. angustifolium*) can form vast stands in some areas of the eastern United States. They are often "managed" and sold as wild blueberries. Notable for their intense coloration, they are about half the size of their tall cousins and can take less warmth. The third variety, rabbiteye blueberries (*V. virgatum*), are the most heat tolerant of all and produce a true blue fruit with a distinctive "eye" on the blossom end.

## Characteristics of Selected Blueberry Varieties

| Variety | Type | Harvest Time | Comments |
|---|---|---|---|
| Earliblue | Northern Highbush | Early season | Large, light blue berries |
| Jersey | Northern Highbush | Late season | One of the oldest and most popular cultivars |
| Emerald | Southern Highbush | Midseason | Large, mildly sweet fruits on plants adapted to mild winters |
| Oneal | Southern Highbush | Very early season | Said to be tastiest of all southern highbush types |
| Northblue | Half High | Midseason | Among the hardiest cultivars |
| Briteblue | Rabbiteye | Midseason | Vigorous; bears all at once for canning or freezing |

Elderberries are found in both hemispheres, but the one best adapted to growing in eastern North America is the American elder (*Sambucus canadensis*). Growing to about 8 feet in diameter, it is often seen along roadsides and in old fields. In the West, it is replaced by the blue elderberry (*S. caerulea*). Showy white flower umbels appear in summer and are followed in early autumn by clusters of berries. The berries can be used for winemaking, or the flowers can be washed, patted dry, dipped in batter, and fried. They are served with a dusting of powdered sugar and cinnamon. One cultivar often recommended is Adams, which produces more and better fruit than the wild type. Another is York, a late-bearing, vigorous plant with large fruits. Plant the two together, as individual plants are not self-fertile. Elderberry plants can be hard to find, as demand is low.

Serviceberries include several species, also known as shadbush. In the eastern United States, the species *Amelanchier canadensis* has been used for food since ancient times. The berries resemble blueberries in flavor, and the seeds have a taste similar to almond extract. Both pies and jams have been made from serviceberries since European colonists arrived on American shores. Two popular cultivars are Honeywood and Northline. The plants can easily top 10 feet, so give them room.

One advantage to growing elderberries and serviceberries is their attractiveness to butterflies and other pollinating insects that will also visit your other plantings.

Honeyberries are highly regionally specific, with cultivars available for zones 2–8. They are undemanding plants that reach a height and spread of about 7 feet. The fruits, which resemble blueberries, are borne on 1-year old wood, so the plants must be pruned annually.

## Culture

For all shrub fruits, pruning is the key to maintaining health. Some high-bush blueberries, for example, lose a significant amount of productivity after the fourth year. Therefore, many references recommend pruning out all 5-year-old canes. Low-bush blueberry types, on the other hand, fruit best on canes produced directly from the roots, rather than from buds on aboveground wood. Pruning is therefore done to encourage the former at the expense of the latter, by removing older canes all the way to the base.

All shrub fruits need well-drained soil, plenty of air circulation, and abundant moisture. Soil fertility is best maintained by regular additions of compost. Blueberries are a special case, as they require acid soil, at a pH of 5.5 or below. If your soil lacks natural acidity, you may need to prepare special beds for blueberries, keeping them well-supplied with acidic components like pine needles and peat moss. Smaller cultivars of highbush blueberries make excellent container plants. Growing these plants in containers also allows you to provide the proper soil conditions without affecting adjacent plants. A 5-gallon container is an appropriate size for a single plant.

## Harvest and Yield

You won't get quick results from the shrub fruits. Most need at least two seasons, and some blueberries need four, before they produce fruit. Once established, however, a well-grown stand of these plants can provide food each season for many years. Yields of course depend on many factors. For highbush blueberries, for example, expect anywhere from 4 to 8 quarts per plant.

Blueberries are extremely winter hardy and need little protection from cold. Move container plants to a sheltered location away from drying winds, however. Although a few cultivars are evergreen, most blueberries are deciduous, losing their leaves after putting on a brilliant fall display of red-purple foliage.

## Uses for Shrub Fruits

Shrub fruits can be eaten fresh or made into jellies and preserves. Gooseberries have been used as a digestive remedy, and can also be used for wine. The flavor of blueberries and currants can be captured in vinegar.

## Blueberries with Greek Yogurt and Lavender Sugar

For four servings

1 pint blueberries
½ cup sugar
1 pint Greek-style yogurt
Lavender sugar (see page 166)

Place the blueberries in a small saucepan with the sugar and ¼ cup water. Bring slowly to a simmer and cook gently until the berries begin to pop. Remove from the heat and cool to room temperature. (Can be prepared ahead and stored, refrigerated, for up to a week. Bring to room temperature before serving.) To serve, place ½ cup Greek yogurt in a serving bowl, top with berries, and sprinkle with lavender sugar.

---

# Vine Fruits

## Grapes

Grapes (*Vitis* sp.) have been consumed since ancient times and growers have developed countless cultivars. Although all grapes can be put to multiple uses, some varieties, Thompson Seedless, for example, are better for table grapes. Others, such as Cabernet Sauvignon and Chardonnay, lend themselves to winemaking and still others, like Concord, make the best jelly. Grape cultivars are also the most regionally adapted of all food plants. Some will grow well in a given location, while others may not produce a crop at all. Therefore, it is essential to research varieties suitable for your location before you start a grape arbor.

### Culture

Grapes require full sun and need two to three years from transplant to harvest. They also require trellising and careful pruning to obtain maximum yields. On the plus side, a grape arbor can be an attractive addition to the landscape, and being able to create your own wine is a terrific luxury. A double-wire fence trellis or an arbor is necessary to provide support for the vigorous vines. Arrange support so the longest axis runs east-west, for maximal sun exposure. Wine grapes are typically trained on a trellis, while table and jelly grapes are often supported by an arbor. The choice does not matter, as long as it is convenient to your needs and fits the space you have available.

Work the soil as deeply as possible to accommodate the extensive root system. Incorporate liberal amounts of compost and sand to create a fast-draining loam that ideally reaches a depth of 3 feet. The compost will provide a nutrient boost to get the plants off to a good start and will help to retain soil moisture until the roots become established. Later, only about 15 pounds of compost per 100 square feet per year provides sufficient fertilization. Fruit production will suffer if the soil is too rich. Because they despise poor drainage, grapes can be grown on a gently sloping site.

Grapes grow and fruit much like brambles—that is, fruit is produced on growth that develops on 1-year-old wood. This wood has smooth bark, while older bark is rough. Plants are typically vigorous and need rigorous pruning to keep them in bounds and to remove nonproductive wood. Major pruning should be done in winter when the plants are dormant. During the growing season, new growth should be shortened to keep it within bounds, bearing in mind that this is the growth that will bear next year's crop.

Mulching grapes with organic material at the beginning of each season is not a good idea. Excessive organic matter content in the soil may result in abundant foliage production at the expense of fruit. Grapes prefer a pH between 6.5 and 7.0 (slightly acidic). Cultivars adapted to soils of higher pH are available and should be sought out if your soil is alkaline.

Grapes do not feed heavily, and will fruit best on lean, mineral-derived soils. (Consider that the first domesticated grapes originated in arid Turkey!) To help control weeds, mulch with pebbles, or use wood chips, which will decompose very slowly. An application each autumn of compost and either greensand or granite dust should provide all the nutrients your grapes need.

### Harvest and Uses

The yield from your arbor will depend on the cultivar, age of the plant, growing conditions and pruning. Healthy mature plants can yield 20 pounds of fruit or more. Making wine (see page 273), the time-honored way to preserve grape juice, may also lead, possibly inadvertently, to making vinegar. Grape jelly is a pantry staple, and grapes can be used in numerous dishes both savory and sweet. French recipes with the word *Veronique* in the name have grapes lurking in them somewhere. While different cultivars are best suited to one of these uses, all can be used interchangeably with reasonable success.

The literature on grape production and winemaking is extensive indeed. If you want more than a vine or two for table use, it pays to do some careful research before building the arbor or laying out the vineyard.

Discover how versatile the grape can be by making roasted grape chutney.

## Roasted Grape Chutney

For four to six servings

2 cups grapes, halved, seeds removed if necessary
1 tablespoon extra-virgin olive oil
1 tablespoon wine vinegar (match the color of the vinegar to that of the grapes you are using)
1 tablespoon fresh thyme leaves
½ teaspoon salt
½ teaspoon freshly ground black pepper

Preheat the oven to 425°F. Combine all of the ingredients in a bowl. Transfer the mixture to a baking sheet and bake 20 minutes, or until the grapes start to shrivel. Cool and store in a tightly capped jar in the refrigerator for up to one week. Serve warm or at room temperature with cheese or as a condiment with roasted pork or chicken.

The chutney is excellent with havarti. Top ¼-inch slices of cheese with chutney and place in a 400°F oven for 3 to 4 minutes. Or remove the rind from the top of a round of brie and bake for 7 to 9 minutes at 400°F. Invite diners to scoop out the brie and spread it on seeded crackers with a dollop of the roasted grape chutney.

## Kiwifruit

If you live in an area with at least 150 days per year of frost-free weather, you might consider growing kiwifruit. The kiwi, a native of China, challenges the intrepid gardener, especially if space is limited. Both male and female plants are needed for fruit production. Only the females, of course, bear fruit, but the males will take up just as much space, thus reducing the yield per square foot. One male is sufficient for eight females. All cultivars require well-drained, slightly acidic soil (pH 6.5) in the sun. Afternoon shade is appreciated in the Deep South. Plant out in spring from nursery-grown stock.

The plants are notorious for being hard to pollinate. Attract bees to your garden with flowers blooming alongside the kiwi in May or June. Two to three years are required for a planting to bear a crop. Vines are vigorous and need a sturdy fence or trellis. Harvest season for kiwi is mid-autumn. Cut plants back every three years to renew them and increase fruit production.

The kiwi found in grocery stores is *Actinidia deliciosa*. It is both less hardy and less sweet than the other two species: *A. arguta* and *A. kolomikta*. The latter two withstand freezing temperatures and are more easily cultivated than the commercial species. Hybridization of *A. deliciosa* with other species of *Actinidia,* however, has yielded cultivars hardy all the way to Zone 5. Growers in hot, humid climates may have trouble getting kiwi to set fruit. Expect the best production where summers are cool and winters mild.

## Passionflower

Among the more interesting possibilities for vine fruits is the native passionflower (*Passiflora incarnata*). Found growing wild in the southern tier of states, and naturalized as far north as Delaware, this vigorous vine with unusual flowers produces an egg-size fruit with a unique flavor. Also called "wild apricot" and "maypop," the plant has been used by Native Americans since ancient times. Each fruit contains many large seeds, possibly why the main use has traditionally been for making jelly. Fresh, ripe fruit is delicious raw, also. Having two plants for cross-pollination maximizes fruit production. The vines are extremely vigorous, however, and may not be suitable for smaller properties. Grow in full sun, on lean, well-drained soil.

# Tree Fruits

If you are willing to endure the long wait for the crop, a small orchard can be a rewarding investment. That said, be prepared to learn a lot before you take the plunge. The climate in your area will determine which fruit tree species can be grown there. The main factors determining which species grow well in a given location are *heating hours* and *chilling hours* required by that species. These terms refer, respectively, to the number of hours per year when the temperature is above 65°F or below 45°F. If a fruit tree does not receive its particular requirement of chilling hours, it will fail to break dormancy in the spring and die. If the heating hours are insufficient, the plant fails to thrive, fruit fails to develop, and the tree usually dies after a few seasons.

## ⊞ Columnar Apple Trees

Relative newcomers to the fruit tree scene, columnar trees have been around for only a couple of decades. They are ideal for small space gardens, as they reach only 8 to 10 feet in height and are seldom more than 2 feet in diameter. Yet, they bear full-size fruit. Golden Sentinel apples are similar to Golden Delicious and Northpole mimics a Macintosh. Culture is similar to regular apples. Plant scientists have also developed columnar peaches, although these are not yet widely available.

## Nontropical Orchard Fruits

Before planting a backyard orchard, check with your cooperative extension service to determine recommended varieties for your area. Besides having to choose a species (apple, pear, cherry, peach) and cultivar (Red Delicious, Montmorency), you also choose the size: standard, semi-dwarf, or dwarf plants. Most suburban gardens can accommodate semi-dwarf or dwarf varieties best. Some dwarf fruit trees can be successfully cultivated in containers.

Modern fruit tree stocks are usually grafted. The top portion of the tree, or "scion," is the fruit bearing portion and has the characteristics of the particular fruit cultivar being grown. The bottom portion, or rootstock, determines the size of the tree, the time required for it to mature, and sometimes its disease resistance characteristics. Apples, for example, are grafted on to roughly ten types of rootstocks, ranging in size from 3 feet (dwarf) to 15 feet (standard) at maturity and requiring from two to five years to produce fruit. The nursery that supplies your trees should be able to tell you which rootstock was used and the expected size.

### Culture

Fruit trees need full sun, well-drained soil, and adequate moisture. Soils must be near neutral pH and of average fertility. Most cultivars adapt to a variety of soil types so long as moisture and pH are correct. Avoid above all low, boggy, or poorly drained sites.

### Pollination

Apples, pears, and sweet cherries are usually not self-fertile, meaning they cannot pollinate themselves. Pollen instead must come from a different cultivar, and in many cases not just any old cultivar will do. Even self-fertile cultivars (plums, apricots, most peaches) produce higher yields if

## Characteristics of Selected Apple Varieties

| Variety | Use | Bloom Time | Pollinated By |
|---------|-----|------------|---------------|
| Gala | Fresh | Early to midseason | Golden Delicious |
| Empire | Fresh, cooking | Early | Golden or Red Delicious, Gala |
| Jonagold | Fresh, cooking | Midseason | Gala, Empire |
| Golden Delicious | Fresh, cooking | Midseason to late | Red Delicious, Gala, Empire |
| Red Delicious | Fresh | Early | Golden Delicious, Gala |
| Stayman | Fresh, cooking | Midseason | Gala, Golden or Red Delicious |
| Rome | Fresh, cooking | Late | Fuji, Braeburn |
| Braeburn | Fresh | Midseason | Rome, Fuji |
| Fuji | Fresh | Midseason | Rome, Braeburn |

pollinated by a different individual plant. Thus, you need a minimum of two trees of any given species to produce fruit or to maximize productivity. Catalog listings typically provide recommendations for pairing appropriate pollinators, or see the accompanying tables.

## Pruning

Pruning fruit trees is a skill better developed with the help of a teacher rather than a book, but it is necessary if you expect production. This task adds to your workload and is an annual chore. Pruning is not only done to maximize fruit production but also to shape the tree. Pruning styles include:

- **Cordon**—suitable for small spaces
- **Espalier**—also good for small spaces, requires more work to maintain
- **Bush**—suitable for medium-size gardens
- **Standard**, up to 15 × 15 feet—suitable for large gardens only

Bush and standard pruned trees maintain the normal pyramidal shape of the tree. Apple and pear trees are pruned during dormancy, while plum, peach, apricot, and cherry trees are pruned in the spring. As a general rule, prune to maintain a symmetrical framework of five to six well-spaced main

## Characteristics of Selected Pear Varieties

| Variety | Use For | Harvest Time | Pollinizer |
|---|---|---|---|
| Bartlett, Red Bartlett | Cooking | Midseason | Golden Russet Bosc |
| Buerre d'Anjou | Cooking, fresh eating | Late | Bartlett, Red Bartlett, Golden Russet Bosc |
| Clapp's Favorite | Cooking | Early | Bartlett |
| Golden Russet Bosc | Cooking, fresh eating | Late | Bartlett, Red Bartlett, Buerre d'Anjou |

branches and to prevent the inner branches of the tree from shading each other too much. Broken, diseased, or crossed branches should be removed first, and the tree should then be carefully evaluated to determine what else to remove. Keep in mind that a branch left on by mistake can be removed later, but one removed by mistake can never be replaced. Err on the side of conservatism, until you get the hang of it.

## Tropical and Subtropical Tree Fruits

Growing a few of the frost-tender fruits brings a whole new dimension to the food garden. While these plants are typically thought to require a frost-free location to spend the winter, many cultivars are surprisingly cold toler-ant and can be grown in sheltered locations outdoors. "Sheltered," however, does not equate to "shaded." These plants all need full sun. Even container-grown plants will do better if they spend the least possible amount of time inside, unless "inside" is a sunny greenhouse. If you bring them into the house for the winter, place them in the sunniest spot you have. Cart them out to the terrace when mild weather is predicted and let them bask in the sun. This will improve production later in the year.

### Avocado

Many gardeners have perhaps at some point started an avocado tree (*Persea americana*) from a pit salvaged from the compost after making guacamole. With patience, it is easy to coax the pit into producing a tree. Unfortunately, this approach almost never results in fruit production. For that, you need grafted stock of a known cultivar. Your best bet is to purchase a small tree from a nursery. Choose cultivars carefully, as the mature size of an avocado tree can range from 6 feet to over 40 feet. Plants can be kept in bounds by pruning, but it is wise to start with a variety that naturally remains relatively small. Smaller cultivars are the obvious choice for container growing. Avocados are hardy only in zones 9–10, and can be killed to the ground by a hard freeze. Most of us who live in more northern zones, therefore, will grow them in a container.

Use a potting mix intended for growing cactus or citrus, avoiding both peat and pine-based products. Avocados need a fast-draining, mineralized soil, such as soil found in the American Southwest. Plant the sapling in a roomy container, setting the crown of the plant a little higher than it was growing in the nursery pot, to prevent damage from rot. Firm the soil around the plant carefully and water well. If you received the plant by mail order, place the pot outside in a sheltered spot, protect it from cold temperatures, and gradually expose it to full sun. Shelter any container-grown tree from winds that might topple the pot.

When the avocado is well-established in its pot, you can begin a careful fertilization program. Use a balanced, soluble product such as fish emulsion or kelp extract, for which the label will provide NPK numbers, or the percentages by weight, respectively, of nitrogen, phosphorus, and potassium. Avocados are heavy feeders. A 2-year-old tree consumes about 2 ounces of nitrogen annually, and a mature tree needs about 1½ pounds of nitrogen per year. If your fertilizer is 8-8-8, you will use 25 ounces of it annually for the young tree and 18¼ pounds of it for the mature one. These numbers apply to field-grown trees in commercial production, so you may need to experiment for container-grown plants. High nitrogen products, such as cottonseed meal, blood meal, and composted manure, if incorporated into the potting mix, may give good results. If the tree is not growing rapidly, with glossy, dark green leaves, try feeding it. Otherwise, hold off. Young trees need more frequent applications than older trees do.

Excessive water is the main enemy of container-grown avocados. Water only when the soil feels dry an inch or so below the surface. This may mean every few days during hot, sunny weather, or only once a month indoors in the winter. The size of your container and the composition of the potting mix will also determine how frequently the plant needs watering. Numerous references suggest that erring on the side of too little water is the best insurance against root rot. Because frequent watering will flush out nutrients, fertilization may need to be seasonally adjusted to keep the tree thriving.

With proper culture, your avocado can be expected to yield a few fruits during its fourth year of growth. Thereafter, yields should increase as the tree grows and matures. Avocado trees can easily live to be 25 years old, providing you with a delicious source of healthful fats and other phytochemicals.

## Characteristics of Selected Stone Fruit Varieties

| Variety | Best Use | Pollinizer | Comments |
|---|---|---|---|
| Apricot, Early Blush | Preserves, drying, cooking | Plant two or more apricot varieties for cross-pollination | Matures early, in June; golden fruit with red blush |
| Apricot, Goldrich | Preserves, drying, cooking | Plant two or more apricot varieties for cross-pollination | Matures about two weeks after Early Blush; golden yellow, fine textured fruit |
| Cherry, Montmorency | Cooking, preserves | Self-fertile | The standard commercial sour cherry variety, also good for home gardens |
| Cherry, Regina | Cooking, preserves, fresh eating | Two or more sweet cherry varieties should be planted together | A late season, dark red sweet cherry; hardy and disease resistant |
| Cherry, Ulster | Cooking, preserves, fresh eating | Two or more sweet cherry varieties should be planted together | Midseason, productive, and resistant to cracking; large cherry-red fruit |
| Nectarine, Redgold | Fresh eating, cooking, canning | Self-fertile | Late season, freestone type with excellent flavor |
| Peach, Garnet Beauty | Fresh eating, cooking, canning | Self-fertile | Early, freestone when fully ripe, and good for colder locations; yellow flesh with garnet red skin |
| Peach, Reliance | Freezing, canning | Self-fertile | One of the hardiest cultivars, matures in late July or early August |
| Peach, September Snow | Cooking, fresh eating, canning | Self-fertile | A late maturing, white-fleshed variety for the South |

*(continued)*

## Characteristics of Selected Stone Fruit Varieties (continued)

| Variety | Best Use | Pollinizer | Comments |
| --- | --- | --- | --- |
| Plum, Green Gage | Fresh eating, canning | Self-fertile | Green fruit matures early August |
| Plum, President | Fresh eating, canning | Stanley | Extra late, freestone blue plum with orange flesh |
| Plum, Stanley | Fresh eating, canning | President | August ripening, blue with greenish flesh |

## Avocado Soup

2 avocados
1 lemon
3 scallions, white portion and 3 inches of green, sliced
1 tablespoon vegetable oil
1 quart vegetable stock
Sour cream
1 small red tomato, peeled, seeded, and cut into ⅛-inch dice
Cilantro leaves, for garnish

Peel the avocado, slice it into a bowl, and squeeze the juice of the lemon over it. Toss to coat and set aside. Heat the vegetable oil in a saucepan, add the scallions, cover, and sweat over medium heat until the scallions are soft and translucent but not browned. Add the stock and simmer for 5 minutes. Add the reserved avocado and lemon juice and simmer 1 minute longer. Cool to room temperature. Puree the soup in a blender and chill until very cold. Add additional stock if the soup is too thick. Serve in chilled bowls, garnished with some of the diced tomatoes, a dollop of sour cream, and a few cilantro leaves.

### Bananas

Nothing says "tropical" like a banana tree, with its enormous leaves and fleshy trunk (correctly called the *pseudostem*). Bananas (*Musa acuminata*) and hybrids have been grown for centuries, and consequently many culti-vars exist. Several of these are small enough for growing in containers to winter indoors. Dwarf Cavendish reaches only 6 feet and is a commonly grown variety. Another, similar commercial variety is Williams Hybrid, which also matures at 6 to 8 feet. At 8 to 10 feet, Dwarf Red, also known as Cuban Red, Jamaican Red, etc., provides unusual leaf coloration as well as some cold tolerance.

Culture: Banana trees reach their full size within a single growing season. The underground portion of the stem will send up multiple suckers, only two of which should be allowed to mature. Remove the others while they are small enough to be easily dealt with. Within ten to fifteen months after emerging, the older of the two suckers will produce a flowering stalk and fruit. Thus, as one might suspect from this extremely rapid growth rate, bananas demand plenty of food and water. The other sucker, which will be younger and therefore smaller than the main one, remains after harvest to continue the plant's growth. One reference suggests the ideal spot to plant a banana tree as "right on top of an old compost pile."

The growing medium must be well-drained. Banana trees do not tolerate wet feet. Fertilization with a balanced formula monthly is necessary. Banana trees need about 1¼ ounces of nitrogen per month when young, and double that amount when mature. If your fertilizer is 8 percent nitrogen— that is, the NPK numbers are 8-x-x—you should apply a pound of this fertilizer around the base of the plant monthly, gradually increasing the application to 2 pounds over the course of the season. If the temperature at night is below 50°F, as during overwintering in a garage perhaps, don't fertilize.

While banana plants are generally tolerant of cold down to 28°F, they perform best when grown under constantly warm to cool conditions. If winter storage is a problem, however, you can take several steps to keep your banana plants growing. First, if you have a suitable sheltered spot exposed to southern sun, you can probably overwinter a banana plant outdoors as far north as Zone 4. This is accomplished by cutting it down, covering the base with a bushel basket, and piling leaves on top to protect the underground stem. Do this as soon as frost kills most of the top growth. Check such plants frequently in early spring and remove the covering as soon as shoots emerge. Be ready with a frost blanket in case of a late cold snap.

A more reliable way of overwintering is to dig up small shoots and pot them in containers as houseplants for the winter. Grow in a bright, warm location and fertilize lightly until you are ready to move them outside again.

Uses: Besides fresh eating, bananas can be used in both savory and sweet dishes, depending on their level of ripeness. Greenish bananas work well in savory cooked dishes, perfectly ripe fruits make the best banana pudding, and overripe bananas are preferred for banana bread.

## Thai Curry with Bananas

For two servings

1 can (5.46 oz.) coconut milk
1 tablespoon Thai red curry paste
1 lime
3 scallions, cleaned and trimmed
1½ cups assorted firm vegetables, such as carrots, potatoes, squash, broccoli, celery, peppers, or mushrooms, cut into bite-size pieces and reserved separately; some or all of this can be canned Asian vegetables, such as water chestnuts, bamboo shoots, baby corn, or even extra firm tofu cut into cubes.
1 large slightly under ripe banana, or 2 small ones
2 tablespoons chopped salted roasted cashews or peanuts
½ cup (lightly packed) fresh cilantro leaves

Shake the coconut milk well, open the can and combine it with the curry paste in a large saucepan. Remove the lime zest with a grater, then cut the lime in half. Slice the white part of the scallions into ½-inch pieces. Slice the green part of the scallions on the bias into ⅛-inch slices. Reserve the white and green parts of the scallions separately.

Bring the contents of the saucepan to a simmer over medium heat. Add the lime zest and a sprinkle of salt, then add the juice from one of the lime halves. Add the vegetables, beginning with the firmest ones, such as potatoes and carrots. Cook covered for 5 minutes, then add another batch of vegetables, such as squash, celery, peppers, broccoli or mushrooms, along with the white part of the scallions. Cover and continue to simmer until the vegetables are almost done, then add any canned vegetables or tofu, if using. Cover and cook until heated through.

Peel the banana and halve it lengthwise, then slice into ½-inch chunks. Add these to the pot, along with half of the cashews and half of the cilantro. Cover and cook one minute. Uncover and simmer briefly to reduce the amount of liquid, if necessary. Squeeze the remaining lime half over the curry. Serve immediately over jasmine rice, garnished with the remaining cashews and cilantro.

---

### Citrus Fruits

Citrus trees have a lot to offer, lustrous green foliage, richly fragrant flowers, and of course their delicious fruits. Unfortunately, they are not hardy and must be grown in containers outside the frost-free areas of the country.

Choosing appropriate cultivars for container culture, however, will enable anyone to grow citrus, if you can provide them with a cool, well-lighted space during the coldest weather.

Fruit production in container-grown citrus trees is a function of the size of the container. Therefore, as the tree grows, choose the largest pot that you consider portable enough to be moved inside when necessary. Younger trees, however, should not be overpotted, as this will make controlling moisture levels at the roots more challenging. For 1-year old nursery stock, a 9-inch pot is fine. Increase the container size by 3 inches for each additional year of growth.

Commercially produced citrus tree cultivars are grafted to one of two rootstocks: sour orange or trifoliate orange. Try to locate stock grafted to trifoliate orange, as this rootstock is both smaller and more cold tolerant than the sour orange. The smaller size will adapt better to a container, and greater cold tolerance means you can wait longer to bring plants inside in autumn and take them back outdoors earlier in spring.

Culture: Any good potting mixture is suitable for citrus trees, as long as it drains well, although commercial mixes intended specifically for citrus are widely available and recommended. Avoid both peat moss and pine bark in mixes intended for citrus.

Water citrus when the top 1 inch of growing mix feels dry when you stick your finger into the soil. Feed once when the plants move outdoors, and again about three months later, using a good, balanced organic fertilizer. Glossy, dark green leaves indicate that the plant is receiving adequate nutrition. When in doubt, err on the side of less food and less water. Too much of either one will result in leggy, unsightly growth and poor fruit production.

Harvesting: In the second year after transplanting nursery stock, you should expect a few fruits. Thereafter, fruit production will increase with the size of the tree. Lemons and limes can bear almost at any time of year, but most other varieties bear the best crop after their spring bloom. Leaving the fruit on the tree until you are ready to eat it is the best bet, as the fruit becomes larger and flavor improves with time. Don't wait until the fruit begins to dry out, however, before picking.

Choosing Cultivars: Among the numerous varieties of citrus available, consider one or more of the following. Meyer lemon is a small form with smooth, thin-skinned fruit and reasonable cold tolerance. Kumquats have good cold tolerance and adapt well to containers. Selections include Nagami and Meiwa, both of which bear during fall and winter. Mandarin oranges and tangerines also exhibit good cold tolerance, but with some varieties, such as the Clementine tangerine, you need two plants for successful pollination. Varieties to try include Satsuma, Owari, Clementine, Dancy, and Changsha tangerines, and Minneola and Orlando tangelos. The tangelo is also known as honeybell tangerine, and is a cross between a tangerine and a grapefruit or the grapefruit relative, the pomelo.

Limes are truly tropical plants with no tolerance for cold weather. However, they do remain relatively small in size and thus are worth considering for container production. Mexican and Key limes produce relatively small, rounded, yellow-green fruit, while the Tahitian, or Persian lime bears the familiar dark green, ovoid type. The limequat, a cross between lime and kumquat, bears yellow fruits on a small plant with good cold tolerance.

For an extensive table of dwarf citrus varieties, visit www.fourwinds growers.com/solver/varietyinfo.html.

## Kumquat-Strawberry Jam

1 cup quartered and seeded kumquats
4 cups crushed strawberries, from about 2 quarts whole berries, washed, stemmed, halved, and mashed gently with a potato masher
1 1.75-ounce package powdered fruit pectin
7 cups sugar

Please see the general instructions on canning, found in chapter 8, before you begin. Bring the kumquats and 1 cup water to a boil in a saucepan, simmer 20 minutes, and drain. Combine the kumquats, the strawberries, and the pectin in a large, heavy pot. Stirring constantly, bring to a full, rolling boil. (A full boil is one that does not subside when the liquid is stirred.) Dump in the sugar all at once. Continue stirring and bring to a full boil again. Boil exactly 1 minute, stirring constantly. Ladle the hot jam into hot, sterilized half pint jars, leaving ¼-inch head space. Adjust caps and process in a boiling water bath canner for 5 minutes. Remove jars from canner and cool on wire racks. Makes 8 to 10 half pints.

## Figs

The fig (*Ficus carica*) occurs naturally from Afghanistan to Portugal and has been consumed by humans since prehistoric times. In fact, its cultivation is thought to have been the first instance of agriculture. Needless to say, wherever the Mediterranean climate prevails, such as along the American Gulf Coast, figs have found their way into gardens. Outside these areas, figs can be grown in containers, or can be overwintered outdoors if the roots are protected. Perhaps the most widely grown cultivar is Brown Turkey, although numerous others exist. All are considered easy to grow, with water management being a more important consideration than soil fertility. Poorly drained, constantly wet soil will rot the roots, but trees should not dry out to the point that leaves begin to wilt. Since the tree should be sited in as much sun as possible, water needs during hot weather can be significant.

Purchase nursery-grown stock of a known cultivar, or root a cutting from a tree of known provenance. Cuttings taken in August will root readily and can be transferred to their permanent location the following year. Plant the tree a little deeper than it was growing in the nursery container, using a well-drained mix such as has been previously recommended for growing citrus. Add a little bone meal to the mix at planting time. Figs are not heavy feeders and phosphorus is more important for them than nitrogen. You will need a container holding 15 to 20 gallons of potting mix to accommodate a mature fig tree. Trees can be kept in bounds by thinning the main stems and by root pruning every three years.

Overwintering a container fig is relatively easy. When leaves fall, move the tree indoors to a cool spot. Light is unnecessary while the tree is dormant, so even a closet will do. Water about once a month. As the weather begins to warm up, gradually acclimate the tree to outdoor conditions, and new buds should begin to swell. Thereafter, resume your normal schedule of watering. Work a few tablespoons of bone meal into the top layer of soil when the plants are growing well again.

A fig tree planted in the ground in a sheltered spot can be successfully overwintered if the roots are protected from freezing. When dormant, the tree can be wrapped in a frost blanket until warm weather returns. Gardeners as far north as Zone 5 report success with this technique. Some drape the tree with non-LED Christmas lights connected to a timer, thus providing extra warmth on cold nights.

Figs can be made into preserves, and they dry well. Fresh figs can be incorporated into both sweet and savory dishes.

### Pomegranate

The ancient pomegranate (*Punica granatum*) grows easily in any climate where the temperature remains above 20°F but may not produce fruit unless it receives heat in summer and cool weather in winter. Therefore, for fruit production a container-grown plant will be needed in most parts of the country. A highly ornamental shrub or small tree, the pomegranate comes in dwarf forms that can be accommodated in a 20-gallon container. Purchase nursery stock of a known cultivar, choosing one developed for fruit production rather than one of the several purely ornamental varieties. Two smallish cultivars with reliable fruit production are Early Wonderful and Sweet. Grow them in a light, freely draining soil. Water regularly and deeply. Incorporate bone meal into the potting mix for young trees. Thereafter, apply an annual top dressing of compost to meet the plant's modest requirements for nutrients.

Attractive, fragrant blooms in spring are followed by the glossy red, highly nutritious fruits. The plants flower only at the tips of the new growth, so proper pruning is important for fruit production. When the plant is 2 feet tall, cut it back to 1 foot. Within a few weeks, new shoots should form near the cut tip. Allow no more than five of these to develop. Remove all suckers that form below this framework. In each of the following three years, cut the 1-year-old branches back by one third, encouraging new shoots to develop. Thereafter, remove only dead branches and suckers. The plant should develop a handsome rounded shape with dense branching. It is worth noting that many varieties have sharp spines. Beware.

Fruits have a long storage life, keeping well up to six months if refrigerated in a perforated plastic vegetable storage bag that maintains humidity around the fruit. The flavor actually improves with storage. Pomegranate cuttings root easily, so you can propagate your plant if you have the space to overwinter multiple containers. Take cuttings in winter from wood that is 1 year old. Apply rooting hormone and stick in potting mix. You should get almost 100 percent rooting. Most plants bear in the fourth year after cuttings are taken, and continue to produce for about twenty years. Older plants stop bearing fruit.

## POMEGRANATE JELLY OR POMEGRANATE-WINE JELLY

1 quart pomegranate juice, fresh or bottled; up to 1 cup of this can be a dry red wine, such as Pinot Noir or Cabernet Sauvignon
¼ cup freshly squeezed lemon juice
1 1.75-ounce package powdered fruit pectin
4½ cups granulated sugar

Please see the general instructions on canning, found in chapter 8, before you begin. Combine the liquids in a heavy 8-quart pot. Stir in the pectin, sprinkling it over the surface to help it dissolve. Let sit for 5 minutes, then stir well and place over high heat. Bring to a full, rolling boil, stirring constantly. Add the sugar all at once. Bring to a full boil again, stirring constantly. Boil hard for 1 minute, stirring constantly. Remove from the heat and skim off any foam that has formed. Ladle the hot jelly into hot, sterilized half pint jars, leaving ¼-inch head space. Adjust the caps and process in a boiling water bath canner for 5 minutes. Remove the jars from the canner and cool on wire racks. Allow to stand at room temperature until the jelly has set. Makes 4 to 5 half pints.

# Nuts

Nuts are the seeds of certain trees in which the seed coat forms a hard, woody shell. The endosperm, or kernel, contains large amounts of fats and oils rich in beneficial omega-3 fatty acids. Nuts are also a good source of vitamins and minerals, with the range of nutrients depending on the variety.

Nut trees range in size from about 12 feet for hazelnuts to 40 feet or more for walnuts and pecans. Because all nut trees require at least one other of its kind for pollination, they are best for larger properties. A list of common nut trees follows.

**Almonds** (*Prunus dulcis*) are actually a type of stone fruit with an edible seed. One variety, Reliable, is a hybrid that is not only small (12 feet or less with pruning) but also self-fertile. It will grow in zones 5–8. Other almonds get considerably larger and are suitable only for zones 9 and 10.

⁊⁊ **American hazelnut** (*Corylus americana*) is a bushy shrub that generally remains under 10 feet and will mature in 2 or 3 years from transplanting. Cultivated varieties include Halls Giant, which bears exceptionally large nuts and reaches about 15 feet. It is suitable for zones 4–9.

⁊⁊ **Black walnut** (*Juglans nigra*) trees are found throughout eastern North America. They grow slowly to around 50 feet in height and spread, yielding a fall crop of large, dark walnuts enclosed in a thick, greenish husk. The nuts are notoriously difficult to extract from the hard shells, with all sorts of methods used to first remove the husks. Many people spread the nuts in the driveway and drive the car over them a few times to pulverize the husks. Juice from the husks will stain hands, clothing, and anything else absorbent and is difficult to remove. Despite these difficulties, people harvest black walnuts every fall for their unique, rich flavor. Large wild trees are becoming increasingly scarce, due to their value as hardwood. Growing a tree to maturity takes 10 years or more, and virtually nothing else can be grown under the dripline because the walnut releases into the soil a chemical that inhibits the growth of other plants.

⁊⁊ **English walnuts** (*Jugulans regia*) are borne on majestic trees that reach 50 feet in height and spread. Two or more trees are needed for pollination. English walnuts are suitable for zones 4–8.

⁊⁊ **Hickories,** also members of the walnut family, come in several species. Several of them produce edible nuts, although those of some species taste much better than others. The preferred species is shagbark hickory (*Carya ovata*). Hickory trees reach 80 to 100 feet in height.

⁊⁊ **Pecan** (*Carya illinoinensis*) is a North American native tree related to hickories. Trees can soar to 100 feet tall, with 6-foot diameter trunks. They are hardy in zones 6–9, and can take up to ten years to mature. Once established, pecans can survive and bear for as long as three hundred years.

⁊⁊ **Pistachio** (*Pistacia vera*) is a nut suitable only for the hot, dry regions of the American Southwest, as it is completely intolerant of high humidity. Native to Asia, the tree reaches about 20 feet in height.

The planting of nut trees on the new American homestead is a practice to be encouraged of anyone with sufficient room to accommodate them.

# 7

# Food from Animals

F ew would disagree that plants will account for most of the food production on the typical new American homestead. Furthermore, eating a vegetarian or mostly vegetarian diet is arguably a more sustainable way to live. Nevertheless, many of the vegetarian table's greatest pleasures—cheese, honey, and eggs—are derived from animal husbandry. Furthermore, many people are following the "almost-vegetarian" trend, eating meat occasionally and on those occasions seeking out meat that is local, naturally farmed, and humanely processed. To help you evaluate the wisdom of including animals in your homestead plan, this chapter will explore bees, fish, chickens, and dairy animals. With the exception of fish, production for slaughter will not be considered.

## Bees

The common honeybee is our only domesticated insect. A description of its husbandry offers a splendid introduction to the complexities of caring for members of the animal kingdom.

We humans value honey not only as a sweetener but also for its health benefits. Eating local honey is said to reduce allergic responses to local pollen. However, the main benefit humans derive from bees results from their activities as pollinators, something we don't often consider. Bees perform an essential function in helping plants produce seeds for future generations. About 60 percent of fruits and vegetables, some 130 plant species, rely on bees for pollination. The value bee pollination represents to

American agriculture is about $9 billion annually, according to information posted online by the University of Georgia (http://interests.caes.uga.edu/insectlab/agimpact.html). In addition, bees contribute to the functioning of local ecosystems by pollinating wild plants.

Keeping bees in your backyard poses some potential challenges. Not least among them are local ordinances and deed covenants that may restrict beekeeping or limit the number of hives you may own. Check before you invest. Consider cost also: the investment in equipment and bees can amount to roughly $500 for your first hive. This is offset, however, by the value of the honey produced, which can recoup your investment within a single good season.

It is also worthwhile to assess your neighbors' potential reaction to your bees. Not everyone welcomes stinging insects, no matter how valuable. You may need to educate the people around you about the benefits of beekeeping. Some people (fewer than one in one hundred) are allergic to bee stings, and experience serious symptoms in response to one. If anyone in your family has this problem, you might want to let someone else provide your honey.

## Beekeeping Equipment

Although humans have been practicing apiculture for centuries, the modern beehive was not invented until 1851 by Pennsylvania clergyman, Lorenzo Langsroth. It consists basically of two sections, a lower one in which bees raise their offspring and store pollen and honey for their own use, and a upper section where bees are induced to store honey that the beekeeper will harvest. Within each of the hive sections are frames on which the beekeeper mounts *foundation*, a material that encourages the bees to build honeycomb and brood cells. Both hives and foundation can be made of all natural materials such as wood and beeswax, or of more durable plastic. Bees, claim several beekeepers, prefer all natural hives and foundation.

Besides the hive itself, you need some additional equipment. A veil and gloves protect your hands and face from stings. A smoker produces abundant cool smoke to calm bees and allow the beekeeper to work safely around the hive. To manage all sorts of maintenance, inspection, and harvest tasks, you will need a hive tool. This flat metal bar has a hook on one end and a scraper on the other, and is used to open the hive, lift frames, scrape excess comb from the frames and so forth. As with any other human activity, beekeeping has spawned its own collection of gadgets and tools to make various jobs easier to accomplish. Only you can decide whether you wish to invest in, for example, an electric honey extractor.

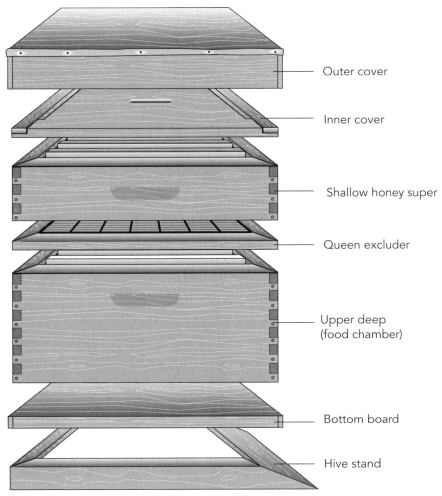

A modern bee hive and its parts.

## Choosing and Installing Bees

Beginning beekeepers frequently choose the Italian strain of *Apis mellifera*. While various other strains have been selected over the years, all with advantages and disadvantages, the Italian strain offers a good combination of productivity, tolerance, and low aggression. Where winters are severe, another strain, such as Caucasian, may be better suited. Recommendations for your area can be found via your cooperative extension agency website. If you locate a beekeeping club in your area, its members will be a treasure trove of advice and encouragement.

Smoker and hive tool.

If you have numerous local beekeepers, you may be able to purchase a nucleus, or *nuc*, colony of bees well established on hive frames. More likely, however, you will need to order your bees online or by phone for shipment via U.S. mail. You should receive a package of about 11,000 insects and the queen in her own little cage. Make certain that the supplier you choose has been inspected by the state's apiary inspector. Newly arrived bees must immediately be cared for and fed. The sooner they are introduced into the hive, the better. Therefore, it pays to have everything prepared well in advance of the bees' arrival.

## Hive Management

Managing a beehive involves everything from properly installing the newly arrived bees to harvesting honey. As with gardening, in beekeeping preventing problems through proper management makes more sense than trying to correct trouble after it arises.

### Introducing Bees to the Hive

Bees are shipped in a screened container, along with a food supply and a small container housing the queen. As soon as your new colony arrives, spray the bees in their shipping container liberally with cool water from a plastic spray bottle. Keep the box in a cool, shady place for an hour or so, then spray the bees with sugar syrup (see recipe below). A light coating is sufficient; you don't want to drown them in it. The bees will lick the syrup from their bodies and begin to regain energy after their journey. You will need additional syrup for feeding the colony during its first weeks.

### Sugar Syrup for Bees

In a large pot, bring 10 cups of water to a rolling boil and add 5 pounds of granulated sugar. Immediately remove the pot from the heat and stir until the sugar dissolves completely. Cool, covered, to room temperature before using.

---

If you feed the bees by spraying them with syrup at least three times daily, you can hold them for about a week before hiving. However, they should be placed into the hive as soon as possible, ideally in the late afternoon of the day they arrive. A clear, warmish day with little wind is ideal. If it is cold, rainy, and dreary, wait a day or two for the weather to improve, but do not leave them in the shipping container for longer than a week. Feed them about half an hour before you plan to open the shipping container, then do the following:

1. Rap the container sharply to jar the bees to the bottom. This does them no harm. Open the lid and remove the food and the queen cage. Loosely replace the lid.

2. Instructions typically accompany the colony. Follow them for opening the package and removing the queen without allowing the bees to escape.

3. After removing some of the frames, suspend the queen cage in the hive and dump in the bees.

4. Plug the cage with a piece of sugary candy that worker bees will consume, thus freeing the queen.

5. Install a hive top feeder and close up the hive, leaving an entrance hole about an inch across.

Do not disturb the hive for at least five days, or the workers may kill the queen. Her purpose is to produce eggs that build the colony's population and to secrete pheromones that regulate the activity of the rest of the hive. Her presence is absolutely essential to success.

> During the first weeks after hiving your bees, spend time observing their behavior as they forage. Read up on the fascinating ecology and behavior of your bees, subjects that lie beyond the scope of this brief introduction to beekeeping. Only by learning what constitutes normal behavior and activity at various times of the season can you develop the skill to recognize problems that may arise early enough to take effective action.

### Inspecting the Hive

Inspect your hive weekly. When you dress for the inspection, remember that bees prefer light colors to dark. Don your protective gear, have your hive tool close by, light the smoker (follow the manufacturer's instructions) and make sure it is producing plenty of cool smoke. Test by smoking your palm. If it does not feel hot, you're fine. Follow these steps:

1. Apply smoke to the entrance, then under the hive cover, and remove the cover.

2. Direct smoke into the hive to calm bees while you remove the hive top feeder. If no feeder is in place, the hive will have an inner cover with a ventilation hole. Direct smoke through the hole, then open the cover with the hive tool, smoke into the hive through the opening, and finally remove the cover completely.

3. Finally, direct smoke down into the hive between the frames until most of the bees have moved into the depths.

Now you are ready to inspect the hive. Carefully remove the frame closest to the outside wall of the hive. Set it aside as you remove each frame in turn and examine it. You are looking for several things:

- Do many cells contain eggs?
- Are many cells of each comb well stocked with pollen and nectar?
- Do the wax caps on the cells look firm and convex?
- Are brood cells close together or scattered?

Few eggs or a scattered brood pattern indicate a sick or aging queen. Perforated or shrunken wax caps indicate potential problems.

Once you have inspected all the frames, carefully return everything to its original position. Use smoke as needed. Do not hurry through the process or you will crush bees and/or get stung. Nevertheless, do not leave the hive open for more than 15 minutes—less if the weather is cool.

### The First Two Months

The first two months after hiving a colony are critical to its long-term success. By the end of the first month, the bees should have built comb on most of the frames in the deep hive body. Add a second deep hive body on top of the first as soon as the bees have filled seven of the first ten frames. At this time, increase ventilation by opening the entrance to the hive to about 4 inches wide.

Near the end of the second month, a healthy colony will have filled the majority of the second-story frames with comb. At this point, you can add a queen excluder to the top of the hive body, followed by a shallow honey super. This process, called *supering*, encourages the bees to store honey that you will eventually harvest. Keeping the queen out of the honey super prevents those cells from being used for egg deposition.

### Completing the First Season

During the first summer, your colony will reach its peak population as nectar production peaks. Inspect hives every other week. Add honey supers as needed. Start harvesting honey as flowering begins to wane in late summer.

Hives in cold winter areas require 60 pounds of honey for winter feeding, and about half as much in milder regions. Make sure to leave sufficient honey for your bees to survive the winter. This may mean you harvest no honey during the first year. Once autumn arrives, the hive must be winterized. Make sure the hive has adequate ventilation and raise the back of the hive so it tilts slightly forward. The tilt allows any moisture that enters to drain quickly away. Wrap the hive in tar paper and put a layer of tar paper over the top, held in place with bricks. The dark paper helps the hive absorb the sun's warmth to overcome winter cold.

Autumn is also the time to medicate the colony. Do this by incorporating medications into sugar syrup fed to the bees. Winterizing syrup contains twice as much sugar as spring syrup. Follow the recipe previously given, adding 10 pounds of sugar instead of 5. During winter, the colony will be mostly inactive, clustered inside the hive and eating stored honey. In late winter, check the frames in the upper hive body for the presence of capped honey cells. If the bees have used this supply, it may be necessary to begin feeding them sugar syrup, a process that must continue until natural food supplies become available once again.

### The Second Year

During its second year, your colony of bees should produce enough honey for an abundant harvest. In order for them to do so, they need a proper head start. Feeding sugar syrup to your bees in spring not only helps them break winter dormancy but also stimulates egg-laying and comb-building activity. As with autumn feeding, medications can be introduced into the syrup in spring. This is generally the time when a new colony is first medicated. If you choose to medicate, make sure to stop six weeks prior to adding honey supers to the hive.

Spring feeding should begin about three weeks before the first blossoms appear in your area, even if the bees still have honey. Wait until the temperature outside is 50°F or warmer to inspect the colony in early spring. Make sure they have honey and that the queen is present. If there is no honey, begin feeding sugar syrup immediately and continue until you see bees returning to the hive with pollen on their legs. Once the season is well under way, follow the instructions given for maintaining the colony during its first year.

Anticipate an abundant harvest of honey in late summer of the second year. Growing conditions during the previous season will influence the availability of nectar and consequently the amount of honey produced.

## Troubleshooting

Bee colonies are subject to several common problems. Most can be avoided through proper husbandry and preventive measures. Problems can be categorized as behavioral issues, husbandry issues, external threats, and diseases.

## Behavioral Issues

The chief behavioral problem is swarming, when half the colony leaves with the queen. The best evidence of an imminent swarm is the appearance of swarm cells, specialized comb structures built near the bottom of the frame by workers in response, it is thought, to overcrowding in the hive. The swarm cells contain developing queens that will lead the new swarm. Swarm cells should be removed each time they are observed in young colonies. Swarming can be prevented by relieving congestion in the hive. One way to do this is to separate the hive into two and purchase a new queen for the daughter colony. A swarm can also be retrieved, sometimes, a task best accomplished with the help of an experienced beekeeper.

## Husbandry Issues

Husbandry issues typically result from inadequate inspection of the hive, according to most experts. Loss of the queen can go unobserved, for example, leading to the eventual collapse of the colony left without a source of eggs. Early detection via routine inspections permits ordering a replacement queen from a supplier. Failure to provide adequate ventilation, especially in hot, humid weather, is another common mistake beginners make.

## External Threats

The following is a list of external threats to bees:

- **Robbing.** This is perhaps the most serious of external threats. It occurs when your hive is attacked by bees from another hive. Bees fighting at the hive entrance indicates with certainty that the hive is being robbed. The guard bees will fight to the death, and a prolonged battle can result in disaster, either from dead bees or lost honey. Reducing the entrance to the hive to the point that only one bee at a time can enter may thwart an attack, or the entire hive can be covered with a wet sheet draped all the way to the ground. Rewet the sheet as it dries in the sun, and leave it in place for no more than two days.

- **Pesticide poisoning.** With widespread use of toxic chemicals, bees can succumb to otherwise well-intentioned spraying. With advance notice, you can protect your hive from nearby applications of pesticide. Ask neighbors to advise you if they plan to spray, and cover the hive with a wet bedsheet to minimize foraging activity that day. Unfortunately, it is possible for bees to ingest pesticides that have been applied to agricultural crops, if the pesticide is of a systemic type that is taken up by the plant. Pollen, for example, can become contaminated in this fashion. The beekeeper has little defense against this type of threat, which has been implicated in the phenomenon known as *colony collapse disorder.*

**Pests.** Two arthropod pests, Varroa mites and tracheal mites, can cause serious problems for a bee colony. The former attach themselves to worker bees and feed on the insect's hemolymph, becoming the bee equivalent of a tick on a mammal. They also attack drone larvae, producing deformities and death. The mites, visible to the naked eye, can be observed directly. Installing a screened bottom board in the hive body as the weather warms up allows for better ventilation and provides the ability to assess the hive's mite population. Mites fall off their hosts and through the screened bottom, below, where a piece of sticky cardboard lies to capture them. By counting the number of mites collected on the board, you can determine the extent of the infestation. A count of more than twenty-five mites per day indicates the need for action.

The available medications must be used with care. Seek professional advice, if possible. Try natural remedies first. Dust the bees very lightly with powdered sugar by opening the hive (apply smoke first) and creating a faint cloud of sugar dust with a shaker. Because the mites prefer drone larvae, you can install a frame with special drone comb foundation. This will cause workers to build drone cells, which will attract the mites. When the cells are capped, they can be removed, killed by placing them in a deep freeze, and uncapped. Workers will clean and reuse the cells, allowing you to repeat the process. Either of these methods effectively reduces the mite population to a point tolerable by the colony.

Tracheal mites, invisible to the naked eye, can infest the bees' breathing tubes and cause severe damage before detection. Recommended control methods include application of menthol to fumigate the hive, and feeding bees a concoction of sugar and vegetable shortening. The rationale behind this traditional remedy relates to the oily coating that the bees acquire when feeding on the mixture. The oil apparently discourages the mites from moving from bee to bee and breaks the reproductive cycle.

Hives sometimes receive invasions of wax moths and small hive beetles. Either is a serious problem and requires help from the state agricultural department's apiary specialist. More conventional invaders such as ants, rodents, raccoons, and birds can also damage hives. Generally speaking, thwarting access by, for example, weighting the hive cover to prevent raccoons from opening it, provides adequate control for such problems.

## Diseases

The "big six" bee diseases are the following:

- **American foulbrood (AFB).** The result of infection by a spore-forming bacterium, AFB causes the death of larvae while in the brood comb. Cell caps take on a shrunken, oily appearance. Dull, brown dead larvae and a strong unpleasant odor characterize the problem. Because the only remedy is destruction of the entire hive and all associated equipment, it is essential to prevent this disease. Administration of the antibiotics tylosin tartrate and oxytetracycline via sugar syrup feeders in spring and fall helps prevent most infections. Manufacturer's directions should be strictly followed when using these products, which can be purchased from beekeeping suppliers.

- **European foulbrood (EFB).** EFB is similar to AFB, but larvae typically die in their cells before capping takes place. The odor, it is said, is not quite so bad, either. This problem does not require complete colony replacement and can be treated with antibiotics. Consult an experienced beekeeper for help immediately, if you think your colony has EFB. Typically, the queen is replaced to slow down brood production, allowing the workers to remove dead larvae, and antibiotics are administered.

- **Nosema.** Caused by a protozoan parasite, Nosema produces symptoms like those of human dysentery. It seems to appear most frequently in the damp, cool conditions of early spring. Prophylactic treatment with the antibiotic Fumagilin-B in the spring and fall is widely recommended.

- **Chalkbrood.** Caused by a fungus, this is another condition favored by springtime's cool, wet weather. No treatment is available, but the appearance of hard, white dead larvae near the hive entrance is a sure sign that the bees are infected. Workers are removing the bodies and dumping them out the door. Remove these to minimize the spread of the fungus and check the hive frames. Usually only one frame will harbor most of the infection. Replacing this frame gives the hive a chance to recover on its own.

- **Sacbrood.** Stressed bees—those undergoing crowding or poor ventilation—may develop this viral disease in which the brood cell becomes a fluid-filled sac. Removing infected cells as they are observed helps the colony recover on its own. No treatment is available.

- **Stonebrood.** An uncommon fungal disease that produces "mummies" from larval bees. Cleaning up the dead larvae dumped by workers is the only action the beekeeper can take to help the hive recover, which it usually does.

## Honey Collection and Storage

The golden reward for all the work of beekeeping, of course, is honey. In a good year, you may be able to harvest 100 pounds of honey from one hive. In other years, you may only get half as much. Regardless of the size of the harvest, you must determine whether to extract the honey from the comb or to collect comb honey. Extracting honey requires additional equipment, while coaxing the bees into producing comb honey requires skill and a measure of good luck.

For extracted honey, you will need the following tools, an investment amounting to as much as $1,000.

- Honey extracting machine, hand or electric
- Uncapping knife
- Honey strainer
- Collecting tank or bucket
- Storage jars
- Labels

You will need labels only if you plan to sell part of your harvest. Check with your county extension agent regarding labeling requirements. Note, also, that in some jurisdictions you may need a health permit to sell honey.

For comb honey production, you will need special supers, frames, and a foundation. You also need to be blessed with a lush and abundant season with strong nectar production. Such conditions encourage bees to produce comb honey. Therefore, most beekeepers opt to extract honey rather than produce comb honey, despite the added costs involved in extraction. Some of this money can be recovered from sales of excess honey.

Regardless of whether you are putting up extracted or comb honey, bottles or jars and their lids must be sterilized with boiling water before use. The use of a collection container fitted with a spigot makes filling jars simple. Beeswax may also be harvested from emptied honeycomb, and suppliers offer equipment to make this easier. It has numerous uses.

# Fish

The ancient Romans kept fish in artificial ponds called *piscinae*, and in Asia the practice of raising fish in ponds dates back even earlier. Although not every new American homestead site will accommodate a pond sufficiently large for efficient fish production, even a small garden pond can provide benefits. A small pond offers water and habitat for wildlife, a focal point, and a resource for both rainwater management and plant production.

## Aquaculture Pond Design and Filtration

For sustained production of fish on a homestead scale with minimal intervention or energy inputs, a pond covering approximately one acre or larger is needed. For fish production on a micro-scale, in a pond that could be built in a suburban backyard, both filtration and aeration will be needed. This will require electricity to drive a pump.

Home-scale aquaculture can be attempted within a completely artificial environment. Indeed, this method is most often employed for small-scale, high-efficiency production of food fish. Growth tanks, situated within a temperature-controlled greenhouse, receive filtration and aeration from automated equipment. Baby fish eat a carefully formulated diet to maximize their growth. Obviously, such an elaborate operation would demand considerable expense and require careful planning.

For the homestead aquaculturist, an outdoor pond makes the most sense. Filtration via a pumped, recirculating system removes biological wastes and provides aeration. With proper care, natural ecological cycles develop, and the pond becomes able to sustain a small population of fish, produce plants both ornamental and edible, and contribute markedly to the overall diversity of the landscape.

### Siting and Construction of a Garden Pond

The pond should be located in a low-lying, level spot that receives full sun. Siting a pond on top of a hill, or on a sloping site looks incongruous. Choose a spot where a natural pond might logically form. You will need to supply electricity if you plan on having a pumped filtration system. Consult with a licensed electrician for safe installation of an outdoor outlet near the pond. Generally, the electrical supply cable will be buried in conduit to meet local building codes. It is essential to include any necessary trenching for the electrical line in the overall plan for the pond.

A prefabricated pond can be sunk in an appropriately sized hole, but the most versatile material for sealing the pond is a flexible PVC liner. Neoprene rubber roofing membrane can also be used. Each of these pond sealers has advantages and disadvantages in terms of availability, cost, and durability. PVC offers a reasonable combination of low price and reasonable durability. Properly installed, a PVC liner should last fifteen years.

Regardless of the type of liner you choose, you will follow the same basic procedure for installing the pond. Lay out the pond on the site, using stakes, landscape paint or a length of hose to mark the perimeter. Use strings and a line level to find level points along the edge. You may have to compensate for slight differences in grade by removing soil from one area and using it to build up another. Establishing a level perimeter, however, is the single most important aspect of pond construction. Once that task has been accomplished, the rest is mere excavation. When you have determined where the level perimeter of the pond will lie, begin excavating. The hole should be about 3 inches deeper than the maximum pond depth. The bottom should be flat. If you plan on growing emergent plants, such as arrowhead or water celery, create a shallow area on one end, or encircling the entire pond. The deepest portion of the pond should be about 2 feet, or 6 inches deeper than the frost line, where winters are severe. The shallow area(s) need not be any deeper than 1 foot.

When the hole has been dug, line it with 2 inches of damp sand. Place a pond liner underlayment fabric sheet on top of the sand, smoothing it to fit the contours of the hole. You may find it easiest to remove your shoes and work from the center of the pond outward while standing on the fabric. The fabric should extend beyond the maximum water level (your level perimeter line) at least 1 foot all around.

Unfold the PVC liner and allow it to warm in the sun. This will make it more flexible and easier to install. Move the liner into the hole, again working outward from the center to smooth it out. Take care not to puncture the liner. Sticks or pebbles that might fall in should be carefully removed before you step on one and push it thorough the liner. When the liner is more or less in place, you can begin filling the pond with water from a garden hose. As the water presses the liner into place, you can smooth and fold it for a precise fit. The liner should extend at least 1 foot beyond the waterline all the way around the pond. Secure the outermost edges of the liner with galvanized landscape pins. When the liner is secure and the pond is almost full, you can turn off the water and begin installing the decorative coping around the pond's edge.

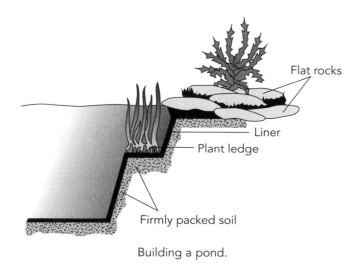

Building a pond.

Three possibilities for coping a pond exist: sod, natural stone, or architectural pavers. Sod can be combined with either of the others to good effect, but the pond will look best if you choose either natural stone or pavers but not both. If you are installing a waterfall filter, natural stone looks best. Coping simply hides the edges of the pond and blends it with the rest of the landscape. Where lawn abuts, allowing the grass to grow right up to the water's edge looks good, especially if emergent plants are growing in the adjacent area of the pond.

### Rainwater

The garden pond can act as a rainwater collection and storage reservoir, provided you take precautions to prevent siltation, flooding, and erosion. Siltation is best avoided by lining drainage channels leading to the pond with compacted sand, gravel, and pebbles to prevent water from picking up soil. Screening debris from the pond is also a good idea. One way to accomplish this without detracting from the pond's appearance is to place several large rocks at the point where channels empty into the pond. The rocks trap leaves and sticks where they can be easily removed.

Avoid flooding during heavy rains by installing an overflow drain at one edge of the pond. Locate the drain just above maximum water level, and direct it away from the pond. A buried section of 4-inch corrugated pipe works best. The water can be directed toward a cistern or storm sewer. To prevent erosion, use corrugated pipe for all outflows, or line any open channels with a layer of compacted sand and gravel.

Drainage systems may require permits from your local codes enforcement office. Check first before beginning construction.

## Installing a Waterfall Filter

If you opt to install a recirculating filter in your pond, you can increase its capacity for fish while maintaining clear, clean, and well-oxygenated water. The simplest filter involves a pump, a length of hose, and some carefully placed rocks forming a waterfall. You can also purchase complete filtration systems for a garden pond, but a carefully designed homemade one will do the same job. Basically, you want the water from the pond to pass over a layer of filter material before being returned to the pond. A good choice of filtration medium is crushed lava rock, sold in bags at DIY centers. To contain the lava rock, select a heavy plastic tub that holds about 5 gallons. A submersible pump in the bottom of the pond moves water up to the tub, where it flows over the gravel before draining through holes in the tub and back into the pond. Larger pieces of debris remain on top of the lava rock, where they can be periodically removed. Bacteria growing on the lava rocks detoxify the pond water. Five gallons of lava rock provides sufficient filtration for a 1,500-gallon pond, assuming the pond is not overcrowded with fish and contains healthy, vigorously growing plants.

## Natural Ecological Cycles and Maintenance

The importance of working with natural ecological cycles to establish a healthy garden pond cannot be overemphasized. The pond should never require medication for the fishes nor a chemical control to prevent algae growth. Rather, when the plants, fish, and filtration system bacteria are present in a proper balance, the pond actually maintains itself.

Even a very large pond may be crowded, in terms of the number of fish per gallon of water, compared with a natural lake or river. The carrying capacity of the pond will be determined by three factors: the number of gallons of water, the number of square feet of surface area, and the efficiency of the biological components of the filtration system.

The filtration system removes particulate matter and debris. Periodic cleaning of the filter takes these materials out of the pond, where they would otherwise decay and release nutrients into the water. Bacteria and other organisms comprising the biological components of the system carry out the important work of metabolizing fish wastes and decaying plant material into the pond equivalent of compost, known as *mulm*. Fish waste consists primarily of ammonia. This compound is toxic to fish, but can be absorbed from the water by certain algae. It is also converted to nitrate in the filtration system by bacterial activity. The nitrate, in turn, is absorbed by green algae and higher plants. Therefore, a pond with all the major components working in harmony will have very little nitrate in the water. Another major plant nutrient, phosphorus, is released into the water when plant and animal debris decomposes. This is why keeping leaves and other debris out of the pond make sense. Mulm may also contain high concentrations of phosphorus, slowly releasing it back into the water where it fuels algal growth. Periodic cleaning of the filtration system and an annual siphoning of the entire pond helps to reduce the amount of mulm and keep the pond's ecosystem in balance. Mulm and pond water are both excellent fertilizers and should be applied to your garden whenever the opportunity arises.

## Choosing Fish to Stock

Rainbow trout and catfish dominate the commercial market for pond-raised freshwater fish, although tilapia are also an option. Trout require clean, cold running water and present significant challenges to home-scale cultivation. Catfish, on the other hand, tolerate warm water and crowding, and offer the best option for homestead production.

### Catfish

The most commonly produced catfish is the channel cat, *Ictalurus punctatus*. It is widespread in the eastern and northern United States. Although experts recommend ponds of at least a quarter acre for catfish production, a small garden pond can yield a few fish. Channel catfish fingerlings often appear in aquarium shops. Placing a few of these in an established garden pond in spring should, with proper feeding, yield a few fish big enough to eat by the end of the season. The same supplier should also stock an appropriate pelleted feed.

### Sunfish

Many beloved American game fishes belong to the sunfish family. However, only a few species of sunfishes adapt sufficiently to small ponds to make keeping them worthwhile. Hardy and aggressive, sunfish need plenty of room to establish territories if you expect them to reproduce. More likely, your garden pond can accommodate only a single pair. They are, however, a superb choice for a larger pond. Check with your local agricultural extension agent regarding pond construction and stocking if you have the real estate available. Not only can a stocked fish pond enhance a property's value, it will provide hours of enjoyment as you harvest dinner with a pole and line. In the central South, such ponds typically have largemouth bass, sunfish, and catfish as their major denizens.

### Tilapia

Tilapia, a tropical cichlid, is the freshwater fish of choice for intensive, warm-water aquaculture. In a home-scale system, a breeding group of one male and six females is maintained in an aquarium. When a brood is produced, the young fish are transferred to a grow-out tank until they are large enough to sex. Only males go into the pond to be raised to harvestable size (about 6 inches). Including females in the pond will result in repeated spawnings, filling the pond with many small fish that will not grow to marketable size. Optimum temperature for tilapia growth is 82–86°F. They are unable to tolerate water cooler than 50°F. The majority of aquacultured tilapia in the United States are the species *Oreochromis niloticus*. Unlike catfish, which require a diet containing added protein, tilapia are vegetarians. This makes them much easier to manage, as some of their food supply will come from the natural productivity of pond plants and algae.

## Other Pond Products

While it may prove difficult to harvest an abundance of fish from a small garden pond, edible aquatic plants can be highly productive. The most familiar aquatic edible is water chestnut (*Eleocharis* sp.). Some additional hardy varieties and their edible parts are:

- **Arrowhead** (*Sagittaria latifolia*)—potato-flavored tubers
- **Cattail** (*Typha* sp.)—spring shoots and pollen
- **Lotus** (*Lotus* sp.)—tubers and seeds
- **Pickerel rush** (*Pontederia cordata*)—young leaves, seeds
- **Taro** (*Colocasia* sp.)—tubers
- **Water celery** (*Oenanthe javanica*)—stems and leaves
- **Water spinach** (*Ipomea batatas*)—leaves
- **Water hyssop** (*Bacopa caroliniana*)—lemony herb

Some other moisture-loving edibles, discussed elsewhere, are celery, lemongrass, and watercress. Several less commonly seen plants, such as perennial rice (*Zizania* sp.), grow well in wet soil and are thus potential candidates for a backyard water garden of edibles.

# Poultry

Any depiction of the iconic American family farmhouse will include a few chickens scratching in the side yard. Without a doubt, chickens are the most popular small space food animal. Keeping a few chickens requires less equipment than does keeping bees or fish. Chickens need far less space than dairy animals. Hardy and adaptable, chickens may also do double duty as garden pest control experts.

## The Coop

The size of the chicken coop you require depends on the number of chickens you intend to keep. In the typical backyard, five or six birds will constitute the flock. (In some locations, the number of birds you can keep is limited by local codes.)

Regardless of its size, the coop needs to be easy to clean, well-ventilated, and inaccessible to predators. Chickens don't mind a bit of crowding when they are on the roost for the night. Three to 5 square feet of indoor space per bird is the typical recommendation. Vents at each roof peak help to carry off moisture. They should be protected with ¼-inch hardware cloth, to prevent access by rodents and snakes. Room for feed and water inside the coop should be provided.

> The floor of your chicken coop, especially underneath the roost where the chickens sleep, should be cleaned on a regular basis. Chicken manure is some of the stinkiest and is too "hot" to use directly on the garden. Add it to your compost pile instead. A smelly coop will almost certainly raise an outcry from a neighbor.

One of the coop's long walls can be hinged along the midline, allowing the bottom portion of the wall to be raised for access to the entire floor, and roosts should be removable. These two features will make cleaning the coop less of a chore, and therefore more likely to be done regularly. This access door must be securely latched to thwart predators. Raccoons can figure out quite complicated devices. A small padlock is your best insurance against unwanted entry. Spilled feed may attract rodents. Remove it on a regular basis. Store feed in a metal container with a tight-fitting lid.

There are many designs for DIY chicken coops—permanent and mobile—online, including A-frames, hoops, and "chicken tractors" to name just a few. You can also buy preconstructed chicken coops; these can be obtained from poultry supply catalogs, farm stores, magazines, and online.

## Outdoor Spaces

Chickens also should have access to outdoor space. They will happily scratch for their own food, removing insects and weed seeds and aerating your lawn. Coops designed to be portable allow you to move the birds to a new spot each day. With flocks of six birds or fewer, a coop can be small enough to be easily portable. While you can purchase a ready-made coop, anyone who is handy with tools can build one from materials available at any DIY store.

> Take care that your chickens cannot gain access to your vegetable garden. They will happily eat tomatoes, squash, and cucumbers, and will pluck any variety of seedlings from the row. Six chickens can wreak absolute devastation in only a few minutes, so take appropriate precautions.

With enough room at your disposal, you can fence off a chicken yard, locate a non-movable coop in one corner of it, and let the chickens have free run during the daytime. This was my grandfather's approach. The fenced area, accommodating about two dozen chickens, was roughly half an acre. A cross fence restricted the birds to one half of the space, allowing the other half to recover. Apple trees also grew in these spaces, providing shade and fallen fruit for the chickens along with apples for Grandma's kitchen. All reasonable care should be taken to prevent access to the yard during the day by dogs. Chickens kept outdoors in this manner need their wing feathers clipped, to prevent them from simply flying over the fence and out of their enclosure.

## Raising Chicks

Start your flock in late spring, when the weather settles and extremes of temperature are unlikely, so that five months or a bit longer will have passed before the chicks start laying eggs. Egg production depends on day length, so you do not want your flock to mature in mid-winter. Otherwise, they will wait until the following spring to begin laying, unless you are willing to go to the trouble and expense of extending the day artificially with added lighting.

If you plan on having only two or three birds, you should probably purchase them as ready-to-lay hens. You should visit the breeder's facility to pick out your birds, affording you the opportunity to inspect conditions there. For a larger flock, ordering chicks may be the best approach, as you not only spend much less per bird but also have a wider selection of breeds from which to select. Mail order suppliers have responded to the demand for backyard birds by lowering their minimum order quantities. Nevertheless, you might want to combine your order with other people's to save on shipping or to take advantage of quantity discounts. You can easily find like-minded folks in your vicinity via home gardening clubs or online.

Baby chicks need attention as soon as they arrive, so you should prepare their quarters ahead of time. A large cardboard box will suffice for a few chicks. Outfit it with water, starter feed made for baby chicks, and some kind of litter. Do not use hay or straw, but otherwise whatever natural materials are available will be fine. Cat litter made from natural materials will do, for example. Cover the litter with some crumpled newspaper to keep the chicks from eating the litter. Remove the paper after a few days. Cut some 6-inch wide strips of cardboard and use it to make the corners of the box curved by taping it in place in each corner. This prevents the chicks from crowding into the corners. Use a desk lamp with an incandescent bulb to keep the temperature of the box at 95°F. Monitor this carefully. After a week has passed, lower the temperature by 5°F, and continue to lower it weekly until you reach the outdoor temperature.

As you remove each chick from the shipping container and transfer it to the box, dip its beak in the watering dish. This lets the chick know where water is to be found. (Note: It is important to purchase a watering dish made for baby chicks. They can drown otherwise.)

Your best defense against problems at this stage is cleanliness. Keep the feeder only about one fourth full to avoid wasting feed, change the litter frequently, and wash the feeder and water dish daily.

Provide feed that contains 20 percent protein, universally sold at farm centers as *chick starter*. Chicks need a feeder that provides 1 inch of space per bird or more. As they grow, they will need a larger feeder and a bigger watering dish. By the time they are six weeks old, they should be switched to a feed type specifically for *pullets*. After another twelve weeks, they will be ready for laying mash. All these feeds have been carefully formulated, and it is a mistake to try to substitute a homemade product. Organic feeds are becoming more widely available, and should be used whenever possible. Once the weather warms up reliably, pullets can be moved outside to a secure enclosure. Set up the coop when you begin feeding laying mash.

Chickens also need grit, which helps them digest their food by substituting for teeth. Birds have a gizzard, in which grit and food are mixed together to help break down tough seeds and such. Grit should be available to the birds as they choose. Ditto with calcium, which can be supplied via crushed oyster shells or as part of a commercial formulation for laying hens.

## Egg Production

For the purposes of this book, egg production is the goal of chicken keeping. And although the traditional fate of the stew pot awaits a hen past her prime, the techniques and equipment required for humane and sanitary slaughtering and butchering lie outside the scope of our discussion. Consult the resources for additional reading regarding meat production for chickens and other species discussed in this chapter.

Hens need a proper diet for maximal egg production. Switch them to laying mash when they are old enough to begin laying. Feed your chickens commercial products sold as a complete diet for them, and allow them to scratch in the lawn for supplemental feeding.

A widespread misconception exists that a rooster is required for egg production. This is not the case. The rooster is needed only for the production of *fertilized* eggs, and ultimately baby chicks. He is otherwise completely extraneous. So don't worry about that darned rooster waking the neighborhood every morning. You don't need him around. If you live out in the country and want a rooster anyway, bear in mind that they are territorial and can be aggressive. You can only keep one per flock, or they will fight.

## Chicken Breeds

For laying hens in the backyard, Bantams offer many advantages. They seldom weigh more than 2 pounds but lay eggs almost as large as a standard type, such as White Leghorn. True Bantams have no standard counterpart, but there are Bantam varieties of many standard breeds. Bantams have less appeal as meat animals than their larger cousins. Leghorns and other layers are usually inferior when butchered. For homesteaders interested in both eggs and meat, consider the all-purpose breeds, such as Plymouth Rock, Rhode Island Red, and Orpington.

As with heirloom vegetables, there are many heirloom chicken breeds, some of them with characteristics that would make them ideal subjects for a backyard coop. The problem with these old breeds is their relative rarity.

Additional information on poultry breeds can be located via the sources suggested in the resources.

# Dairy Animals

Although they require more space than chickens do, dairy animals provide an enormous quantity of high-quality food in exchange for the effort to maintain them. However, their demands are significant, and you should

## Characteristics of Selected Chicken Breeds

| Breed | Adult Weight (lb.) | Appearance | Comments |
| --- | --- | --- | --- |
| Bantam | 2–5 | Miniature version of larger breeds, or "true" Bantams with no larger counterpart; various colors | Often chosen for backyard coops due to small size and good egg production; seldom suitable for meat |
| White Leghorn | 3–4 | White, sometimes other colors | Excellent producer of white eggs, though high-strung |
| Rhode Island Red | 3–5 | Deep red-brown color | Lay lots of brown eggs; hardy and active |
| Plymouth Rock | 3–5 | White, buff, or black and white | Good for both meat and brown eggs; calm and easy to handle |
| Orpington | 3–5 | Buff, blue, black, or white | Good for both meat and brown eggs; good brooders; calm and easy to handle |
| Araucana | 4–7 | Large, many color variations; no tail feathers | Lay blue or blue green eggs; calm; good brooders; an heirloom breed |

give careful consideration to the nature of those demands before including a dairy animal in your lifescape plan.

## Barns and Pastures

The need for protected housing can create the primary obstacle to dairy animal production. Goats, for example, require 20 square feet per animal of indoor space. Cattle require at least five times as much. In addition, animals require outdoor space in which to exercise and to graze upon fresh vegetation.

Animals will also produce manure that requires composting prior to its use on the garden, resulting in the need for additional space. Manure composting must take place under the proper circumstances (and in a suitable location) to avoid objectionable odors.

## Characteristics of Selected Dairy Goat Breeds

| Breed | Avg. Daily Yield (lb.) | Color, Weight,* and Appearance | Comments |
|-------|------------------------|-------------------------------|----------|
| Alpine | 7 | Front end color differs from the back end, erect ears; 130 pounds | Good for cool climates |
| LaMancha | 6 | Many colors, but no visible ears at all; 130–135 pounds | Considered the calmest breed |
| Nubian | 5 | Can be any color. They have floppy ears and Roman noses and can weigh up to 135 pounds | The most popular breed, producing less milk but with higher fat content |
| Oberhasli | 6 | Bay and black coloration like a deer, ears erect; weighs 120 pounds or less | Moderate milk producer but remains smaller in size |
| Saanen | 7 | White, with erect ears and a flattened snout; large, about 130 pounds | Generally considered good milk producers |
| Toggenburg | 6+ | Brown with white face and rump, erect ears; 120 pounds | An old breed long popular in North America |

*Weights indicated are for a mature doe. Bucks in all cases will be about 25 to 30 percent larger.*

## Goats

Goats have been domesticated for centuries and remain the first choice for a dairy source where space is at a premium. Their shed should provide ample space, depending on the amount of time they will be inside during the winter months. The farther north you live, the bigger the shed you will need. A dirt floor is fine. Other materials may encourage too much moisture to accumulate. Make sure the shed is ventilated at the roof peaks. You will need a manger, which can be time-consuming to maintain, because goats are messy eaters. Besides the main outdoor pen, you will need an additional pen for kids. Unless the female goats periodically have offspring, you won't get any milk.

Kids absolutely must have colostrum, a special form of milk produced by the mother goat, for their first twenty-four hours. After that, if necessary they can be switched to cow's milk until they are large enough to forage. Kids do better, though, if kept with the herd and allowed to feed naturally. After about two weeks, the mother will cease to produce colostrum and you can milk her. Reducing the amount of milk available from the mother will help encourage the kids to learn to eat like their parents.

Milk production in goats varies with the breed and also depends on husbandry and feed quality. Like chickens, goats living on the new American homestead will fare best on a commercially prepared diet that provides complete nutrition, supplemented with goodies from the exercise pen.

Breeding typically occurs between September and January. The homesteader with limited space will want to consider a stud service, as keeping a male goat (buck) can pose some problems, not the least of which is the smell he produces during the rutting season. This may mean transporting the female (doe) a long distance for breeding. Timing is important, as the female may be receptive for only a short period. Following a successful pregnancy, of course, you must be prepared to deliver the kid and raise it to maturity.

The payoff for all this trouble is high-quality milk, produced on average at the rate of about a gallon a day. Goat milk can be made into a wide variety of delectable products. More about that in chapter 8.

## Sheep

Although eight sheep can be accommodated on the same space as one cow, they are generally not recommended for the small farm. Sheep provide less milk than goats do; the milk yield, however, varies by breed, and can range from 100 to 1,100 pounds of milk over the course of the lactation period, which can be anywhere from three to eight months in length. Sheep must also be shorn annually, generally in early spring before lambing. While it does not hurt to have the wool, and while sheep are hardier and less demanding than goats, as author Jerome Belanger puts it, "For a couple of sheep, the fencing will cost far more than the animals unless you are in it for the long haul." For the suburban homestead, keeping sheep makes little sense.

On the other hand, some homesteaders may find wool production sufficient justification for keeping sheep, with milk as a side benefit. Lambs can also provide additional income if sold for slaughter.

## Characteristics of Selected Sheep Breeds

| Breed | Coloration | Milk Production | Comments |
|-------|-----------|-----------------|----------|
| Dorset | White; may or may not have horns | Moderate, but breeds easily | Very gentle disposition. Can produce lambs in late summer and autumn; average quality wool |
| Polypay | White face, darker body, no horns | Best milking sheep, and superior for lamb production | Good mothers; average quality wool |
| Romney | White with black nose and hooves | Average milk production, breeds easily | Excellent wool; best suited to cool locations |
| Tunis | Reddish tan with lopped ears, no horns | Good breeders, high milk production | Best suited to warm climates; average quality wool |

## Cows

The average milk cow produces 6 gallons of milk a day. Obviously, the first thing you must take into account if you are considering adding a cow to your homestead is what to do with all that milk! Chapter 8 has some suggestions to get you started, should you decide a milk cow is in your future.

Cattle are not too picky in terms of feeding. They will eat hay or grain, although the latter is not a natural food for them. If you have pasture, you can allow cows to forage for themselves. You should allow about an acre of pasture per animal, although the quality of the forage grass will determine the amount actually needed. Supplemental feed will be necessary unless you have a large spread and are an expert at both growing forage and producing hay for winter feeding. Given that cows typically exceed 1,200 pounds in weight, you can envision their need for abundant food and plenty of water.

Milk production is a function of lactation stage (a cow does not produce milk all year long), the health of the animal, and the quality of the feeds she receives.

You do not, in most regions of the country, require a barn to keep cattle, but they do require shade. Trees are fine, but most homesteads will need

## Characteristics of Selected Dairy Cow Breeds

| Breed | Coloration | Size (lb.) | Comments |
| --- | --- | --- | --- |
| Ayrshire | White and roan to dark brown | 1,200 | Long lived and hardy, high-quality milk |
| Brown Swiss | Brown or gray | 1,400 | High butterfat and protein content in milk |
| Guernsey | Yellow brown and white | 1,100 | Rich in butterfat, milk is yellow in color; quick to mature |
| Holstein | Black and white or red and white | 1,500 | Large volume of low butterfat milk produced |
| Jersey | Yellow-brown, brown or gray with white markings. | 1,000 | Best milk producer for its size; milk high in butterfat |
| Shorthorn | Red, red and white, or roan | 1,500 | Hardy, high-volume producers; milk is of average butterfat content |

a roof and two walls to provide shade in summer, as well as relief from winter winds and cold. In addition, you must construct fencing to confine your cows to their pasture. If they gain access to the garden, for example, they may wreak havoc.

As long as you have a good veterinarian with whom you can consult, cows present few problems when their simple needs are met.

# The Bottom Line

As I completed this chapter, it occurred to me that many would-be homesteaders might be discouraged by all the caveats and warnings I have included. It has not been my intention to dampen anyone's enthusiasm for including animal food production in their lifescape plan. In presenting a broad overview of the essential facts of animal husbandry, I have necessarily erred on the side of caution in warning beginners about common mistakes. That said, plenty of people raise animals on small acreage with great success.

To conclude this chapter, here are the basic pros and cons for each type of animal we have discussed:

## Pros and Cons of Animal Types

| Animals | Pros | Cons |
|---------|------|------|
| Bees | Honey, pollination, beeswax, potential income generation, small space requirement | Large initial investment, require careful and frequent care, stings, can swarm and abandon your premises |
| Fish | High-quality protein and essential fats, easy to feed, pond enhances property value and appearance | Large initial investment, need large pond for significant productivity, some species not winter hardy, need to understand water chemistry and filtration techniques |
| Chickens | Easily accommodated in small space, egg production can be matched to family needs, provide free weed and insect control | Moderate initial investment, manure stinky and requires composting, require purchased commercial feeds, attractive to predators and rodents |
| Goats | Easily accommodated in small space, milk production reasonable for typical family use, manure low odor and can be spread directly on garden | Breeding essential for continued milk production, require purchased commercial feeds, must have both an outdoor pen and covered indoor space |
| Sheep | Wool as well as milk, undemanding and hardy, can forage on land unsuitable for crop production, simple shelter and fencing needs, many breeds for varied climates | Must be kept in small flocks due to social nature, need hay and grain for winter feeding, require food supplementation year round, must be sheared, only certain breeds are good milkers; large initial investment in fencing required |
| Cows | Abundant milk production, tolerant of inclement weather, pasture forage produces best milk, calving generally easy | Large size, high food demand, large initial investment in fencing and shelter required |

# 8

# In the Homestead Kitchen

When settlers first moved into the western Appalachians, only hunting trails traversed the rugged mountains. The manufactured goods that found their way into the region had to fit into a saddlebag. Otherwise, the settlers had only local materials and their own ingenuity with which to provide themselves the necessities and a few of the comforts of life. Even as railroads spread across the continent, the mountains inhibited commerce. Today, practitioners of the home crafts that our ancestors depended on regularly gather to celebrate the old art of making things for themselves. For example, the annual Craftsmen's Fairs in Gatlinburg, Tennessee, have been drawing visitors from all over the world every summer and fall for thirty-six years. A quick Web search will turn up dozens of other events that showcase homestead crafts from brewing beer to furniture making. It is in the spirit of those celebrations that I offer in this chapter an overview of basic home crafts. As with the remainder of this book, food is the primary focus, but the homestead kitchen, no matter how small, can also turn out remedies and other products.

Entire books have been written on each of the major topics of this chapter. I hope this necessarily brief overview whets your appetite sufficiently that you will seek out additional information and develop your skills. Also, I urge you to look for craft celebrations in your area to expand your home craft horizons.

## The Homestead Pantry

The art of food preservation has evolved over centuries, but the basic techniques remain unchanged. The goal of any preservation technique is to avert spoilage by one of several means. The most common approach is to reduce the amount of available water present in the food, either by dehydration or indirectly by the addition of salt or sugar. Another way to inhibit the growth of undesirable organisms in nonacid foods is to increase their acidity. Pickling and various fermentation processes utilize that method. Killing organisms in food by applying heat, as in canning and pressure canning, constitutes another approach. Freezing, made possible by technological advances in the twentieth century, is perhaps the most commonly used method of home food preservation, and certainly the simplest.

## Drying Foods

Undoubtedly, our Paleolithic ancestors learned by accident that food left to dry in the sun would remain edible longer than fresh food. Where the climate is suitably hot and dry, sun drying presents a way to preserve many types of foods while utilizing solar energy. The gentle heat of the sun dries the food, placed on racks or screens, while air circulation around the food helps to carry away moisture. Cover the food to protect it from the depredations of insects. My grandmother used window screens and thin fabric (similar to today's floating row cover material) for drying June apples. Even so, when the humidity was high, she lost a portion of the crop to mold. Nevertheless, a similar approach will work on a sunny balcony, for small amounts of food.

> Chili peppers and green beans can be strung on heavy thread with a sewing needle and hung up to dry. As soon as they reach the leathery stage, they should be transferred to airtight jars and stored in a cool, dark place. Leaving them hanging somewhere may be decorative, but their quality will rapidly deteriorate and they will accumulate dust.

A far less risky approach than drying foods directly in the sun is the use of an electric dehydrator. Typical models have a stack of perforated racks on which the food is placed. Warm air is circulated around the food by means of a fan and the temperature is controlled by a thermostat. You can choose models with additional features, depending on your budget and needs. For my household of two adults, a simple, inexpensive model has been adequate.

Simply using your oven on its lowest possible temperature setting to dry small amounts of food spread out on a cookie sheet works fine, but uses a lot of electricity. Try leaving the oven door open after baking something, and placing a sheet with food to be dried in the cooling oven. Some, but by no means all, ovens have a built-in setting for food drying. This is a feature worth looking for when you shop for a new range.

### Preparations for Drying

To ensure thorough drying, food must be properly prepared. Vegetables and fruits should be washed and carefully dried, then trimmed and sliced into pieces of uniform thickness. Tomatoes, figs, grapes, and plums should be pierced or cut in half to allow them to release water properly. Blackberries, cranberries, pitted cherries, raspberries, strawberries, and pineapple should be sliced or coarsely chopped.

To prevent discoloration, apples, apricots, bananas, peaches, and pears need to be treated with an ascorbic/citric acid mixture, available wherever food preservation products are sold. Simply dissolve the proper amount (see package label) in water or fruit juice and dip the fruit pieces in it before drying. You can also use a sugar syrup (see recipe below) or pineapple juice as a predrying dip.

## SYRUP FOR DRIED FRUITS

½ cup honey
½ cup sugar
1½ cups hot water

Combine the ingredients in a small bowl and stir until the sugar is dissolved. Use any leftovers as a marinade for fresh fruit. Store covered in the refrigerator for up to 3 days. Bring to room temperature before using to dry fruit.

---

Vegetables should be blanched in boiling water for thirty seconds, drained, then plunged into ice water. Drain well again and dry with kitchen towels before placing on the dehydrator racks.

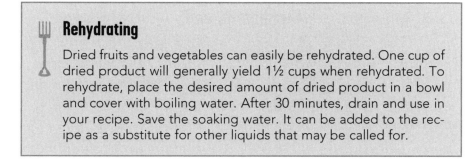

### Rehydrating

Dried fruits and vegetables can easily be rehydrated. One cup of dried product will generally yield 1½ cups when rehydrated. To rehydrate, place the desired amount of dried product in a bowl and cover with boiling water. After 30 minutes, drain and use in your recipe. Save the soaking water. It can be added to the recipe as a substitute for other liquids that may be called for.

Drying time varies with the type of product being dried, the dehydrator settings, and the ambient temperature and humidity. You can judge whether the food is dry enough by its texture. Vegetables (except tomatoes), strawberries, and bananas should be crispy. All other fruits will be wrinkled, leathery, and chewy when they are done.

## Drying Herbs

Many herbs are easy to dry. Cut them when their flavor is at its peak, wash, and spin dry in a salad spinner. Remove the leaves from the stems and chop finely if needed. Place in a shallow layer on the dehydrator rack and dry until the leaves are crumbly. Lavender, marjoram, oregano, rosemary, sage, and thyme are among the best culinary herbs for drying. Lemon verbena, lemongrass, and catnip also dry well. Basil, chives, cilantro, and parsley seldom dry well.

## Dried Herb Mixture 1

Use for seasoning poultry or vegetables before roasting or grilling.

2 tablespoons crumbled dried sage
1 tablespoon dried thyme
1 tablespoon dried marjoram or oregano
1 teaspoon ground black pepper
¼ teaspoon ground cloves

Combine these ingredients in a small jar and store in a cool, dark place.

## Dried Herb Mixture 2

Use for seasoning mushrooms, tomato dishes, and beef.

1 tablespoon dried rosemary leaves, crumbled
1 tablespoon dried oregano leaves, crumbled
1 tablespoon dried thyme leaves
1 teaspoon ground black pepper

Combine these ingredients in a small jar and store in a cool, dark place.

### Drying Garlic and Onions

Garlic and onions can also be dried successfully, using the same techniques just described for other vegetables. Finely chopping the bulbs before using speeds drying and enables you to grind them more finely when they are dry. Ground dehydrated garlic and onions form the basis for two classic seasoning blends: Creole and Tex-Mex.

## CREOLE SEASONING

1½ teaspoons paprika, sweet or smoked
1 teaspoon ground dried onion
1 teaspoon ground dried garlic
½ teaspoon dried oregano, crumbled
½ teaspoon ground white pepper
¼ teaspoon dried thyme leaves
¼ teaspoon dried hot pepper flakes or ground hot pepper (or to taste)

Grind the ingredients together in a mortar or spice grinder and transfer to a small jar.

## TEX-MEX SEASONING

1½ teaspoons paprika, sweet or smoked
1 teaspoon ground dried onion
1 teaspoon ground dried garlic
1 teaspoon dried oregano, crumbled
1 teaspoon ground cumin seed
1 teaspoon ground dried chili powder (see "Handling Dried Chili Peppers")
½ teaspoon ground coriander seed
¼ teaspoon ground dried hot pepper (such as cayenne) or to taste

Combine the ingredients in a small bowl and transfer to a clean jar. Note: if possible, use powder made from a single type of dried chili, such as ancho.

### Handling Dried Chili Peppers

All types of chili peppers contain capsaicin, an oily substance that gives chilies their heat. It can also burn your skin and eyes. Always wear plastic gloves when handling chili peppers, whether fresh or dried. Eye protection is also a good idea. If you plan to grind dried chilies, it is best to have a dedicated spice grinder just for them. Otherwise, you risk introducing heat into every dish containing anything ground in that appliance for months thereafter. If you will be working with a large quantity of hot peppers, it is wise to work outside, to avoid getting capsaicin all over the kitchen. This is especially true if anyone in your family is particularly sensitive.

## Freezing Foods

In contrast to the ancient technique of drying, home freezing is the most recent innovation in food preservation, and one of the simplest. Vegetables can be trimmed, cut to the desired size, and blanched in small batches as they are harvested from the garden. Among the best vegetables for freezing are green beans, broccoli, Brussels sprouts, carrots, cauliflower, collards, kale, kohlrabi, peas, peppers, rhubarb, and spinach. These all need to be blanched thirty seconds to three minutes (depending on the size of pieces) in a large pot of rapidly boiling water. The vegetables are then drained, plunged into ice water to stop the cooking process, drained thoroughly, and packed into freezer containers.

> Make sure to leave enough head space at the top of the container to allow for expansion of the food as it freezes. Some types of freezer containers are marked with a maximum fill line.

Okra, along with both sweet and hot peppers, is among the easiest of foods to freeze. Simply wipe the pods or fruits with a clean kitchen towel, cut into pieces, and pack into freezer containers. No blanching or other treatment is required. Peppers should have the seeds and membranes removed, however.

Fruits typically require additional preparation before freezing. After washing and drying them, they should be combined with sugar or sugar syrup before packing into freezer containers. Peaches, apricots, and pears should be treated to prevent darkening. Combine ⅔ cup sugar and ¼ teaspoon ascorbic/citric acid mixture. Layer this in a bowl with 1 quart prepared fruit. Allow to sit thirty minutes, stir well, and pack into freezer containers. You can omit the ascorbic/citric acid and treat strawberries, blackberries, and raspberries with plain sugar.

If you prefer fruits frozen in syrup, use 50 percent strength. Combine equal parts sugar and water and stir over heat to dissolve the sugar. Keep the syrup hot, but do not allow it to boil or it will become too concentrated. You will need about a cup of syrup for each quart of fruit. Four cups water and 4 cups sugar will produce about 6 cups syrup. Orange juice can be substituted for the sugar syrup, if you prefer. It will also prevent darkening, so the ascorbic/citric acid mixture can be omitted. Add ½ cup sugar to 1 cup orange juice, stirring to dissolve. Use this mixture for about 1 quart sliced fruit.

> Contrary to popular belief, home-frozen food retains its best quality for only about three months. Frozen vegetables and fruits can be safely eaten after six months but should be composted thereafter.

## Canning Foods

Home canning requires some additional equipment. In addition to ordinary kitchen utensils, the list includes:

- Jars
- Lids
- Water bath canner
- Jar funnel
- Jar lifter
- Pressure canner (for some foods)
- Ascorbic/citric acid mixture (for some foods)
- Pectin (for some foods), both liquid and powdered

High-acid foods, such as tomatoes and pickles, can be canned using a water bath canner. So can high-sugar foods like jam. Low acid foods such as potatoes, green beans, and meats require the higher temperature achieved in a pressure canner. You may want to practice home canning with only acid foods at first, because the process is simpler and more foolproof. Later, you can "graduate" to pressure canning.

### Water Bath Canning

The most commonly canned high acid foods are tomatoes and peaches. They are prepared for canning in much the same way, using the raw pack method. Plan on canning about 6 or 7 quarts of either one at a time. A typical canner will accommodate this amount.

> For up-to-date information on home canning, contact your county extension agent or download the USDA Complete Guide to Home Canning from www.uga.edu/nchfp/publications/publications_usda. html.

Preparing Your Jars: Start by inspecting your jars to make sure none have cracks. Run your fingertip carefully around the rim to locate any imperfections. Jars with damage to the rim will not seal properly and should not be used for canning. Save them for storing dry foods. Cracked jars should be recycled. Wash the jars in hot, soapy water, rinse well, and leave them in a sink of hot water until you are ready to use them. Place lids and bands in a saucepan of water, bring to a boil. Remove the saucepan from the heat, keeping the lids in the hot water until you need them. If using reusable lids and gaskets, follow the same procedure.

Preparing Your Fruits: Select firm, fully ripe fruits that are free of blemishes and wash them carefully. Drain well. For tomatoes, slash an *X* on the blossom end to make the skins easy to remove. Both peaches and tomatoes are skinned before canning by immersing them in a boiling water bath for thirty seconds to one minute. Transfer them to cold water, slip off the skins, and treat as follows.

Peaches. For peaches, do the following:

1. Cut them in half, remove the pit, and transfer the halves to a bowl of water to which an ascorbic/citric acid mixture has been added. (Follow package directions.)

2. Prepare a 40 percent syrup by combining 3¼ cups sugar with 5 cups water over medium heat. Stir just until the sugar completely dissolves, then keep hot. (You can also use 1 cup sugar, 1 cup honey, and 4 cups water, if you prefer.) Adding a cinnamon stick and a couple of whole cloves while heating the syrup is optional.

3. Place the sliced peaches, seed side down, into the jars, overlapping them so as many as possible fit in. Cover with hot syrup, leaving ½ inch head space.

Meanwhile, fill the canner about half full of water and set it to heat.

Tomatoes. For tomatoes, do the following:

1. Core the skinned fruits and cut them in half, if you desire.
2. Place them in a saucepan and cover with water. Bring the saucepan to a simmer and cook gently for 3 to 5 minutes.
3. Pack the hot tomatoes into hot jars. Add ½ teaspoon citric acid and 1 teaspoon canning salt to each quart.
4. Cover the tomatoes with their cooking liquid, leaving ½-inch head space.

Meanwhile, fill the canner about half full of water and set it to heat.

Canning: Follow these steps:

1. When each jar is packed, run a wooden spoon handle or plastic spatula between the food and the sides of the jar to release any trapped air bubbles. Add additional liquid if needed to maintain ½ inch head space.
2. Carefully wipe the rim of each jar with a clean kitchen towel. Remove a lid or gasket from the hot water and align it with the top of the jar. Install the band or reusable lid, securing the latter with its clips, and tightening the former until just hand tight. Place the jar on the rack in the canner of hot water.
3. When all the jars are in the canner, add enough boiling water to cover the jars at least an inch above the tops. Cover the canner and bring the water to a boil. Peaches should be processed 30 minutes, tomatoes 45 minutes, for quarts. Pints need 5 minutes less.

These guidelines for peaches and tomatoes can be applied with few modifications to other acidic foods. Apples, apricots, berries, cherries, grapefruit, grapes, nectarines, pears, pineapple, plums, and the juices of these fruits and tomatoes are all good choices for home water bath canning. Various flavorings such as cinnamon, brandy, cloves, citrus peel, and so forth can be added to personalize the taste of your canned creations.

Tomato juice can be spiced up with peppers and other vegetables before canning, and tomato sauce—with or without herbs and seasonings—can also be canned using these methods.

Always look for a tested recipe when home canning. If you choose to modify it, do not exceed the quantities of nonacid foods, such as onions or carrots, that the recipe calls for. Otherwise, your product may spoil.

> Take care to add citric acid when the recipe calls for it. Some recipes may call for lemon juice instead of citric acid. If you use lemon juice, it must be the bottled, from-concentrate variety (such as ReaLemon), which has been adjusted to a uniform level of acidity by the manufacturer. Fresh lemon juice will not give predictable results and should not be used for home canning.

### Pressure Canning

With the purchase of a pressure canner, you can broaden your horizons for home-canned products. The basic procedures for cleaning and handling jars and lids are the same as described for water bath canning. Jars must be inspected for cracks and uneven or damaged rims that would interfere with proper sealing. Similarly, vegetables should be washed well before trimming, then trimmed and cut into the desired pieces. Select only perfect, properly ripened produce for canning projects.

Always read and closely follow the manufacturer's recommendations for the operation and care of your pressure canner. Failure to do so can result in improper processing and potentially dangerous food spoilage. Meat, poultry, nonacid vegetables, fruits, and seafood can be preserved by pressure canning because all spoilage microorganisms are destroyed by the high heat applied. However, it is absolutely essential that you follow directions for processing exactly as written, or dangerous spoilage may otherwise occur.

Cooked dried beans and green beans are popular subjects for pressure canning. Other vegetables that can well are beets, carrots, corn, and potatoes. You can also pressure-can foods containing a mixture of acid and nonacid vegetables, or vegetables and meat. Soups, stock, and pasta sauce all pressure-can well.

## John's Best Ever Vegetable Soup for Canning

6 cups beef stock, preferably homemade
6 cups chicken stock, preferably homemade
3 cups diced potatoes (use a low starch potato such as Yukon Gold)
3 cups diced carrots
1 quart broken green beans
1 cup fresh shelled peas (optional)
2 teaspoons salt plus more to taste
3 tablespoons olive oil
4 medium, red ripe tomatoes, peeled, cored, and chopped
3 medium zucchini, trimmed and chopped
2 medium onions, chopped
3 cloves garlic, chopped
1 stalk celery, chopped
½ teaspoon freshly ground black pepper plus more to taste
1 quart canned tomatoes, chopped, with juices
1 large handful fresh herbs, basil, chives, oregano, and parsley, in any combination, washed, dried, and finely chopped

In a large stockpot, combine the stocks over medium heat. Add the diced potatoes, carrots, green beans, and peas, if using, along with a teaspoon of salt. Bring to a boil, reduce the heat, and simmer until the vegetables are barely tender, about 5 minutes. Meanwhile, in a large skillet, heat the oil over medium heat until it shimmers. Add the tomatoes, zucchini, onions, garlic, celery, remaining teaspoon salt, and half of the pepper. Sautè the vegetables until the onions are translucent, then add to the soup in the kettle. Stir in the canned tomatoes and their juices. Bring the soup to a simmer, add the herbs, turn off the heat, and stir well. Taste and add the remaining ¼ teaspoon pepper, or more if necessary, and adjust the salt as necessary as well. Thin the soup as needed with additional hot stock, water, or tomato juice.

Ladle the hot soup into hot jars, leaving 1-inch head space. Process quarts 1 hour and 15 minutes and pints 1 hour at 10 pounds pressure. Yields 7 to 9 quarts.

You may substitute water, tomato juice, or vegetable stock for any portion of the meat stocks suggested in the recipe.

---

**Green Beans:** Perhaps the most popular low acid food for home canning is green beans. While freezing them is easier, green beans just taste different when canned. It is worth noting that different varieties of beans will give different results with the various means available for preserving them. Some varieties freeze well, others are better if canned, and still others are best used fresh. If you want a crop of beans to can for the winter, choose a cultivar recommended for the purpose, such as Blue Lake or Kentucky Wonder.

Processing times given in recipes for canned beans usually assume you are working with tender, young pods. If you grow "shelly" beans and want to can them, increase the processing time by 20 minutes at 10 pounds of pressure. Two good varieties of shelly beans to try are Dwarf Horticultural and White Half Runner. These are somewhere between bush and pole beans in size, and need a trellis about 4 feet tall. They can also be grown on cornstalks. Shelly beans are usually harvested late in the season and are sometimes called "October beans."

## Canned Green Beans

6 quarts broken fresh green beans
Boiling water
Canning salt

Place a teaspoon of salt in the bottom of each hot quart jar. Pack the beans into the jars, leaving 1-inch head space. Pour boiling water over the beans, again leaving 1-inch head space. Use a spatula or wooden spoon to release any trapped air bubbles from the jars. Wipe the jar rims, apply lids, and process 25 minutes at 10 pounds pressure.

## Jams, Jellies, and Preserves

Jams, jellies, and preserves are similar in that a combination of sugar and heat are used to preserve the food. The main "trick" in making these three foods involves judging when the proper consistency has been reached. The exact timing of this depends on the type of food, the amount of sugar used, and the volume of water in the pan. Anywhere from eight to thirty minutes are required.

You can use the spoon test (described under "Jams and Preserves") or a thermometer to determine the consistency of your product. When the firm jelly stage is reached, a candy thermometer will read between 220°F and 222°F. At a slightly lower temperature, the consistency of the product will be softer.

As a rule, cook all products over medium heat until the sugar completely dissolves, stirring to combine the ingredients. After the sugar has dissolved, cook the mixture rapidly to the proper consistency without stirring. Butters, which contain less water, are the exception (see "Marmalades, Butters, and Conserves"). They should be cooked slowly and stirred frequently to prevent sticking or burning.

**Jams and Preserves:** In the case of jam, the prepared fruit is combined with sugar and cooked rapidly until the mixture will hold its shape and remain in a spoon when the spoon is tilted sideways.

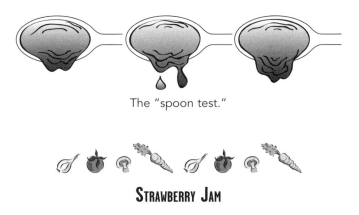

The "spoon test."

## STRAWBERRY JAM

1 quart strawberries
3 cups sugar

Crush or coarsely chop the strawberries. Combine them with the sugar and bring the mixture to a boil over low heat, stirring to dissolve the sugar. Boil rapidly until the mixture is thickened, stirring toward the end to prevent sticking. Transfer to pint or half pint jars, seal, and process 15 minutes in a water bath canner.

---

Preserves are the elegant cousins of jams, and are frequently made from whole fruits. The fruit is permitted to sit in the sugar solution for a period of time before cooking. This step not only infuses the liquid with the flavor of the fresh fruit but also helps to preserve the shape of the fruit for a pleasing presentation. Small, perfect fruits, such as raspberries or Alpine strawberries, make the best tasting and prettiest preserves. Preserves may be made with a sugar syrup, or may rely on dry sugar to release the juices from the fruit, producing an intensely flavored syrup as in the recipe that follows.

## Raspberry Preserves

1 pound perfect, ripe raspberries
12 ounces sugar

Combine the fruit and sugar in a large bowl. Turn gently with a wooden spoon to distribute the sugar evenly, taking care not to break the fruit up. Allow to sit at room temperature until the juice has been released, about 2 hours. Alternatively, cover and place the bowl in the refrigerator overnight. Bring slowly to a boil, stir just to dissolve the sugar, and cook until a candy thermometer registers 218°F. Immediately transfer into hot, prepared jars, apply lids, and process 15 minutes in a water bath canner.

**Marmalades, Butters, and Conserves:** These are all relatives of the basic three, and differ primarily in consistency and the nature of the ingredients. Marmalades, for example, often contain fruit peel, while conserves can include nuts or raisins. Butters are fruit purée, cooked with sugar until the consistency is thick enough to spread. These sugar-preserved products are some of the simplest home-canned products to make.

## Orange Marmalade

10 oranges
Sugar

Peel the oranges, reserving the peel. Thinly slice the peel and chop the pulp, discarding any seeds. Cover the fruit with 6 cups water in a large saucepan, bring to a boil, and then simmer 5 minutes. Remove from heat and let stand, covered, overnight. Transfer to the refrigerator after the mixture reaches room temperature. Return the mixture to the heat, bring to a boil, and cook 1 hour. Measure the resulting fruit purée and add an equal volume of sugar. Bring to a boil again, stirring to dissolve the sugar. Cook until the mixture reaches the "sheet" stage, or 220°F, stirring now and then to prevent sticking. Watch carefully or it may scorch. Remove the pan from the heat and ladle the marmalade into prepared jars. Seal, then process 10 minutes in a water bath canner.

## Apple Butter

3 pounds apples
1½ cups sugar
½ teaspoon cinnamon (or more to taste)
¼ teaspoon ground cloves (or to taste)

Coarsely chop the apples, peeling core and all, and place them in a saucepan with 1 cup water. Bring to a boil and simmer until tender. Pass the apples through a coarse sieve or food mill. Return the apple purée to the saucepan and cook until it will hold its shape in a spoon, a little thicker than applesauce. Then add the sugar and spices, stir until the sugar dissolves, and cook over low heat until thick, stirring frequently to prevent sticking. Ladle into prepared jars, seal, and process 10 minutes in a water bath canner.

---

**Jellies:** Jelly is made in essentially the same way as jam but is generally prepared from strained juice or other clear liquid and pains are taken to keep the finished product clear.

Jelled products often require the addition of pectin, a gelling agent that occurs naturally in fruits. Some recipes may depend on the natural pectin present in the fruit, and may call for the use of underripe fruits that contain more pectin that mature fruit. Similarly, you may be instructed to leave peelings in fruit preparations because pectin is concentrated in the skin. Apples are an excellent source of pectin. One medium apple cooked in a little water until softened will yield enough pectin-rich juice to thicken a quart of fruit. For repeatable results, store-bought pectin is recommended in most recipes. It is available in either liquid or powdered form. Use the type that your recipe calls for.

If you alter the pectin content of a recipe, cooking times may have to be adjusted and the yield will be different than if the recipe is followed precisely. The final product will nevertheless be delicious. Do not, however, substitute commercial liquid pectin for the powdered product or vice versa, or the recipe may be disappointing.

## Apple Juice for Jellies

Choose perfect, barely ripened fruits. Tart apples work best for this recipe. Remove the stem and blossom ends but leave the cores and skins in place. Chop the apples and measure their volume. Add water equal to half the volume of chopped apples. Cook, covered, over low heat until the apples are soft and have released their juices, about 25 minutes. Cool slightly, then strain through a colander lined with several thicknesses of dampened cheesecloth. Use immediately or bring to a boil, transfer to hot jars, seal, and process 10 minutes in a water bath canner .

To make flavored jellies, combine 1⅓ cups juice with 1 cup sugar, along with the flavoring agent (see next recipe). Bring slowly to a boil, stirring to dissolve the sugar, then cook slowly to 220°F. Transfer to prepared half pint jars, adjust the caps, and process 5 minutes in a water bath canner.

---

## Mint or Basil Extract for Jelly

Collect 1 cup (packed) fresh mint or basil leaves and place them in a shallow bowl. Pour 1 cup boiling water over them. Allow to steep for 1 hour, then strain. Two tablespoons of extract will flavor 1 cup of apple juice.

You can experiment with other fresh or dried herbs. The extract must be a strong tea but not so strong that bitterness develops.

---

You can make this grape jelly recipe with products from the grocery store. It is a great introduction to jelly making.

## Water Softening Method

1. Boil water in an open kettle for 15 minutes.
2. Remove from the heat and let stand for 24 hours.
3. Ladle water from the kettle without disturbing sediment.
4. Pour water through a coffee filter to trap surface scum or dust.

## GRAPE JELLY

3 cups commercial grape juice
1 package powdered pectin
4 cups sugar

Bring the juice and pectin to a boil in a large pot. Stir in the sugar and bring to a boil again over high heat. Boil strongly, stirring constantly, for 1 minute. Remove from the heat and skim off any foam that has formed. Transfer to prepared half pint jars, leaving ¼-inch head space, seal, and process for 5 minutes in a water bath canner.

These are but a few examples of homemade goodies made from fruit, sugar, and flavorings. Try these, then find some appealing recipes elsewhere and try them. With experience, you will be able to devise your own unique creations.

## Pickling Foods

Fruits and vegetables can be turned into pickles by immersing them in a liquid consisting of water, salt, vinegar, and sometimes sugar, in varying ratios depending on the recipe. The quality of the finished pickle will depend on several factors, the primary one being the quality of the fruit or vegetables being pickled. Water is also important. Hard water will negatively affect the quality of the pickles. Purchase distilled water, or reduce the hardness of tap water by the procedure presented in the sidebar on page 246.

Attention must also be paid to the vinegar, salt, and sugar used for pickles. Follow these guidelines:

- Use refined cane sugar, not brown or unrefined sugar.
- Use pickling salt, not iodized table salt, kosher, or sea salt. Doing otherwise may impart discoloration or off flavors to your pickles.
- Use only distilled white vinegar or cider vinegar adjusted to 5 percent acidity. Imperfect preservation may result with other vinegars. Cider vinegar should not be used, however, if you wish to avoid any brownish coloration in the final product.

Because of the corrosive nature of the ingredients, you must use only stainless steel, glass, ceramic, or food grade plastic containers and utensils for making pickles and relishes.

Pickles may be classified into three groups: brined pickles, raw-packed pickles, and relishes. Brined pickles are actually fermented products, and will be considered in the next section "Salting and Fermenting Foods." Raw-packed pickles actually "pickle" in the jar. Sometimes the food is brined before pickling, but in all cases the pickles are covered with a fla-vored vinegar solution, then processed in a water bath canner. Relishes are pickled products made from chopped ingredients. Apart from this, recipes and procedures for relishes are similar to those for pickles.

### Refrigerator Pickles

Pickles need not be canned to be enjoyed. Virtually any pickle recipe can be scaled down and a small batch kept in the refrigerator. Refrigerator pickles will easily keep for a month in good condition.

## UNIVERSAL PICKLING SOLUTION

1 cup distilled white vinegar
1 tablespoon pickling salt

Combine 1 cup water, the white vinegar and pickling salt in a bowl. Use this mixture for refrigerator pickles or to create your own canned pickle recipes.

---

## RAW-PACKED DILL PICKLES

4 pounds cucumbers
½ cup plus 2 tablespoons sugar
¼ cup pickling salt
2 cups white vinegar
4 teaspoons mixed pickling spices (recipe follows)
Dill seeds or dill flower heads

Wash and dry the cucumbers, then slice in half lengthwise. Pack into prepared hot pint jars. Combine the sugar, salt, vinegar, and 2 cups water in a pot that can hold at least 3 quarts. Bring to a boil, watching carefully. It will foam up vigorously and may boil over if the pot is too small or you are careless. The result is a sticky, hard-to-clean mess on the stove top and counter. Reduce the heat and add the spices, tied into a cheesecloth bag for easy removal later. Simmer the mixture gently for 15 minutes, then remove from the heat. Place a head of dill or a teaspoon of dill seeds in each jar. Ladle the hot liquid over the cucumbers, leaving ¼-inch head space. Apply the lids, then process 15 minutes in a water bath.

## Mixed Pickling Spices

2 tablespoons yellow mustard seeds
1 tablespoon coriander seeds
1 tablespoon allspice berries
4 large bay leaves, broken into pieces
1 teaspoon white peppercorns

Select only fresh, whole spices and combine well. Store in a tightly closed container in a cool, dark space. Use within one year.

## Dilled Green Tomatoes or Green Beans

Small, hard, green tomatoes no larger than 2 inches in diameter, or mature, well-filled green beans
1 batch Universal Pickling Solution (recipe on page 248)
Fresh, whole garlic cloves, peeled
Dill seeds or dill flower heads, fresh or dried
Bay leaves
Whole small hot red peppers, fresh or dried

This recipe is a great way to use up the end of the season tomatoes or beans. Select only perfect vegetables for the best-quality pickles. Tomatoes can be used whole if they are as small as a golf ball or can be halved or quartered if larger. Just make sure there is no trace of ripening, or they may become mushy. Beans should be washed, then blanched in boiling water for 3 minutes. Drain, then plunge into cold water to stop the cooking and set their color. Drain thoroughly before continuing.

Bring the pickling liquid to a boil, remove from the heat, and keep hot.

Pack the vegetables into pint jars, adding along with them 1 garlic clove, 1 bay leaf, 1 teaspoon dill seeds (or one head of dill), and 1 whole pepper per jar. Cover with pickling liquid, leaving ¼-inch head space. Apply lids and process 15 minutes in a water bath, or store in the refrigerator without processing.

For either green tomatoes or green beans, wait about two weeks for the flavor to develop fully before consuming them. Hot pack pickles, such as the beet pickles in the following recipe, can be used immediately.

## BEET PICKLES

12 beets, about 1½ inches in diameter, cooked and peeled (see recipe)
1 cup sugar
1 stick cinnamon, about 3 inches long
1½ teaspoons allspice berries
¾ teaspoon pickling salt
1¾ cups distilled white vinegar
¾ cup distilled water

Beets are easiest to peel after cooking. Wash them well, cut off the tops to about an inch above the crown, and trim all but ½ inch of root. Cook the beets either by boiling them in water to cover until they are easily pierced with the tip of a knife or by drizzling with a little olive oil, wrapping them in aluminum foil, and roasting in a 400°F oven until tender, about 30 minutes. Drain boiled beets in a colander, or remove the foil packet from the oven and allow to cool before continuing. When the beets are cool enough to handle, slice off the ends and slip off the skins. Pack them directly into hot jars. While the beets cool, combine the remaining ingredients in a large saucepan, bring to a boil, and then simmer 15 minutes. Ladle the hot liquid over the beets, using a small strainer to remove the whole spices. Apply lids, then process in a water bath canner for 30 minutes.

### Fruit Pickles and Relishes

Relishes, fruit pickles, and chutneys are all related products. Fruit pickles are the simplest to prepare. The typical recipe involves making a flavored syrup of vinegar, sugar, and spices and cooking the fruit gently in this mixture. Fruit pickles, once cooked, are then left standing in the liquid overnight to absorb more flavor. On the following day, the fruit is transferred to prepared jars, covered with the liquid (heated again to boiling), and processed in a water bath canner.

For relishes, the ingredients are first cut into uniform size pieces, salted briefly, then cooked in a flavored pickling solution before canning and processing.

## PICKLED PEACHES

4 pounds small cling peaches
Ascorbic/citric acid mixture
1½ pounds sugar
2 sticks cinnamon, each about 3 inches long
1 tablespoon whole cloves
1 piece fresh ginger about the size of the end of your thumb, chopped
2 cups cider vinegar

Wash the peaches, peel them, and drop into a bowl with the ascorbic/citric acid mixture, using the amount specified on the label. Combine the remaining ingredients in a large stockpot and bring to a boil. Watch carefully to prevent the liquid from boiling over. It helps to use an extra large pot. Carefully drop the peaches into the simmering liquid and cook them until you can just barely pierce one with a fork. Err on the side of undercooking; overcooked fruit will become mushy. Take the pot off the heat, cover, and let stand overnight at room temperature.

The next day bring the pot to a simmer again, remove the peaches with a slotted spoon, and transfer them to prepared hot jars. Cover with boiling hot liquid, leaving ¼-inch head space, adjust the lids, and process 20 minutes in a water bath canner.

Relishes can be made with fruits or vegetables or a combination. They differ from fresh pack pickles in that the ingredients are cooked in the pickling liquid before packaging.

I make chow chow every summer with whatever I have on hand and can find at the farmer's market. It is delicious as an accompaniment to beans, chili, roast meats, or sausages.

## Chow Chow Relish

2 cups chopped cabbage
5 cups chopped mixed vegetables, such as cauliflower, onions, green tomatoes, green or colored bell peppers
4 teaspoons pickling salt
1½ cups vinegar
¾ cup sugar
1 teaspoon dry mustard, such as Colman's
1 teaspoon celery seed
½ teaspoon ground turmeric
½ teaspoon yellow mustard seed
½ teaspoon coriander seed
½ teaspoon grated fresh ginger root

Combine the vegetables and salt in a large bowl, stirring well to mix thoroughly. Cover and let stand overnight in the refrigerator. Drain well in a colander. Combine the remaining ingredients in a large stockpot. Bring to a boil and simmer 5 minutes. Add the drained vegetables and simmer 5 minutes longer. Pack immediately into hot jars, adjust lids, and process 10 minutes in a water bath canner.

---

Chutney recipes start out much like relishes, but the ingredients, which can include fruits, vegetables, spices, and even nuts, are cooked to a thick consistency before canning.

## "Major Great" Chutney

1 Meyer lemon, seeded and chopped
1 clove garlic, chopped
3 cups chopped firm green tomatoes
2 cups cored and chopped tart apples
2 cups brown sugar

2 cups seedless raisins
¾ cup chopped fresh ginger root
1½ teaspoons pickling salt
1 small green hot pepper, such as Serrano, chopped
2 cups cider vinegar

Combine all the ingredients in a large saucepan. Bring slowly to a boil, stirring until the sugar is completely dissolved. Reduce the heat and simmer gently until the vegetables are tender and the mixture is as thick as you want it, watching carefully near the end and stirring to prevent sticking. Transfer immediately to hot jars, apply lids, and process 5 minutes in a water bath canner. For more heat, increase the quantity of Serrano pepper.

## Salting and Fermenting Foods

Salt has been used for centuries to preserve food. Ancient techniques can be applied in the modern kitchen to prepare all sorts of delicious, healthy products. Salting preserves food by reducing its water content. The process often also involves fermentation, which lowers the food's pH and prevents the growth of spoilage organisms.

### Sauerkraut

One of the simplest fermented foods to prepare is sauerkraut.

- Nonreactive vessel (since the whole thing needs to be refrigerated, choose accordingly)
- Clean kitchen towel
- Dinner plate or saucer
- Glass jar
- Cabbage
- Pickling salt

All that is necessary to make your own sauerkraut is to:

1. Finely shred the cabbage and mix it with salt, about 2 teaspoons of pickling salt for each pound of shreds.

2. Pack the mixture into a nonreactive vessel to within about 2 inches of the rim and spread the clean kitchen towel across the surface, holding in place by the dinner plate or saucer. (Obviously, you should select an appropriate container and plate combination before you begin.)

3. Weight the plate with a glass jar of water, adjusting the weight so that brine rises to the top and completely covers the cabbage.

4. Leave the sauerkraut in the refrigerator for a month. Each day, remove the cloth along with the surface scum that forms, then replace with a clean cloth and plate.

5. After a month, transfer the finished sauerkraut to a nonreactive pot and heat until a candy thermometer registers 180°F. Remove with a slotted spoon to prepared, hot quart jars, packing firmly. Cover the sauerkraut with the hot brine, leaving ½-inch head space. (If you do not have enough brine, make some more by combining 2 tablespoons salt with 1 quart water and heat to dissolve the salt.)

6. Process in the water bath canner for 30 minutes.

## Kimchee

Kimchee is an Asian condiment made from fermented vegetables. It is somewhat like sauerkraut but more complex, owing to the greater variety of ingredients it typically includes. It can accompany a main dish in the same way sauerkraut accompanies frankfurters, or can shine on its own right out of

### Gochu Garu

Many recipes for kimchee call for *gochu garu*, authentic Korean red chili flakes. I have found that a mixture of good quality sweet paprika and Italian-style hot pepper flakes works just as well and offers the additional advantage of complete control over the level of heat, not to mention being far easier to find in the average market. I have been happy with the results obtained using three parts sweet paprika to one part hot pepper flakes. Simply vary the ratio as you deem appropriate, keeping the total amount of spice equal to that called for in the recipe.

the jar with a little rice and soy sauce. Kimchee can be prepared in numerous ways and appears in many versions throughout Asia, but it is most often associated with Korean cooking. Besides being delicious, kimchee offers a simple way to preserve leafy greens. You can experiment with variations on the basic recipe by using different greens, different combinations of seasoning ingredients, and different levels of heat.

Bear in mind as you tinker with the ingredients that flavors will become more pronounced as the kimchee ferments. A long fermentation, for example, can result in mustard greens too "mustardy" to eat. Nevertheless, with this in mind you can turn any of the mustards, cabbages, and radishes discussed elsewhere in the book into delicious kimchee.

The first of the following recipes demonstrates how easy the technique for kimchee actually is. The second recipe is a refined version that produces a deeper and more complex flavor and is a modification of one by Debra Samuels that appeared in the February/March 2011 issue of *Fine Cooking*.

## Simple Kimchee

2 pounds Napa cabbage, washed, cored, and cut crosswise into 1-inch ribbons
1 bunch green onions, sliced into 1-inch pieces
4 cloves garlic, chopped
1-inch piece ginger, grated
1 cup gochu garu (or substitute a mixture of paprika and hot pepper flakes as described on page 254)
2 tablespoons fish sauce, or substitute soy sauce for vegan kimchee

Place a layer of cabbage into a large bowl and sprinkle some salt onto the cabbage. Repeat until all of the cabbage and salt have been used. Place the cabbage mixture covered in the refrigerator for 4 hours. Transfer to a colander, rinse briefly under cold water, and drain well. Combine the cabbage with the remaining ingredients in a large bowl. Mix well, then place the mixture into a sealable plastic storage container and allow to ferment at room temperature for 3 days. Place the container in the refrigerator and let ferment for a few more days or begin using immediately. It will keep a month or more in the refrigerator.

# Fancy Kimchee

4 cups Napa cabbage, cored and chopped into 2-inch rectangles
1½ teaspoons kosher salt
2 scallions, chopped into 1-inch pieces
1 clove garlic, chopped
1-inch piece fresh ginger, shredded
5 tablespoons Kimchee Paste (recipe follows)

In a large glass or stainless-steel bowl, combine the cabbage with the salt. Set in the refrigerator for 2 hours. Rinse briefly in cold water and drain well. Combine the cabbage with the other vegetables in a large bowl. Add the Kimchi Paste to the vegetables and mix well. Transfer the mixture to a 1-gallon resealable bag.

Beginning at the bottom of the bag, roll the cabbage forward, pressing the air out of the bag as you go. Once you reach the top and the air has been released, seal the bag. Leave the bag at room temperature for 24 hours, then transfer to the refrigerator. It can be eaten immediately or will improve after a few more days of fermentation.

---

# Kimchi Paste

3 tablespoons sweet paprika
1 tablespoon hot red pepper flakes
5 teaspoons turbinado sugar, or brown sugar
¾ teaspoon kosher salt
½ cup chopped unpeeled Fuji apple
¼ cup chopped yellow onion
1 clove garlic, minced
1 piece fresh ginger about the size of a quarter, ⅛ inch thick, minced
2 oil-packed anchovy filets, drained on paper towels

In a bowl combine the paprika, pepper flakes, and 2 tablespoons water and set aside. Place the other ingredients in a food processor and process until you have a uniform paste, scraping down the sides of the bowl as necessary. Combine this with the pepper mixture. Cover and refrigerate overnight to blend the flavors before using. Store tightly covered in the refrigerator for 3 months. To prepare a vegan version, substitute 2 oil-packed sun-dried tomato halves for the anchovies. The paste will keep for 3 months in the refrigerator, and can also be used as a sandwich spread or as a condiment for steamed or grilled vegetables or meats.

## Brined Pickles

My all-time favorite fermented food is long-brined pickles. Cucumbers sit in a salt solution as their flavor and texture are altered by the activities of naturally occurring yeasts and bacteria. Old-fashioned dill pickles require the least trouble to make, but be sure to try my recipe for long-brined sweet pickles. They are cucumber candy! As long as you maintain the same ratios, you can increase these recipes to accommodate a bumper crop.

Always remember to use Kirby, or pickling, cucumbers when making pickles, either raw packed or brined. They are usually no more than 6 inches long, slightly curved, and prickly on the surface. Long, smooth dark green salad cucumbers will develop an unpleasant texture when used for pickles. Select only perfect fruits for making pickles and harvest them the day you intend to use them. A plastic 5-gallon bucket with a lid makes a fine fermentation container for homemade pickles. Wash the container with a mixture of hot water and baking soda, then rinse thoroughly. Soap may adversely affect your pickles.

### Use Your Leftover Pickle Juice!

Leftover pickle juices, whether homemade or store-bought, can be used to make other kinds of refrigerator pickles. For example, the brine from the raw-pack dill pickle recipe in the previous section can be used to preserve hard-boiled eggs. Just place the eggs in a jar, cover with brine and store in the refrigerator for a month. Beet pickle juice can also be used to pickle hard-boiled eggs, and imparts a pretty color to the egg white.

Try using any syrup left over from the long-brined sweet pickles to make coleslaw. Combine chopped cabbage with the syrup and place in the refrigerator. When ready to serve, stir in enough prepared mayonnaise to give the slaw the texture you desire. Don't forget to add plenty of black pepper, if you wish.

## Long-Brined Dill Pickles

6 tablespoons mixed pickling spices (see recipe on page 249)
1 bunch dill, fresh or dried

5 pounds cucumbers
¾ cup pickling salt
1 cup vinegar
1 gallon distilled water

Place half the spices and dill on the bottom of the container. Add the cucumbers, leaving at least 4 inches of head space. Place the remaining spices and dill on top. Combine the salt, vinegar, and water and stir until the salt dissolves. Pour the salt-vinegar mixture over the cucumbers. Lay a plate on top of the cucumbers and weight it with a canning jar of water. Adjust the weight so that the brine just covers the plate. Each day, remove the plate, skim off the surface scum, and cover with a clean plate. Allow the pickles to ferment for 21 days at room temperature.

Pack the pickles into hot jars. Strain the pickling brine into a large pot and bring it to a boil. Pour the brine over the pickles, leaving ¼-inch head space. Process 15 minutes in a water bath canner.

## Grandma Boswell's Sweet Chunk Pickles

3 pounds pickling cucumbers
1¾ cups pickling salt
1 tablespoon alum
2 cups cider vinegar
4 cups sugar
1 stick cinnamon, about 3 inches long
1½ teaspoons whole cloves
½ teaspoon ground mace

Wash the cucumbers and place in a clean fermentation container. Combine 6 cups water and salt, stir to dissolve the salt, and pour the water over the cucumbers. Place a plate on top of the cucumbers and weight it down with a canning jar of water. Let the cucumbers sit in the brine undisturbed for 14 days. On day 15, drain the cucumbers, wash well under running water, and cut crosswise into 1-inch chunks. Wash the fermentation container and return the pickles to it. Cover with cold water and add the alum, stirring gently to dissolve. Let stand overnight.

Drain and rinse the cucumbers and transfer them to a large heatproof container. Combine the vinegar, sugar, and spices in a large stockpot. Bring to a boil, stirring until the sugar dissolves. Use a large pot and heat slowly, or the mixture will boil over and make a huge mess. Pour the boiling hot liquid over the cucumbers. Cover loosely and allow to sit overnight.

Drain the cucumbers, reheat the liquid to boiling, and pour it over the cucumbers again. Allow to sit overnight, then repeat the procedure a third time, once again leaving the pickles to sit in the liquid overnight.

The next day, drain the pickles again, then pack them into hot jars. As you work, pick out the cinnamon stick and discard it. Distribute the cloves evenly among the jars. Bring the liquid to a boil and pour over the pickles, leaving ¼-inch head space. Apply the caps, then process 15 minutes in a water bath canner.

Oftentimes these recipes will not yield a precise number of full cans. You may have a few pickles or some liquid left over. Just toss them in a spare container and place in the refrigerator, where they will keep for a month.

## Smoking Foods

Smoking is a variation on drying. Food dried over a smoky fire is not only preserved but also acquires the delicious, smoky flavor. Meat products are most often smoked, but you can also smoke cheeses, chili peppers, and various other vegetables and fruits.

Chipotle chilies are jalapeños that have been allowed to ripen and then are smoked over a mixture of materials, including mesquite and tobacco, until they are dry and leathery.

Smoked sea salt imported from Spain costs a fortune, but you can make an inexpensive substitute with the recipe below.

## Fake "Spanish" Smoked Salt

1 cup coarse, gray sea salt
½ cup distilled water or bottled spring water

Mix the salt with the water until you have a slurry. Spread this in a skillet and place over low heat with a smoke source. Cover the smoker and cook slowly until the water has evaporated and the salt has returned to its crystalline state. Cool, then store in a sealed container at room temperature. Using spring water will add additional minerals to the salt and subtly alter the flavor of the finished product. Smoked salt is best used as a condiment, to add a finishing note of smokiness to grilled or roasted meats or vegetables. Adding it as a seasoning during cooking may result in a finished product that is too smoky tasting.

---

Unless you have a commercial grade range hood, smoking will need to be done outside. Although the most intense smoked flavor can be obtained with a slow wood fire, excellent results can also be had by smoking foods on a gas or charcoal grill, using wood chips as the smoke source.

The choice of smoking wood has an effect on the flavor of the finished product. Hickory wood smoke has been valued throughout the South for the flavor it imparts to barbecued meats. In the Southwest, mesquite provides a unique flavor that goes especially well with chicken and fish. Other good choices are woods from fruit trees, especially apple and cherry, along with branches pruned from old, woody specimens of rosemary, sage, or thyme. Smoke sources are limited only by the imagination. Take care, of course, that you do not use wood from poisonous plants for smoking purposes. Azaleas and rhododendrons, for example, should never be used.

When using wood chips or dry branches, soak them in water for an hour, then drain well before placing them in the smoker. This will increase the smoke output. Fresh herb branches need not be soaked.

As a rule, a little smoke goes a long way. If you are cooking over a wood fire, the smoking time will equal the cooking time, although you can finagle this a bit by starting out with a really hot, smokeless blaze, searing the food before taming the fire. With a gas or charcoal grill, you have more control over the duration of smoking, and thus the

> intensity of flavor imparted to the food. I have found the best flavor is achieved on a grill by cooking the food until it is within half an hour of being done. I then place the smoking wood on the heat and cover the grill to finish cooking. You may find that a longer or shorter smoking time suits your taste.

Smoked meats require refrigeration to preserve them, or they can be pressure-canned. Smoked, dried vegetables or fruits, which should be wrinkled and leathery when they are removed from the heat, will keep best if frozen.

# The Homestead Bakery and Brewery

Bread and beer have sustained humankind since the dawn of civilization. In fact, some authorities suggest that we learned how to make beer before we learned how to make bread. Archaeologists have translated Egyptian hieroglyphs that read, "Happy is he whose mouth is filled with beer." Regardless, either is one of life's great pleasures, all the more so if homemade.

## Homestead Grain Production

Contrary to popular belief, you do not need vast acreage to produce a worthwhile quantity of grain. What you do need, however, is the proper climate for the grain you intend to grow. The grains most often used in baking and brewing are wheat, barley, rye, oats, and corn.

### Climate Requirements

Wheat may be either the hard winter variety or soft summer type. The former makes good yeast bread flour, while the latter produces flour better suited to pastry and shortbreads.

> Soft summer wheat grows better in warmer climates, which is one reason Southern cooking places more emphasis on biscuits, dumplings, and pie crust than on yeast bread.

Barley, the essential ingredient for beer, and hops, barley's trusty companion, both like to grow in cool summer areas. Hence, some of the world's great beers come from central Europe. Rye and oats are also cool season crops. Both are difficult to thresh, making them less suited to small-scale production. Corn grows wherever summers are long, sunny, and hot with warm nights. It requires more careful cultivation than the other grains, but the yield of golden (or other colors) kernels keeps well and can be turned into a variety of products in the kitchen.

### Yields per Acre

When most of us think of baking, we think of wheat bread. It takes a pound of wheat to make a loaf of bread. Therefore, if your family consumes a loaf of bread per week, you will need about 50 pounds of wheat flour. Such a yield is possible from a remarkably small area. One acre of field will easily yield 50 bushels of wheat on average. (In Tennessee, for example, which ranks twenty-third in wheat production in the United States, typical yields are from 60 to 75 bushels per acre.) Since a bushel of wheat weighs roughly 60 pounds, you need less than 1 bushel to meet your needs for a year. If the expected yield is 50 bushels per acre, you need only 43,560/50 or 871 square feet to produce a year's worth of bread. Call it 800 square feet. With careful, intensive cultivation and excellent weather, you can probably wring enough grain from half this much space.

Five pounds of barley will make 5 gallons of beer. Barley production for malt can be as high as 120 bushels, or 5,760 pounds per acre. Therefore, to make 100 gallons of beer, you would need 43,560/57.6 or just over 750 square feet devoted to barley production.

Corn of the varieties used for making cornmeal can yield as high as 6 tons per acre. For 100 pounds of cornmeal, you will need 43,560/120 or 363 square feet or more devoted to corn.

Oat production averages about 65 bushels per acre in the United States, while the equivalent figure for rye is 30 to 50 bushels.

Rice production has not been discussed because only a small portion of the country enjoys a suitable climate. However, typical yields are greater than 5,000 pounds per acre. If rice is produced commercially in your area, you can probably grow your own. The practice of flooding rice fields has been questioned by some experts and may not be necessary for home-scale production.

## An Honest Loaf of Bread

Nothing surpasses home-baked bread for flavor and texture. The simple magic of flour, yeast, and water combining to yield a soft, chewy loaf with a crispy brown crust never fails to amaze me.

## The Science Behind the Loaf

Turning a pound of flour into a pound of bread is much easier if you understand how the process actually works. Yeast is a microscopic fungus that feeds on the sugars in the bread dough, producing carbon dioxide that causes the bread to rise, along with alcohols and other compounds that give bread its distinctive flavor and aroma. Because yeast is a living organism, its needs must be addressed in the recipe. Baker's yeast is *Saccharomyces cerevisiae* of a strain selected by the producer to give the best results in the bakery. Brewer's yeast is the same organism, but the various strains have been selected for beer and winemaking. Using baker's yeast to make beer or wine will result in a lower quality product, as a rule. However, using brewer's yeast to make bread may produce a loaf with exceptional flavor.

The other important component of flour, besides the sugars that feed the yeast, is gluten, or grain protein. Different grains and different varieties of the same grain contain varying amounts of gluten. Because gluten content determines the sturdiness of the dough, high gluten flours produce high-rising breads with large interior holes, because the gluten can stand up longer as the bread is baked. Low gluten flours give the opposite result.

One aspect of bread making has undergone rethinking in recent years. Kneading the dough in a certain way was once thought essential to gluten development, but modern cooks have discovered that traditional kneading can be avoided. Stretching and folding the dough, however it is accomplished, will change the texture of the finished product, but bread made with no kneading at all will also turn out fine and be delicious.

Because flour characteristics such as the starch content or amount of moisture present influence the nature of the finished bread, it is impossible to give a precise recipe that will turn out perfectly every time. Rather than becoming recipe-dependent, learn to make bread with the simplest ingredient and little handling, then experiment for yourself. Seldom will your work result in something totally unusable.

It is helpful to remember that the best flavor develops when the yeast takes a long time to ferment the dough. Therefore, cool working temperatures and long rising times produce the most flavorful breads. Using warm water and a rising temperature above 75°F will speed up the whole process if you are pressed for time. But the bread won't taste quite as good.

# Ultra-Basic Bread

1 pound bread flour
1 teaspoon active dry yeast
1 teaspoon salt

Combine the flour, yeast, and salt in a large bowl. Run in enough cool tap water to make a slightly sticky dough, a bit more than 1 cup. Cover and let sit at room temperature overnight. Wet your hands, turn the dough out onto a wet surface, and stretch it 3 or 4 times, folding it back on itself until roughly spherical. Return it to the same bowl and allow to rise at room temperature until doubled in bulk. Turn it out onto a work surface and stretch and fold the dough again until it forms a ball. Place in a well-floured bowl, dust the top of the ball with more flour, and cover the bowl with a kitchen towel. Allow the dough to rise until nearly doubled again. Transfer the dough to a cookie sheet that has been preheated in a 425°F oven. Bake about 30 minutes, or until the loaf sounds hollow when tapped. Remove from the oven and invert the loaf on a rack to cool.

---

## Sourdough Bread

Baker's yeast can be purchased but is not necessary for bread making. Sourdough bread is made using the wild yeasts and bacteria normally found in the environment. Typically, flour is mixed with a small amount of water and the resulting paste allowed to ferment at room temperature. This "starter" is then used to leaven bread.

> The particular strains of wild organisms in San Francisco or Brooklyn are responsible for the special (and irreproducible) flavors of sourdough breads made in those locations. In other words, sourdough breads made in Tennessee or Chicago or Indianapolis will each have their own unique and subtle flavor.

Sourdough starter will keep for three days at room temperature, or a week in the refrigerator. It may be rejuvenated indefinitely by adding equal parts of lukewarm water and flour every two to four days. Sourdough starter will have a slightly pungent aroma, but no discoloration should be evident. If the starter develops an off-color, discard it and begin again. Transfer the starter to a clean container every week. Save the water used for boiling potatoes to add to sourdough starter.

## Sourdough Starter

2 cups flour
1 teaspoon salt
1 tablespoon sugar
2 cups water or potato water

Combine all the ingredients in a bowl. Cover with a kitchen towel and let stand in a warm place for three days. One cup sourdough starter equals approximately one package dry yeast.

---

### Multi-Grain Breads

Rich, hearty breads can be made by substituting whole wheat and other whole grain flours for some or all of the bread flour in the recipe. Breads can also be enriched by the addition of fat in the form of oil, eggs, or milk. Adding more yeast or increasing the rising temperature will produce bread with a soft crumb and beginning with more liquid (hence a stickier dough) will produce bread with a finer texture. Use these simple rules to develop bread recipes that reflect your tastes and preferences.

The following recipe illustrates a more complex bread recipe. I have found no other bread that is better for grilling than this one.

## Amaranth Oatmeal Bread

1 cup oatmeal (not quick cooking)
2 teaspoons salt
1 packet dry yeast
½ cup very warm water
3 tablespoons honey
¼ cup vegetable oil
1 cup amaranth flour
4 cups whole-wheat flour

Put the oatmeal and salt in a saucepan, add 2 cups water, and bring to a boil. Cook until the oatmeal is thick and creamy. Remove from the heat and cool to room temperature. Combine the yeast in a large work bowl with the warm water, the honey, and the oil and let stand until foamy, 5 to 10 minutes. Then add the flours. Stir with a wooden spoon until the mixture forms a ball, then turn out on a floured surface and knead a few times. Place the dough in an oiled bowl, cover with a kitchen towel, and let rise for 1½ hours in a warm place. Punch down the dough, knead again, let rise a second time, punch down again, and form into two loaves. Let rise again until almost doubled, then bake at 350°F for 1 hour, or until the crust is nicely browned and the loaves sound hollow when tapped.

---

Any type of bread can be gussied up. For example, you can slash the tops of the unbaked loaves with a razor blade to produce interesting patterns of "open" crust. A soft powdery crust will result if the loaf is brushed with milk or butter before baking. To make a shiny, hard crust, brush with a wash made of one egg beaten with 1 teaspoon of water.

Egg wash or milk can be used to adhere garnishes to the top of the loaf. Seeds, nuts, or a mixture traditionally are used to garnish bread. Try the amaranth oatmeal bread recipe topped with chopped sunflower kernels and flax seeds. Press the seed mixture gently into the surface of the dough after brushing it with milk. Then bake as directed.

Bread can also receive additions of chopped nuts, seeds, cheese, or herbs. You can use about a tablespoon of additions for each cup of flour in the recipe. Add to the dough after it is mixed but before the first rise.

Besides bread, you can also make pasta at home. Directions and dozens of recipes can be found in books or online.

### Cornbread

Corn can be ground into cornmeal, which is used for making cornbread or polenta. Cracked corn is also the starting point for whiskey, recipes for which will not be included here, since making it is illegal. The southern Appalachian region in which I reside is famous for homemade whiskey. I can confidently assert that the product is worth the effort, though not, perhaps, the legal risks.

---

### ⅏ Makin' Moonshine

If you really want to learn how to do it (make moonshine, that is), I suggest locating the Neal Hutcheson documentary, *The Last One*, about Marvin "Popcorn" Sutton, a regionally famous moonshiner who committed suicide rather than go to jail for making whiskey. In the film, Sutton reveals just about everything you'd want to know to make your own corn squeezin's.

For the less adventurous, here's my family's tried and true recipe for old-fashioned cornbread. If possible, find a cornmeal prepared from 100 percent organically grown flint corn of a named variety. Flint, or "dent" corns varieties differ from the sweet corn most home gardeners grow. They have low sugar content, a dense texture, and a distinctive indentation on the top of each kernel. The preferred local flint corn is Hickory King. Other types, such as Floriani's Red Flint, also give good results. Cornmeal made from these types of corn also makes excellent polenta.

## John's Cornbread

½ cup unbleached all-purpose flour
1½ cups cornmeal
¾ teaspoon salt
2½ teaspoons double-acting baking powder
2 large eggs
2 tablespoons vegetable oil, plus more for the skillet
1½ cups 2% milk

Preheat the oven to 425°F. Pour enough oil in the bottom of a 10-inch cast iron skillet to coat it well. Place the skillet in the oven to heat while you make the cornbread. In a bowl, combine the dry ingredients and whisk to produce a uniform mixture. Whisk the remaining ingredients in a separate bowl until they are well combined. Make a well in the center of the dry ingredients and pour in the liquid. Whisk just enough to fully incorporate the liquid. Carefully remove the hot skillet from the oven and pour the batter into it. The skillet should be hot enough that the batter sizzles. Return the skillet to the oven and bake until the top is golden brown and the cornbread has pulled away slightly from the sides of the skillet, 30 to 40 minutes.

## Brewing Beer at Home

If you are one of the many Americans who has given up on factory-made beer in favor of small batch craft brews, you really should try brewing your own beer at home. It is not necessary to grow and malt your own barley, you can make beer from purchased ingredients very inexpensively. Or, you can make your own malt from purchased barley and work from there. The beauty of home brewing is that like so many other homestead crafts, you can experiment and develop your own special creations once you learn the basic techniques.

Beer brewing requires six ingredients:

- **Spring water** with low hardness and a slightly acidic pH makes the best beer. Tap water may be conditioned with a commercial product, Burton Water Salts, to condition it for brewing.

- **Malt concentrate** contains the sugars that will feed the yeast. It is prepared from malt, barley that has been partially germinated, and has a syrupy consistency. Amber, dark, and light malts make different styles of beer.

- **Hops,** an herb traditionally used to flavor beer, adds bitterness. An ounce and a half, up to 3 ounces per 5-gallon batch, is typically used, depending on the degree of bitterness desired.

- **Brewer's yeast,** usually sold in an amount suitable for 5 gallons of brew, should always be used in preference to baker's yeast.

- **Crystal malt** is malt that has been toasted and stored in granular form, rather than having the sugar extracted from it. You can make your own if so inclined.

- **Corn sugar** is added at bottling time to assist in carbonating the beer.

Besides the ingredients, you need some specialized equipment, including the following:

- Stockpot
- Spoon
- Mason jar
- Aluminum foil
- Grain bag
- Siphon hose
- Primary fermenter with cover
- Fermentation lock
- Secondary fermentation carboy (a large bottle holding about 5 gallons) with stopper
- Bottling bucket with hose and wand
- Bottles
- Caps
- Capper

Shops selling home-brewing supplies have cropped up all over the country, or you can order brewing supplies online.

## Sanitize!

A special sanitizing solution is used to prevent bacteria from spoiling the brew. Everthing that will come into contact with the beer must be sanitized. Although you can use a solution of household bleach and water, it is best to purchase a commercial product and mix it according to the package directions until you have obtained some beer-making experience. Take care to thoroughly rinse all sanitized items in almost-boiling water after they are sanitized. Be especially careful with plastic items, as they may absorb a "swimming pool" flavor and transmit it to the beer if left in the sanitizing solution for too long.

## Primary Fermentation Process

During the primary fermentation, the yeast will begin the process of converting the sugars in malt extract into alcohol and carbon dioxide. The carbon dioxide escapes the fermentation vessel via a special valve, or *lock*, and the alcohol remains behind in the *wort* or brew. As with breadmaking, the yeast is first proofed by mixing it with sugar and a small amount of water. Then the mixture is added to the wort and the whole thing is placed in the fermentation vessel for up to a week.

Making the wort for the primary fermentation is analogous to making herbal tea, albeit in a much larger quantity. Flavoring agents are steeped in hot water to extract their components. You have the opportunity to choose flavoring agents that affect the taste of the final product. The flavoring agents are malt extract, crystal malt, and hops. Numerous selections of each of these are available and you can even produce your own crystal malt or hops. Experienced brewers also add other flavors, such as coriander or citrus peel, during this stage. The many choices and endless combinations are what give hand-crafted beers their unique characteristics. Malt extract is the basic sugar source for the wort and is simply combined with the brewing water and heated. Hops contribute a bitter character that renders the finished beer more refreshing. Hops are added near the end of the steeping process and remain in the wort when it goes into the fermenter. Crystal malt, which is dried, partially sprouted barley, comes in a variety of flavors and is steeped in the wort at different stages of the process. It is placed into a grain bag, the equivalent of a tea bag, though much larger. The bag moves around from pot to pan to pot to fermenter during preparation of the wort but does not remain in the fermenter when the yeast is added, so be sure to carefully read through the following directions before you begin the procedure.

The basic procedure for making home brew is described below. It is important that you read and understand all procedures and prepare all the equipment well in advance. Failure to do so will likely result in a spoiled batch. Tragedy!

1. Start by sanitizing the Mason jar, the primary fermenter, its cover, and the fermentation lock. Sanitize a piece of aluminum foil large enough to cover the top of the jar. Next, prepare the food for the yeast.

2. In a saucepan, place 2¼ cups brewing water and heat until steam begins to rise. Add 1 tablespoon malt concentrate and 1 teaspoon corn sugar. Simmer for 10 minutes, stirring just until the sugar dissolves. Remove from the heat and allow to cool until you can hold your hand on the bottom of the pan. Transfer the warm liquid to the Mason jar, add 1 package brewer's yeast, swirl to mix the contents, and immediately cover the mouth of the jar with the piece of aluminum foil. Set the jar aside at room temperature to allow the yeast to begin growing.

3. Place 1 pound crystal malt in the grain bag and tie off the top. Place 1 gallon brewing water in the stockpot over low heat and bring it to the point of simmering. Lower the grain bag into the pot, then remove both from the heat. Take the grain bag from the pot and set it aside in a clean pan. This step extracts a little flavor but mainly softens the crystal malt, preparing it for flavoring the brew later in the procedure.

4. Add 2 cans (about 4 pounds) amber malt concentrate to the hot water in the pot. Return the pot to the stove, stir until the malt concentrate has dissolved, and adjust the heat until the liquid is almost boiling. Now return the grain bag to the pot, stirring frequently but gently. You want to steep the crystal malt without letting the liquid actually boil. This will take some care until you have done it a few times. This procedure adds another layer of flavor from the crystal malt to the wort.

5. Pour 4 gallons chilled brewing water into the fermentation carboy, agitating it as much as possible in the process. Keep the fermenter covered. Before the liquid in the stockpot reaches the boiling point, remove the grain bag from the stockpot and place it into the fermenter. Replace the fermenter cover quickly. This cold soaking of the hot crystal malt extracts yet another layer of flavor from it.

6. Add 2 ounces hops pellets to the hot liquid in the stockpot. Stir well and increase the heat to high. As the liquid approaches the boiling

point it will begin to foam, and when it does boil it will foam up more than twice its original volume. Use an appropriately large vessel to avoid this problem, as was described previously under the topic of pickle making. The hot foam can cause serious skin damage, not to mention the mother of all messes in the kitchen. When this crucial point has passed, the liquid in the stockpot will boil along merrily without further problems. Allow it to do so for 20 minutes after the foam subsides.

7. Remove the pot from the stove and transfer it to a sink full of cold water. Add ice to the water in the sink, if you wish. **Take extreme care to prevent water or other contamination from reaching the contents of the stockpot.** Meanwhile, remove the grain bag from the fermenter and discard its contents. Wash the bag immediately, to preserve it for future use.

8. When the pot is cool to the touch, remove it from the sink, dry the outside, and pour the contents into the fermenter. The cool water already in the fermenter will further lower the temperature of the mixture, which should be at about 120°F or lower when the yeast is added. The liquid brew in the fermenter is now called the wort. The Mason jar (see step 2) will by now contain a foamy mixture of rapidly growing yeast and sugar water. Mix the contents by swirling them gently and pour into the fermenter.

9. Cover the fermenter and install the fermentation lock, following the manufacturer's directions.

At room temperature, the yeast should become active in 24 hours. At that time, move the fermenter to a location that remains between 45°F and 50°F and allow the primary fermentation to continue. You will see bubbles passing through the fermentation lock. After anywhere from a couple of days to a week, the bubble rate will slow to less than one bubble every minute and a half.

It is now time to move the wort to another container for the secondary fermentation.

## Secondary Fermentation Process

The secondary fermentation process develops more flavor in the brew and finishes the conversion of sugars to alcohol. This process also clarifies the beer, as sediment settles to the bottom of the secondary fermenter. Unlike the primary fermentation vessel, which has a wide opening to allow for adding the grain bag, the secondary fermenter is a carboy, a big bottle with a narrow mouth. You simply siphon the beer from the primary fermenter in to the carboy, install a fermentation lock, and wait. The secondary fermentation will stop by itself, and the beer can be left in the carboy until you have time to bottle it.

1. Sanitize the secondary fermentation carboy, its stopper, the fermentation lock, and a siphon hose.

2. Open the primary fermenter and use the siphon to transfer the wort from one container to the other. Fill the siphon with water, keep the ends closed with your thumb, and place one end under the surface of the wort in the primary fermenter. Release your thumb from the other end, allowing water to flow from the hose into a waste container. When the wort reaches the end of the hose, transfer it to the secondary fermenter. If you do not have enough wort to fill the secondary fermenter to within an inch of the shoulder, add more brewing water.

3. Install the stopper and fermentation lock, and return the beer to an ambient temperature of 45°F to 50°F. Cover the carboy to prevent light exposure.

Leave the secondary fermenter sitting for up to six weeks. Check it periodically after two weeks have passed. When a ⅛-inch-wide ring of bubbles has formed at the surface of the wort, the fermentation is done. Let the fermenter sit for another week or two before bottling. This allows sediment to settle out, and permits you to bottle when it is convenient.

## Bottling

Now that your beer is ready, it is time to bottle it. At this stage, you will add a small amount of sugar to the beer. Yeasts that have been sitting in the finished beer, dormant because they have consumed all the sugar, will now regrow, creating carbon dioxide that gives the beer its head.

Get your bottles, caps, and bottling supplies ready well in advance of bottling day. It also helps to have a friend lined up, because bottling can seem to require the talents of a juggler.

1. Sanitize the bottles and caps just before using them.

2. Prepare a sugar solution by combining 1 cup of brewing water with ½ cup of corn sugar in a small saucepan. Bring to a boil, stirring until the sugar is dissolved, then remove from the heat and allow to cool, covered, to room temperature. This sugar shot will cause dormant yeast to carbonate the beer in the bottles.

3. Sanitize a bottling bucket and siphon and use the siphon to transfer the beer from the secondary fermenter to the bucket, leaving the sediment behind. Pour the cooled sugar solution into the beer and stir without introducing air into the mixture.

4. Sanitize the spigot on the bottling bucket, the bottling hose, and the plastic wand that attaches to the end of the hose. Attach the hose and wand to the spout of the spigot.

5. Place the wand all the way to the bottom of the first bottle, open the spigot, and allow beer to fill the bottle without overflowing. Remove the wand. The level of beer will drop to just above the shoulder of the bottle when you do so, leaving the appropriate amount of head space. I suggest practicing first using plain water. Once you get the hang of it, you can fill each bottle precisely every time.

6. Cap the bottle and position it on the capper. Press down on the capper handle and seal the bottle. Set the bottle aside, and repeat until all the beer has been bottled. Ideally, have a friend hold the bottle while you fill it, then hand you another bottle. He or she can then cap the first bottle while you fill the second one. This leaves you free to manage the filling wand and will make the whole process smoother and faster.

7. Wash everything off with clean water, dry the bottles, and place them in crates in a cool dry place.

The beer will be ready to drink in about six weeks and will improve with additional time. This 5-gallon batch should produce two cases (48) 12-ounce bottles of amber lager similar to, but much better than, commercial beer.

> You can find hundreds of homebrew recipes online, but the best way to learn to craft really good beer is to join your local homebrew club. Check out the Fermenters International Trade Association and the Brewers Association (see resources) for a wealth of information and to locate a club near you.

# The Homestead Vineyard

Few pleasures of the table compare with those derived from good wine. Even if your climate will not support classic grapes, like Chardonnay or Cabernet Sauvignon, you can grow some type of grape or other fruit that will make acceptable wine. By using purchased grape concentrates, anyone can make fabulous wine without the trouble of planting a vineyard.

## Growing Grapes

There is truth in the old adage that "Grapes must suffer to make good wine." Grapevines flourish in poor, mineralized, and well-drained soils, and do not yield well when the soil is rich. Composted cow manure, applied at the rate of 15 pounds per 100 square feet in the autumn, is all the fertilization any vineyard requires. Prepare the soil to the greatest depth you can manage when grapes are planted, to allow for the deep roots. Wine grapes need plenty of sun and heat. Plant them on an east- or south-facing slope and/or where the natural topography or shelter from buildings will create the warmest microclimate possible. Once established, a properly maintained vineyard will bear fruit for at least fifty years.

## Building and Maintaining a Small Vineyard

Pruning and trellising are both essential for good grape production, and I recommend the widely employed 4-cane Kniffin system (described below) for all grapes.

Set wooden posts about 48 inches above grade and 8 feet apart. Attach a 10 gauge galvanized wire to the posts about 30 inches above ground level and another wire about a foot above the first. Center a single grapevine between the posts, then follow the 4-cane Kniffin system pruning schedule:

1. **First year:** Allow the grapes to grow at will, which will help them produce a vigorous root system.

2. **Second year:** Begin in earliest spring and cut the vine back to a single stem, removing all side branches. When the new buds begin to swell, allow only four to grow into branches. Train these to the wires, two in each direction; they will produce next year's crop of grapes.

3. **Third year:** Allow only four new branches to grow, removing all others of this year's growth. Let them trail on the ground below the wires. This year, you will harvest grapes from the second-year vines that were trained to the wires last year.

4. When the vines are dormant again in winter, remove the branches that bore fruit and replace them with the four that grew along the ground. These will provide the next crop. In subsequent years, repeat steps 3 and 4.

In areas with high humidity and abundant rainfall, proper pruning is essential to maintain air circulation around the vines. Unpruned grapes may develop fungal diseases and suffer extreme reductions in productivity.

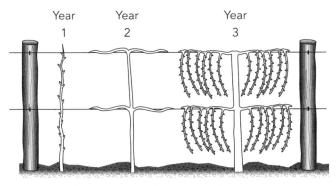

Year
1

Year
2

Year
3

The 4-cane Kniffin system of pruning.

Different varieties of grapes perform best in different areas of the country. Locate those that are recommended for your area by consulting your local agricultural extension agent.

## Winemaking at Home

Making wine involves a double fermentation process not unlike that used to produce beer. You can start with any fruit; grapes are merely the most popular raw material for winemaking. As you might suspect if you enjoy wine and have developed any knowledge of winemaking, a vast array of subtle factors affects the finished product. I'll give you a basic overview, and you can develop your own creations as you gain experience.

### Equipment and Ingredients

You need the following essential equipment, available online or through your local winemaking shop:

- Primary fermenter (a plastic bucket with cover)
- Siphon hose
- Plastic fermentation vessel(s)
- Fermentation lock
- Wine bottles
- Corks
- Mallet
- Strainer

You will also need the following ingredients, again, available locally or online:

- Fruit
- Yeast
- Yeast nutrient
- Pectic enzyme (optional)

- Acid blend, commercial
- Campden tablets
- Tannin

Fruit can consist of fresh produce from the farmer's market, or you can buy concentrates of wine grape varieties like Pinot Noir. Winemakers often guard their yeast strains jealously. It is important to use a yeast intended for winemaking. Other varieties of yeast, while they will technically work, may produce unexpected flavors. The pectic enzyme is needed only when certain fruits, such as apples, are used. Their high pectin content leads to cloudiness, which is avoided by treating the wine with the enzyme. The acid blend provides substances essential to proper fermentation. Campden tablets release sulfur dioxide and are used for sanitization and to prevent the growth of wild yeasts that would spoil the fermentation process. Tannin gives the wine dryness and improves its keeping qualities. All these products are modern inventions. Tradional vinters used orange juice instead of the acid blend, and tea leaves instead of tannin.

### Preparing to Make Wine

The steps in making wine are simpler than those for beer, but must nevertheless be performed out with care. Proper sanitization of all equipment is absolutely essential. To make a homemade sanitizing solution, do the following:

1. Combine 1 part chlorine laundry bleach with 9 parts water.
2. Wash equipment with a solution of hot water and baking soda, rinse with the bleach solution, and then rinse three times with the hottest water your tap will yield.
3. Drain containers upside down to prevent airborne yeasts and bacteria from falling in.

Work quickly when preparing the wine for fermentation, to avoid introducing contaminants.

If you want to make a totally traditional batch of wine, do the following:

1. Start with 3 pounds fresh wine grapes (available at specialty produce markets or by mail order), crush them by hand into the primary fermenter, and add 1 gallon water (boil to soften it as described on page 246, or use bottled spring water) plus the other ingredients as directed below.

2. To the fruit and water in the primary fermenter, add one Campden tablet. Let sit, covered, for 24 hours.

3. Next, prepare the yeast, much as you would for baking. To 1½ cups lukewarm orange juice, add 1 package wine yeast and 1 teaspoon yeast nutrient. Let this sit for a couple of hours until it becomes foamy. This is your starter.

4. Dump the starter into the prepared fruit juice, now known as *must*. Cover the bucket and install the fermentation lock. Let the must sit for three to five days. A little longer won't hurt anything, as the fermentation will cease by itself. The must will bubble and fizz, and will separate into a cap (on top) and lees (on the bottom) and the wine.

5. When the must is done, use the siphon hose, carefully sanitized, to transfer the wine to the secondary fermentation vessel. Take care not to get any of the cap or lees into the liquid. Fill the vessel almost to the rim, but leave room for a closure and the fermentation lock, neither of which should touch the wine.

6. Place the secondary fermenter in a cool, dark place and allow the wine to continue to develop until it becomes clear. This takes anywhere from two weeks to several months.

When the wine is ready, do the following:

1. Sanitize the bottles and siphon tube.

2. Use the siphon to transfer the wine from the secondary fermenter.

3. Insert corks about a quarter of the way into the bottle, then set the bottles aside for two weeks.

If any of the corks pop within the two-week interval, return the wine to a clean fermenter and allow it to ferment longer. (The timing of the fermentation process is one of those skills best learned by experience, as it is impossible to offer precise guidelines.)

---

**⫿⫿⫿ Making a Batch**

To practice, you can make wine using purchased grape concentrate and rehydrate it according to label directions, or start with a gallon of commercial grape juice, which will produce a sweet, though drinkable wine. You can temper the sugar by mixing 1 quart cranberry juice with 3 quarts grape juice, if you prefer. Then proceed with step 2 in the instructions for making a traditional batch of wine.

---

If the corks have not popped after two weeks, use a mallet to tap them all the way into the bottles, cellar the wine, and wait at least six months before opening it. Wine, as we all know, improves with age and can keep getting better for years before it should be consumed.

# The Homestead Creamery

As I pointed out in chapter 7, one of the main drawbacks to keeping dairy animals is deciding what to do with all that milk, especially if you have a cow. But you do not need to keep livestock to enjoy delicious homemade dairy products. You can purchase whole milk from grass-fed animals at the grocery or farmer's market and convert it into butter, cheese, or yogurt in your home's kitchen.

If you have very fresh cream, simply allowing it to sit at room temperature for a day or two will cause it to thicken, or *clabber*. Clabbering not only improves the taste of the finished butter but also makes it easier to churn.

To make butter from clabbered cream, use a 1-gallon churn, available from home supply stores or online.

## Butter and Buttermilk

Nothing could be simpler than creating sweet creamery butter from heavy cream. Do the following:

1. Chill the cream, then fill a jar half full with it and drop in a clean small, smooth pebble or marble.

2. Cap the jar and shake it for about half an hour. It helps to have assistance, as your arm will get tired.

3. When the cream begins to thicken, continue shaking, but more gently. Like magic, the butter will suddenly come together in a ball.

4. Drain off the buttermilk, reserving it for cooking. Wash the butter by kneading it in several changes of cold water. Milk left behind will cause the butter to spoil, so keep kneading and rinsing until the water runs completely clear. A small wooden or rubber spatula makes kneading the butter easier.

5. Remove the butter from the container and form it into a ball with your hands. With the spatula, flatten the ball of butter by pressing it onto a cutting board or plate while rinsing with water. Use the spatula to fold the flattened butter onto itself, rinse, then flatten again, rinse and fold. Keep this up until no more milky solids are rinsed out.

If the jar method involves more exercise and time than you'd prefer, pour the chilled cream into a chilled food processor bowl and process for about 15 minutes, or until the butter separates from the buttermilk. Scrape down the sides of the bowl periodically, as required. Pour off the buttermilk and wash the butter in cold water as just described.

## Sour Cream and Yogurt

Sour cream, yogurt, and crème fraiche are cousins. All are made by mixing milk or cream with cultured buttermilk, which provides a source of good bacteria for fermentation. The mixture is then allowed to sit, with added warmth in the case of yogurt, until thickened. Sour cream differs from crème fraiche in that the latter is made only with heavy cream with the highest butterfat content, while sour cream can be made with cream of a lower fat content, such as "coffee" cream. Yogurt can be made with nonfat milk, 2 percent milk, skim milk, or whole milk.

### Sour Cream

Cream can be soured, or "ripened" prior to making butter, or the sour cream can be used as is. To ripen fresh cream, heat it to a temperature of 86°F and add about 2 tablespoons of commercially made cultured buttermilk or cheese starter. Allow the mixture to sit at room temperature overnight. It should be thickened and have a slightly acidic flavor.

### Crème Fraiche

To prepare crème fraiche, follow the instructions for sour cream, but start with heavy whipping cream. Make sure the label says "heavy" to get the highest amount of butterfat. Add the buttermilk as directed above, allow to sit at room temperature for twenty-four hours, then move to the refrigerator for twenty-four hours before using. This product will have the consistency of grocery store cream cheese but will taste much better.

### Yogurt

Yogurt is made not from cream but from milk. You can use whole milk, 2 percent milk, or nonfat dry milk as the starting point. Yogurt depends on the protein component of the milk for its texture, not the fat component. The basic procedure is simple.

Heat 1 quart milk to a temperature of 100°F and add ¼ cup plain yogurt. If using a commercial yogurt starter, add the quantity recommended on the label. Mix thoroughly and place the container in a location that will remain at about 100°F for six hours. Alternatively, place in a warm spot, such as on the back of the stove after the evening meal has been prepared, and allow to sit overnight. You can experiment with different ways of keeping the yogurt warm, or resort to a commercial yogurt maker. The yogurt will thicken if merely placed in a jar in the sun for a few hours. Too much fermentation will result in a sharper flavored product with a thicker texture.

## Cheesemaking

Cheese starts out like sour cream, butter, and yogurt but ends up so, so much differently. Like winemaking, cheesemaking is an art that has evolved over centuries. Variables, such as the type of milk used and how it is treated before and after the curds and whey are separated, determine the texture, flavor, and keeping qualities of the huge variety of cheeses made throughout the world. All of them can be sorted into three basic types: cottage cheese, soft cheese, and hard cheese.

### Cottage Cheese

Cottage cheese is the simplest variety and is typically made as needed from whole or skim milk.

## Rennet

Rennet is a slaughterhouse byproduct. Vegetarians who eat dairy products and who wish to make their own cheese can use vegetable rennet instead of the standard variety used in cheesemaking.

## COTTAGE CHEESE

To 1 gallon skim milk at room temperature, add ½ cup commercial cultured buttermilk. Allow to sit at room temperature until clabbered, about 12 hours. Gently break up the curd with a sharp knife, leaving it in rough 1-inch cubes. Allow to rest for 10 minutes, then add 2 quarts warm (98°F to 100°F) water.

Place a rack in a large pan such as a water bath canner. Set the pan of milk on the rack and heat the water on the stove until the curd reaches a temperature of 99°F. Maintain the temperature of the water bath for an hour, stirring gently about every 5 minutes, until the curd has settled to the bottom of the pan. Test for doneness by removing a small amount of the curd and pressing it between your fingers. It should crumble and not release any milky liquid.

Carefully strain the finished cheese through several thicknesses of moistened cheesecloth in a strainer. Allow to drain until it ceases to drip liquid, but do not allow the surface of the curd to dry out. Transfer the finished cheese to a storage container and refrigerate. Cottage cheese is often combined with fresh heavy cream before serving.

### Soft Cheese

Soft cheese is the starting point for hard cheese but is often eaten immediately, without aging. It can be made either from whole or skim milk. One of the simplest soft cheeses is crème fraiche, described previously.

Commercial cream cheese is similar but typically contains additives to create a creamy consistency with lower fat content. However, these cheeses are not produced by separating the curds from the whey after the initial fermentation, and no rennet is involved in the process.

Neufchatel cheese dates to the sixth century and is one of the oldest French cheese styles. The Americanized version, sometimes known as *farmer cheese*, was invented in the nineteenth century and has about a third less fat than the traditional French Neufchatel. The following soft unripened Neufchatel cheese recipe provides a good introduction to techniques that are used for both soft and hard cheeses.

## NEUFCHATEL CHEESE

Warm 1 gallon fresh whole milk with ½ cup cultured buttermilk in a large heatproof bowl until the temperature reaches 85°F. Have ready a water bath with rack in which to place the bowl to maintain this temperature throughout the process. Dissolve a rennet tablet, available at most well-stocked markets, in ¼ cup cold water and add this to the milk. Stir gently until the first sign of thickening, then stop stirring and transfer the container to the water bath. Allow to sit until the curd pulls away from the sides when the bowl is tipped slightly. Cut the curds into 1-inch cubes, using a knife or curd cutter.

Carefully transfer the curds to a colander lined with several layers of dampened cheesecloth. Allow the curd to drain until it appears dry, then mix in 1½ teaspoons kosher salt or cheese salt. Transfer the salted curd to a cheesecloth lined mold, place cheesecloth over the top of the curd, add the mold's follower, and weight it with bricks or cans of food. Depending on the weight used and other factors, the cheese should be firm enough to slice within an hour. Remove it from the mold and refrigerate. It will be best if eaten within 1 week.

Goat Cheese has so many fans that special equipment and supplies are available for making it at home. You will need liquid rennet and special goat cheese starter culture, along with some little goat cheese molds, for the following recipe. You can purchase everything online, unless you have a cheesemaking supply shop in your area. Goat milk is available in many grocery stores. If you are lucky, someone at your farmer's market sells fresh, local goat milk.

You can make your own molds, if you like, from 3-inch long sections of 1¼-inch diameter PVC pipe. Cover one end of the pipe with several layers of cheesecloth, held in place with a rubber band. Fill the molds with the cheese and set them on a rack over a pan to drain.

## CHEVRE

Heat 2 quarts goat milk to 72°F. Add 1 ounce goat cheese starter. Dilute the liquid rennet by combining 1 drop of it with 4 teaspoons water in a glass measuring cup. Add 1 tablespoon diluted mixture to the milk, discarding the remainder. Stir the milk well, cover, and allow to sit at room temperature for about 18 hours, or until the milk coagulates completely.

Transfer the curd to the prepared molds and set them where they will remain at 72°F. Cover loosely with a kitchen towel. Allow the cheese to drain for 48 hours. Remove the cheese from the molds and wrap in plastic wrap. The surface of the cheese can be salted, if you desire, or it can be rolled in cracked pepper, fresh herbs, or even fresh sifted white wood ashes. The chevre will keep for 2 weeks in the refrigerator.

---

Mozzarella: By adding other components that affect the character of the milk, other types of soft cheese may be produced. Classic mozzarella involves the use of lipase, an enzyme that breaks down some of the milk fat into fatty acids that contribute flavor to the cheese. The name *mozzarella* derives from the Italian verb meaning "to tear apart." This cheese is "little torn bits" as you will see from the recipe. Traditional mozzarella is often made with water buffalo milk or sheep's milk, but cow's milk works just fine, too. Besides the lipase, you will need citric acid and liquid rennet. All of these products are available from well-stocked markets or online.

## MOZZARELLA .

Dissolve 1½ teaspoons citric acid in 1 cup cold water. Dissolve ¼ teaspoon lipase powder in a small amount of cold water and allow to sit for 20 minutes before using. Dilute ¼ teaspoon liquid rennet in ¼ cup cold water.

Place 1 gallon pasteurized whole milk into a large pot and add the citric acid solution while stirring. Add the lipase solution and stir vigorously to incorporate everything completely. Place the pot on the burner and stir gently while bringing the temperature up to 90°F over low heat. Take the pot from the heat, gently stir in the rennet solution without introducing air into the milk, cover the pot, and allow to sit undisturbed for 5 minutes, or until a clear separation between curds and whey can be discerned when you inspect the contents of the pot.

Cut the curd, using a curd cutter or a knife that will reach all the way to the bottom of the pot, ensuring all the curd is cubed. Return the pot to low heat and stir very gently while heating the curd to 110°F. Pour off and reserve the whey, removing as much of it as possible from the curds without handling them too much. Heat the whey to 175°F, add ¼ cup salt and keep hot. Shape the drained curd into one or more lumps and place them in a basket strainer. Dip the strainer into the hot whey for a few seconds. Take them out and knead, using a pair of spoons or your hands if protected with heavy gloves, until the cheese is warm throughout and stretches without breaking. This point will be reached just before the cheese becomes too hot to handle with bare hands. Exercise caution to avoid scalding yourself. If the cheese does not become elastic, heat it for a few more seconds in the hot whey.

Once it reaches the desired consistency, tear the cheese into those little bits, roll them into balls between your palms. They are ready to eat immediately, or can be tossed into a bowl of ice water for half an hour, then drain and refrigerate for up to 3 days.

---

The classic dish for fresh mozzarella could not be simpler. Slice the cheese, arrange it on a plate with fresh tomato slices, torn fresh basil leaves, and a few grinds of black pepper. Drizzle with extra virgin olive oil and enjoy with crusty bread.

## Hard Cheese

Hard cheese involves the most work, takes the longest time, and yields the most interesting aromas and flavors from whole milk. To make a hard cheese, you will need commercial USDA-approved cheese coating in addition to the starter, rennet, and salt we have already been using to make soft cheese. The process, however, is essentially the same as that described for making unripened cheeses: First, the milk is clabbered, rennet is added, the curd is cut, then heated, and then separated from the whey by draining. The curd is then salted, pressed in a cheese press until firm, coated with the appropriate coating product, and aged until the desired flavor and texture is achieved.

Blue cheeses are prepared by introducing an appropriate fungus during the curing process, while other types of cheeses ripen under the influence of wild bacteria and yeasts present in the environment. The special character of certain famous cheeses develops because the ripening rooms have been used for the purpose for decades and have thus acquired a collection of microorganisms unique to them. The following recipe for cheddar illustrates how treating the curd in various ways affects the cheese.

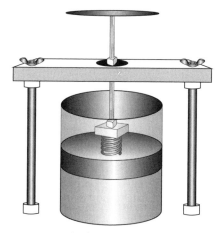

A cheese press.

# White Cheddar Cheese

2 gallons whole milk
2 cups cheese starter
½ teaspoon liquid rennet
1 tablespoon kosher salt
8 ounces USDA-approved cheese coating

Gently heat the milk to 86°F and add the cheese starter. Stir for about 2 minutes, cover, and allow to stand at room temperature overnight. The next day add the rennet, stir well for 2 minutes, cover, and allow to sit undisturbed until the curd has separated from the whey. When whey appears on top of the curd and the curd is firm to the touch, cut it into 1-inch cubes using a knife or curd cutter. Place the container in a larger pan of water and bring very slowly to 100°F, taking about an hour to do so. Then hold the curd at this temperature until it has reached a firm state. Stir gently now and then to keep the cubes from sticking together.

Transfer the curd to a colander lined with several thicknesses of dampened cheesecloth. Drain thoroughly, then transfer to a heatproof container and place in a water bath at 100°F. Heat until the curd coalesces into a solid mass. Carefully remove the curd to a work surface, cut it into strips about 1 inch each way and as long as convenient, and keep cooking them in the container at 100°F until they are thoroughly dry, about 1 hour. Add the salt, mix thoroughly, and transfer the strips to a cheesecloth-lined cheese press. Press, adding more weight as needed, until no more whey is exuded, about 1 hour. Take the cheese out of the press, reshape it as needed, and put it back in the press, lined with fresh cheesecloth for another 24 hours. Remove the cheese from the press, wipe dry carefully, and press closed any cracks or holes. Set it on a rack in a cool, dry place to dry for about 5 days. Check daily, wipe off any liquid, and observe for the formation of a dry, hard rind. When the rind has formed, you are ready to coat the cheese for aging.

Prepare the coating according to the manufacturer's directions, brush it on the cheese to completely cover, and place the cheese in a cool, dark, dry location to age. Six months will be required for a medium-sharp cheddar. Longer aging produces a sharper cheese.

The variations on this basic recipe are endless. Besides different approaches to drying and aging the cheese, various flavoring agents ranging from spices to certain green molds, can be introduced into the cheese at different stages during its production. Each of these imparts a distinctive touch. You can attempt to imitate the classics, or devise your own creations, all with procedures more or less equivalent to those just described.

## Yogurt Cheese

You can also make quick cheeses from commercial or homemade yogurt.

## YOGURT CHEESE OR PANEER

Place 1 quart homemade or good quality commercial plain yogurt into a bowl lined with several thicknesses of dampened cheesecloth. Gather the cloth around the yogurt, forming a sack, and secure the corners with kitchen string. Suspend the sack over a stockpot by tying it to the handle of a wooden spoon and laying the handle across the rim of the pot. Allow the yogurt to drain overnight in the refrigerator. Gently squeeze the cheesecloth to express as much whey as possible, then transfer the cheese to a clean container and use as called for in your recipe.

## Tofu

No discussion of cheese would be complete without including the vegetarian version, tofu. Tofu is prepared from soy milk in much the same way that cheese is made from dairy milk, by the application of heat and a coagulating agent. Not rennet, in this case, but calcium sulfate. I have found no better instructions for making tofu than those posted at www.brenda jwiley.com/making_tofu.html.

All the explanations on this website are clear, complete, and unambiguous. As for what to do with the finished product, here is a suggestion that may suit the needs of reformed carnivores.

# Tofu Bacon

1 pound extra-firm tofu
1 tablespoon vegetable oil
1 teaspoon liquid smoke seasoning
Sea salt
2 tablespoons soy sauce
2 tablespoons nutritional yeast

Slice tofu on its long side into ⅛ to ¼ inch slices, like bacon. Heat a large skillet, add the oil, and fry the tofu strips over medium heat until they are crisp on the outside. This will take about 10 minutes on one side. Then turn the strips and fry them another 10 minutes. Meanwhile, in a bowl, mix the liquid smoke, salt, and soy sauce,. Remove the skillet from the heat, pour the liquid smoke mixture into the pan, and stir gently so that all sides of the tofu are coated, then sprinkle the yeast over the tofu. Return the pan to low heat and cook gently until the liquid has evaporated. Cool, transfer to a storage container and refrigerate, covered, for up to a week.

# 9

# Putting It All Together

To maximize your savings from, and enjoyment of, your new American homestead, you need a plan that can take into account such things as your family's eating habits, the space available, the needs of crops and livestock, location of accessory structures, water management, and the overall impact on the appearance of your property.

Armed with an understanding of the basic principles of urban/suburban homesteading, you can proceed to create such a plan. A good plan will contain timelines, sketches, notes, and a journal, and will evolve with each passing season as experience dictates and the needs of the household change. Your plan will guide you in developing a homestead that is well integrated into the local ecology and able to generate the maximum possible share of your family's needs from the space you have available.

## Creating a Lifescape Plan

This approach to managing your property is much more than landscaping, it should be called *lifescaping*. To create your own lifescape plan, I recommend starting with a walking tour of your property, during which you sketch out the property boundaries and mark the location of buildings, large trees, and other important features, such as utility lines and fences.

Using the sketch, proceed to create a scale drawing of your homestead, using a computer or graph paper, pencil, and ruler. This drawing will give you the basic information about your lot, enabling you to allocate appropriate parts of the property for the various things you envision: garden site, orchard, workshop, or whatever you decide on.

To accompany the sketch, you should make a list of goals for your homestead. A typical goal might be: "We will produce half of our fresh vegetables this year." For each goal, you then list the steps, or tasks, needed to achieve the goal. Tasks associated with producing vegetables might include:

- Locate and mark garden site
- Build raised beds
- Create crop plan
- Purchase seeds
- Start transplants indoors
- Sow seeds outdoors
- Transplant plants outdoors
- Maintain garden throughout season

Each task should then be assigned a time frame, based on your crop plan. (Remember that the crop plan includes the varieties of crops you intend to grow, their maturity dates, and the amount of each to be planted.) Similarly, your goals should include a "time to completion" note. If you are planting apple trees this year, for example, estimate when the first harvest can be expected and include this in your lifescape plan. Each task will also likely suggest to you the materials you need. For example, "start transplants indoors" implies that you will have containers, germination growing medium, and a warm, well-illuminated spot for the plants to develop.

I like to use a three-ring binder for my homestead plan. I have sections for short-term garden planning, long-term garden planning, construction projects, maintenance memos, and want lists for plants and tools. Reviewing this notebook during the winter helps me to focus on what can be accomplished during the coming year. I also maintain a planting journal by using a spreadsheet program. In it, I record planting and harvest dates, along with yield data for each crop. Each year, the information in last year's journal supplies guidelines for this year's crop plan.

The importance of keeping records specific to your situation cannot be overemphasized. Over the years, your journals will contain a wealth of data that you can use to help make predictions for the coming season. You will quickly discover, for example, that the information in seed catalogs regarding the maturity times for vegetables are often rough estimates only. Your experience with a given cultivar may vary dramatically, depending on the weather and your growing expertise. A good year may result in some crops maturing one or two weeks earlier than predicted by the catalog entry, for example.

# The Initial Site Survey

Growing plants takes room. Do you have enough? How does your land lie? Is there sun or shade? Is it more or less level, or steeply inclined? Do existing features, such as an adjacent house, cast shade? Can you gain more sun by pruning a large tree? The answers to such questions will be site-specific, and can be answered with the help of a site survey.

Start with some stakes, a tape measure, and a sheet of graph paper to make a rough drawing of your lot. Use stakes to set benchmarks, then take a series of measurements from these points, recording the distances on the graph paper. A good place to begin is at a corner of your house. Measure the distance from one corner to the property line. Drive a stake into the ground at this location. Work from that point around the circumference of your lot, taking additional measurements and setting stakes as reference points. As you go, indicate on your sketch the large trees, outbuildings, house, adjacent structures, and other significant features. By taking several measurements of the distance from the house to the line at various spots, you can create an accurate drawing without resorting to a professional survey.

From the rough sketch, prepare a scale drawing, as mentioned earlier. Study your drawing to identify areas that can be used for crop production. If you do a good job with the sketch, you can easily add up the number of square feet you have available. Also locate *activity areas* on your drawing to include such things as a compost bin or a chicken coop.

# What Do We Need?

At this point, you will want to consider which activity areas you will require, based on your goals for the homestead. Activity areas might include:

- Vegetable beds, annual
- Vegetable beds, perennial
- Orchard
- Vineyard
- Bramble
- Berry patch
- Chicken coop
- Beehives
- Pasture
- Barn
- Greenhouse/cold frame(s)
- Composting area
- Pond
- Ornamental plantings (butterfly garden, native plants, etc.)
- Rain barrels

Organizing the space into specific activity areas simplifies maintenance. Fitting activity areas into your site drawing will help you determine
if you can accommodate everything you want. If not enough room is available, you can make the tough choices, or decide how to squeeze something
in. For example, you may not have enough room for an orchard of dwarf
fruit trees, owing to their spacing requirements. But could you grow one or
two trees in containers? Or perhaps espalier the trees against one wall of the
house, instead? Trying out various options on paper lets you avoid costly
and time-consuming mistakes.

> When I was selling garden pond supplies, I was always amazed at how
> many people would come to the store for a pond liner *after* having
> dug a hole. Seldom did we have a liner with the dimensions that
> would precisely fit. Instead, these would-be water gardeners should
> have researched the available precut liner sizes, *then* started digging.
> Considering the back-breaking labor involved in such a project, you
> would think that more people would plan ahead.

## Locating Growing Spaces

You can remedy almost any shortcoming of your property, in terms of crop
production, with the exception of sun exposure. If you haven't enough sun,
some plants simply won't grow, and a great many will perform poorly.
Thus, it behooves you to consider carefully the sun exposure in the areas
you propose to use for growing food. Besides the number of hours of sun a
location receives per day during the growing season, exposure will affect
how quickly or slowly the site's temperature changes with the changing
seasons, its relationship to prevailing winds and consequently its suscepti-
bility to unseasonal weather.

An east-facing slope will warm up earlier in the spring than a west-
facing one. Plants that are subject to damage from late spring frosts may
thus benefit from later emergence when planted on the west side of a house.
When planted on the eastern side, the same species may break dormancy
too early and be damaged by a late cold snap. Raised beds produce similar
microclimatic conditions, they warm up earlier and dry out faster than in-
ground beds. Such differences can determine whether your produce is
ready earlier or later in the season.

As you create your site drawing, locate north using a compass or GPS
device. Note the exposure of each of your proposed growing areas. If you

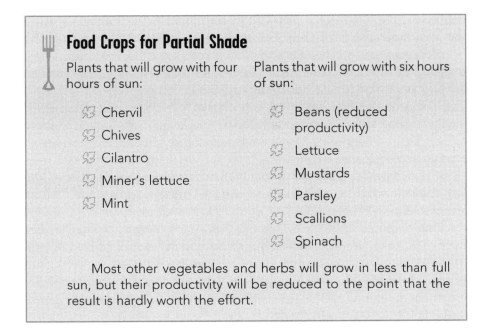

## Food Crops for Partial Shade

Plants that will grow with four hours of sun:

- Chervil
- Chives
- Cilantro
- Miner's lettuce
- Mint

Plants that will grow with six hours of sun:

- Beans (reduced productivity)
- Lettuce
- Mustards
- Parsley
- Scallions
- Spinach

Most other vegetables and herbs will grow in less than full sun, but their productivity will be reduced to the point that the result is hardly worth the effort.

have seasonal shade from a large deciduous tree, indicate the shade line on your drawing. Think about how to exploit conditions in each of these areas to achieve your goals. Some crops, for example, will grow in partial shade, although productivity will not be as high as for the same crop growing in full sun.

## Activity Areas and Structures

Give some thought to locating the various activity areas and structures you decide on. Everything should be placed to maximize efficiency, so you won't be running all over the yard every time you start a project or initiate maintenance. For example, the compost area should be as close as practical to the kitchen door, since you will be making many trips to compost scraps all year long. On the other hand, the composter may not be the most attractive feature of the yard, requiring screening from the neighbors' view, perhaps. I find that I need, in addition to a compost bin holding about a cubic yard of material, a staging area for the compost. This is a spot near the compost bin where I pile materials, such as branches pruned from trees and shrubs, while they await further processing. I like to chop everything up, using the lawnmower, before putting it in the compost bin. This chore is one I prefer to do infrequently, and thus I accumulate a fair amount before dragging out the mower.

Beekeeping experts will tell you that your hives should be under a large tree, facing south, and away from low, cold, windy spots. If you plan on keeping bees, you should search for such a location on your site plan.

Your chicken coop should be in a relatively sheltered spot, and the chickens need access to outdoor space. If you keep goats, they need room to exercise and browse on fresh greens but also need to be kept away from the vegetable garden.

Taking such matters into account when developing your site plan will save many headaches later on. I have provided information on animal space requirements in chapter 7.

Adding buildings such as a chicken coop, greenhouse, or storage shed may entail other considerations. If the structure can be considered permanent, you may need a building permit. If you run electricity to the greenhouse, you may need a building permit. In some jurisdictions, the size of the structure and its setback (distance from the property line or a right-of way) may be prescribed by local codes. Always investigate such matters before you invest in improvements to your homestead. Take setbacks into consideration when drawing your site plan, if necessary.

## To DIY or Not to DIY

Do-it-yourself construction can save a fortune but only if you know what you are doing. Understand the limits of your skills, time, and resources. For example, a greenhouse roof must have glazing that is compatible with the anticipated maximum snow load in your area. Laying sheets of thin plastic between the rafters may work fine during the spring, summer, and fall, but the whole thing can come crashing down after a good snowfall (even in the supposedly "sunny South"). Not only might such an accident mean the loss of a crop, it could seriously injure a member of your family. Electrical wiring can pose all kinds of dangers if you lack the knowledge of how to do it properly.

Take the time to research the demands of any particular project. If it appears that your plans exceed your skills, seek professional help. Some tasks require specialized tools that can set you back several hundred dollars or more, another reason you may need the services of a professional.

You will want cost estimates for any anticipated project. A good place to begin is your local home improvement store. They will provide assistance in developing a bill of materials for your project, along with a quote for the cost, free of charge. Labor costs are another matter. As a rule of thumb, expect the labor charge for a given project to equal at least the cost of materials. For example, if you want to build a storage shed and $1,000 worth of materials are required, expect that the labor cost for such a project will be at least $1,000. Depending on the skill level required, labor can amount to much more than this, however. It is always wise to obtain at least three estimates for any project.

# Managing Water

Only about 2 percent of the planet's freshwater is available for human use. How you manage water in and around your home really matters. From a simple rain barrel to a garden pond to home scale aquaculture, the new American homesteader can "tap into" avenues leading toward greater self-sufficiency.

Growing food requires water in copious quantities. Rain is the ideal water source, but it may not arrive in the appropriate amounts, and at the right times. Sooner or later, you will need to irrigate. Thus, you must consider not only the quantity but also the quality of available water.

If you happen to have a stream or lake adjacent this may be a good source of irrigation water, but check with local authorities concerning withdrawal. Natural waters typically receive close government regulation, and you will probably need a permit. If you have a small pond, a cistern, or other means to capture and store rainwater, this provides the perfect option for low-cost irrigation. For many suburban and urban farmers, however, the municipal water supply is the only option for irrigation.

## Determining Your Water Needs

Your water needs will vary depending on the type of crop and method of cultivation. Vegetables growing in the open in raised beds will need irrigation only to supplement natural rainfall. A greenhouse will have no other water source than the irrigation you provide. Estimate usage by calculating the irrigation needed to equal 1 inch of rainfall per week, a reasonable amount of water for most crop production.

Let's say you have 240 square feet of greenhouse bench space that will receive irrigation. One inch of rain over this space equals 20 cubic feet of water (240 ÷ 12 inches per foot). That equals 150 gallons per week, or 600 gallons per month. If the combined water and sewer charge is two cents per gallon (about what it costs in my town), you will pay $12 per month to irrigate.

## Reducing Your Irrigation Costs

Learn as much as you can from your monthly utility bill. How much do you pay for a gallon of water? How much do you pay for sewer service? The sewer charge can double your cost for a gallon of irrigation water, maybe increase it even more.

> Some utilities provide a way around the sewer charge, in the form of a seasonal watering credit, or sewer charge rebate. Under this arrangement, the utility company compares your winter water use with your summer use, and issues a credit for the difference. The justification is that water used for irrigation does not flow down the drain, so you are not employing the sewer to remove this water. My utility offers such a break but makes no effort to advertise it. Chances are, if you want to find a similar deal in your area, you will need to call the utility company.

Another option is to have a secondary water meter installed. Such a meter provides a separate measure of the water used for irrigation. The utility company reads both meters, and subtracts the secondary meter reading from the sewer bill, so you pay only for the water. Check to see if you can install this meter yourself, which will result in savings of $500–$1,000 in fees charged by the utility company. First determine if the investment is worth it. In my case, I found that only fourteen months would be required to cover the $625 cost of a secondary meter for a greenhouse. Utilities measure water usage either in gallons, cubic feet, or hundred cubic feet. (One cubic foot of water equals 7.5 gallons.) The sewer charge is then based on water usage. Check with your supplier if you need help figuring out your bill.

## Hard Water

A common water quality issue is too much *hardness*. This term refers to the quantity of dissolved mineral salts, particularly calcium and magnesium. Hard water can interfere with the adsorption of critical plant nutrients. A more mundane effect is the appearance of unsightly white or yellowish spots on plant leaves, telltale signs of hardness left behind when the water evaporates. You may find that water purification is needed, especially for greenhouse irrigation systems that can be damaged by hard water.

Reverse osmosis, a process whereby water is forced under pressure through a semi-permeable plastic membrane, provides a practical way to purify irrigation water. For horticultural purposes, reverse osmosis is preferable to deionization, another common method, because the latter introduces sodium into the product water, replacing the hardness components. Plants generally abhor sodium. Reverse osmosis has its drawbacks, however; primarily the production of a considerable amount of waste water for each gallon of product.

The purest, softest, and cheapest water you can get literally falls from the sky. Rather than invest in expensive equipment, consider how you can capture and store rainwater.

## Rainwater Collection Systems

One of the simplest ways to improve water management on your homestead is to install rain barrels below your downspouts. If you reuse salvaged barrels, make sure they previously contained nothing harmful to plants or people. You can use plastic garbage cans, or purchase rain barrels made for the purpose at many garden centers or via mail order. These are usually designed to attach easily to an existing downspout, with a bib near the bottom to connect a garden hose. Desirable additional features include a tight-fitting lid to prevent access by mosquitoes, a base that elevates the bottom of the barrel to allow it to drain completely and built-in fittings that permit more than one barrel to be connected in series.

## Managing Site Drainage

Solving significant water management problems, such as heavy erosion, flooding, or ponding of rainwater on your property may require professional assistance. However, you can effectively direct water flow using a French drain. This is basically a shallow trench, lined with stones, that carries water away from the house and directs it where it will do the most good. This can be a pond or cistern or perhaps a rain garden. A rain garden is a low spot on the property, often where water naturally accumulates, where moisture loving plants are cultivated. This makes use of an otherwise difficult growing area, while also reducing the possibility that water will stand long enough to encourage mosquitoes. The most effective French drains and rain gardens are simply enhancements of natural drainage patterns. Study your site during and after a heavy rain to determine how water naturally flows across it.

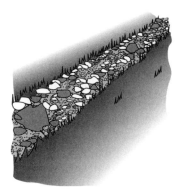

A French drain.

## Graywater Recovery

*Graywater* is water that has been used for bathing, washing dishes, or laundry. While not suitable for drinking or cooking, it does not pose a health hazard as does the water from flushing the toilet. With appropriate plumbing, graywater can be sent not to the sewer but rather directed toward the garden for irrigation. While it is relatively easy to install a separate graywater system during new construction, retrofitting can be costly. You may also run into outmoded ordinances if you direct graywater anywhere other than into the sewer system.

# Reducing Energy Consumption

Fundamental to everything we do, energy rules our planet. How we consume, use, and produce energy affects the entire biosphere via climate change, while also creating more localized problems like smog, acid rain, and oil spills. Despite the promise of new green technologies, our best new "source" of energy comes from improved efficiency and conservation. Saving energy through reduced consumption, repurposing of materials, composting, and recycling are essential skills for greening both the urban and the world's environment. Saving energy also means saving money. Cheap has become the new rich, in the era of global climate change.

Some utility companies encourage conservation by offering free energy audits. An expert inspects your home and makes recommendations for improvements that would save energy. A wide range of options is available to every family, depending on the age of the house, its construction, your location, and the resources you have for the project. Here is a basic list to consider.

- Seal wall outlets and switch boxes to prevent air leaks.
- Seal air leaks around windows and doors.
- Add insulation in your attic.
- Insulate your water heater.
- Install a clothesline to reduce dryer use.
- Wash dishes by hand instead of running the dishwasher.
- Install compact fluorescent or LED lamps to replace incandescent bulbs.
- Replace aging appliances with new, energy-efficient models.
- Replace old windows with energy-efficient ones.
- Install a solar water heater.
- Install a solar electricity generation system.

# Basic Skill Sets to Develop

In order to take full advantage of the opportunities for self-sufficiency that your homestead provides, you'll have to acquire a few basic skills. Here we will cover the basic carpentry, wiring, plumbing, and mechanical skill sets that you will be called on to use from time to time in managing your homestead. Not everyone can easily become proficient at all these crafts, and like other acquired talents, achieving professional quality results requires practice. But to the extent you can learn to meet your own needs in these areas, you will avoid the cost of professional help.

- **Carpentry.** Wood is a renewable resource, and among the most versatile for small scale projects at home. Learning carpentry at a young age from my father has enabled me to build everything from picture frames to a garden shed without having to hire anyone. I have more than one power saw and a chest full of tools, but you can do most outdoor carpentry jobs with a short list of hand tools. Include a hand-held circular saw and a rechargeable drill/screwdriver in your tool box, and you can build almost anything you need with minimal sweat.

- **Wiring.** The reason we have licensed electricians is to prevent shoddy wiring from starting a fire. However, anyone can probably learn to install a ceiling fan, replace a faulty wall switch, or even run a new circuit from the load center to the greenhouse. If electrical projects appeal to you, thoroughly research the techniques involved before you begin. You can find how-to videos online, purchase reference books, or even take a noncredit course. Your DIY home improvement store probably has at least one licensed electrician whose advice will cost you nothing. Despite the learning curve, handling your own basic electrical needs can save you a fortune in labor charges.

**Plumbing.** Having been a homeowner for thirty-five years, I can say with conviction that plumbing repairs can present a greater challenge to the nonprofessional than any other home project. Nevertheless, repacking a faucet or running a water line to the greenhouse can be mastered by anyone handy with tools.

> I had a great plumber for most of those thirty-five years. He has since retired, but he left me with the best piece of advice I can offer regarding his trade. "Drain pipe installation requires more care than installation of supply lines," he said. "If you doubt me, consider which one you'd rather have leak."

**Mechanical Repairs.** Stuff breaks. If you learn how to do repairs at home, you save money and extend the life of your equipment. Life on some suburban homesteads would not be as easy without a lawn tractor, for example. If yours won't start, do you know what to do? Murphy's Law dictates that the failure will occur at the height of the season, when every repair shop in the county has a backlog. Small engine repair skills can serve you well, and you can often learn all you need to know from the owner's manual or the equipment manufacturer's website.

# Essential Tools to Own

No matter which trade skills you choose to learn, you will need appropriate tools. What follows is a basic list. Thousands of specialized tools exist, but you probably can accomplish 90 percent of garden, household repair, and maintenance tasks with a hammer, a cordless drill/screwdriver, a square, a level, and a pair of pliers. For the garden, you will want a spade, a hoe, a rake, a hand trowel, pruning shears, and a small wheelbarrow or wagon. When you discover a need for additional tools, then consider purchasing or renting them.

## Carpentry and Construction Tools

- Hand saw
- Hammer
- Carpenter's square
- Builder's square
- Levels in several lengths
- Hand drill
- Drill bits, both twist type and spade type
- Screwdrivers, flat and Phillips, small and large, in various lengths
- Wood chisels
- Masonry chisels

- Electric circular saw
- Electric drill/screwdriver
- Electric sander
- Table saw
- Drill press
- Clamps, assorted
- Vise
- Nail puller
- Wrecking bar
- Flat crowbar
- Electronic stud finder

## Electrical Tools

- Electronic multimeter or circuit tester
- Diagonal wire cutters

- Standard pliers
- Needle-nosed pliers
- Electrician's pliers

## Plumbing Tools

- Adjustable wrench
- Hand torch, solder, and flux

- Pipe wrenches
- Pipe cutter

## Mechanic's Tools

- Assorted crescent wrenches
- Assorted box end wrenches
- Assorted socket wrenches

- Assorted hex wrenches
- Hacksaw
- Welder (for the truly dedicated DIY enthusiast)

## Garden Tools

- Shovel
- Spade
- Hoe
- Rake
- Hand trowel
- Hand cultivator
- Garden fork
- Knee pads or kneeling pad

- Pruning shears
- Small electric chainsaw with heavy-duty extension cord
- Hand pruning saw
- Wheelbarrow or garden cart
- Small tractor and wagon (again, for larger properties or the enthusiastic gardener

# Recycling

I consider myself a lucky guy when it comes to recycling. My local garbage company offers curbside recycling pickup that is *single stream*, meaning I don't have to sort my refuse into separate bins for glass, aluminum, etc. Every two weeks, I wheel a 50-gallon container to the street and it is whisked away to the recycling center. Before this reasonably priced service was added, I was taking recyclable material to the local convenience center myself. Curbside pickup saves me time and has made our household more recycling conscious because it is so easy. We don't have to separate glass from paper and can just dump everything into one big bin. Our true garbage amounts to less than 10 gallons a week, since we also compost most kitchen wastes.

In other locales, you may have curbside pickup available, but you have to separate everything, or you may have to haul the stuff to the recycling center yourself. Nevertheless, please take advantage of any opportunity to recycle. It is one of the easiest and simplest ways to reduce your household carbon footprint, because recycling materials invariably uses less energy than producing new materials. Recycling also keeps stuff out of sanitary landfills, which are becoming full at an alarming rate across the country. Each new landfill created eats up 50 or more acres of land that would otherwise be farmland or habitat for wildlife. Landfills are seldom located on land that has been developed, because acquiring such property is too costly. Furthermore, in some parts of the country, the underlying geology limits where a landfill can be located.

Many retailers now offer recycling of products, such as rechargeable batteries (loaded with irreplaceable metals such as lithium, cadmium, and nickel), fluorescent lamps (containing tiny amounts of toxic mercury), computers and cell phones (containing rare metals), and those ubiquitous plastic bags. Trillions of the latter are used worldwide each year, clogging landfills and creating hazards for wildlife when they are not properly disposed of. They often end up in local waters or are blown across the landscape like urbanized tumbleweeds. Recycling the darn things is rarely profitable, although companies that offer the service gain a few competitive points with ecology-minded consumers. Instead of contributing to this problem, buy some reusable shopping bags and carry them in your car so you will always have them with you when you shop.

Another class of toxic products should always be recycled: unused drugs. Never dump them down the toilet, as this can create significant problems for local aquatic habitats. Many drugs persist through the processing of sewage and end up in rivers where they can play havoc with the metabolism of fish and invertebrates, not to mention the potential for danger to humans. Antibiotics, in particular, pose a threat because exposure to them helps to select for resistant strains of bacteria in the environment. Always consult your pharmacist regarding proper disposal of unused drugs, whether prescribed by a doctor or purchased over the counter. Sometimes, prescription drugs can be repackaged and donated to charity, not only keeping them out of the environment but also helping a fellow human in need.

## Reusing

Packaging constitutes the bulk of recycled materials in most households. Food and beverage containers and cardboard boxes are the most common items in the recycle bin at my house. We are reducing the number of those every year, too, mostly by preserving our own food in containers that we wash and reuse. We also shop at the local food co-op for items that can be purchased in bulk, in containers that we bring from home. When I run out of, say, almonds, I simply wash the plastic storage jar and take it to the co-op. The clerk weighs the jar for me, and subtracts that initial weight, or *tare*, from the total weight after I fill the jar with almonds. One of these days, I plan to switch to glass jars, and mark the tare on each one with a diamond scriber, merely to save time when I am at the co-op. This approach to the food pantry is one of the best ways to save energy and money through reuse.

Lots of other things around the house can be reused. Many kinds of plastic containers from the grocery store can be used to start seeds, for example. Those clear clamshells that the grocer uses to pack all sorts of foods make nifty miniature greenhouses. Glass jars and bottles, once emptied of the original contents, can be used to store everything from seeds to nuts and bolts. When I shop, I look for items in packaging that I can reuse, and purchase those instead of competing products in wasteful packaging. Some companies make the effort to package their products in containers that can be easily reused. One large distributor of organic herbs and spices wins my business because their jar labels peel off easily and cleanly, for example.

Home food canning has for many decades depended on jar lids designed for one use only. However, you can purchase good quality canning jars with reusable glass lids and rubber gaskets that can be resterilized multiple times without degradation. They are more expensive initially than the more familiar canning jars, but over their lifetime, you save money by not having to replace lids every season. You may be tempted to use empty jars from purchased food products to can your own produce. However, it is dangerous to reuse food containers for home canning. The seals may not work properly, and the food can easily spoil as a result, because air can enter the jar. Commercial food containers are not intended for multiple use or repeated exposure to canning temperatures. Always use products intended for home canning and carefully inspect jar rims for cracks or chips before using them.

I have been trying to figure out just when Americans started purchasing those plastic storage bins rather than reusing empty cardboard boxes. For some things, the bins probably make good sense, but for storing old books or clothing in the attic? Come on. Why spend five dollars on a bin made out of plastic (which in turn was made from oil) when you can get a cardboard box for nothing? Trees are renewable, oil isn't. Besides, plastic bins can retain humidity, a potential cause of mold or mildew damage in some types of stored items, such as books.

Almost anything can potentially be reused for something. The possibilities are limited only by your imagination. I work for a large DIY retailer and frequently scout the trash cart before it reaches the Dumpster. I've used old shipping pallets to fuel a fire for a barbecue, for example. The pallets are made of oak and burn hot and slowly.

I am always on the lookout for "junk" that might fit some need around the house, although I resist the temptation to accumulate more stuff just because I might use it someday. If I run across something and think, "That would be perfect for X project," I grab it. Otherwise, no.

Yard sales and flea markets are prime sources for cheap, reusable goods. Hand tools can often be purchased at a fraction of their new price, and you can usually judge their quality simply by inspecting them. Avoid used gasoline-powered tools unless you are a good judge of small engines, however. Ditto for electric appliances, unless you can repair them yourself. But almost anything else is fair game. One friend of mine has purchased every one of her plant containers from yard sales. She grows herbs in them. Used lumber can be repurposed for all sorts of uses around the house and in the garden. If you need a raised bed, why not build it from salvaged boards instead of buying new? It may rot after a couple of years outdoors, but you can always replace it then.

Never forget this adage from the America of a couple of generations ago: "Use it up. Wear it out. Make it do. Or do without." What made good sense on the frontier where everything manufactured was in short supply, makes good sense today when basic resources themselves are becoming ever scarcer.

When looking for something for a project, do not neglect your own basement, garage, or attic as a source of reusable "finds." Ever clean out a space and find stuff you could have used had you remembered that you owned it? Simply organizing your storage space and labeling boxes can help you repurpose household goods rather than replace them. We all have way too much stuff. Have a major cleaning every year. Sort your stuff into four piles: Trash, Donate, Sell, and Keep. You'll feel a sense of accomplishment every time you complete that process.

# Curb Appeal

Regardless of the exact nature of the changes you make to your suburban or urban property in evolving it into an example of the new American homestead, bear in mind that they can affect the appearance, and ultimately the value, of your property. Apartment or condominium dwellers will be restricted by legal agreements as to the nature and magnitude of home food production that is possible. Homeowners, likewise, may be constrained by deed covenants, but frequently may do as they please. Given that you may one day want to sell your home, it is wise to devise a plan that will increase its value. As the popularity of suburban homesteading grows, having established planting beds with high-quality organic soil, mature fruit trees, and integrated landscaping may be worth more than an extra bedroom or bath.

Some things to consider when creating the lifescape plan for your property include the following:

- Permanent plantings such as fruit or nut trees will increase in value as they mature.

- Growing beds made of durable materials such as masonry, composites, or naturally rot-resistant wood are worth more than beds constructed of less durable materials.

- Landscape elements that feature flowers, fragrance, or fruit should be located where they are visible from the street.

- Whenever possible, integrate kitchen plants such as herbs with otherwise ornamental plantings.

- Experiment with vegetable varieties that offer unusual colors, bold foliage, or other attributes that can be exploited for decorative effect.

- To have the greatest possible diversity, plant dwarf varieties whenever possible.

- Chicken coops, garden sheds, and compost areas are best located out of sight in the backyard.

- Beehives should never be located where normal patterns of foot traffic might intersect with the bees' flight path to and from the hive entrance.

- Keeping a logbook of information relevant to your permanent plantings that can be passed along to potential new owners may earn their gratitude and possibly generate a higher offer from them.

- If you have concerns regarding the impact of your lifescape plans on your property's curb appeal, seek expert advice from a local designer or a Realtor.

Think about some basic principles of design when you create your lifescape plan:

- Consider traffic flow and lay out pathways first.
- Direct the viewer's eye with focal points.
- Borrow the view from across the property line, if possible.
- Identify the main entrance to the house clearly.
- Screen unsightly utility areas appropriately.

※ Keep in mind that straight lines and geometric shapes look formal, while curves and irregular shapes look "natural."

※ Use the sunniest areas for food production.

My book, *Pay Dirt: How to Make $10,000 a Year From Your Backyard Garden* (Adams Media, 2006), considered the possibilities of *micro-farming* or using your homestead to provide a source of income. You can also incorporate income-producing space into your lifescape plan. If you think this makes sense in your case, pick up a copy of *Pay Dirt* to guide you in creating a business plan. For our present purpose, however, suffice it to say that having an ongoing home-based business in place can only enhance the attractiveness of your property in the eyes of a buyer who values self-sufficiency as much as you do.

Armed with some basic skills and a plan, anyone with the motivation can transform a house and lot into a new American homestead.

# 10

# The Future of the American Homestead

The trend toward urban homesteading results from people's motivation to improve their lives and help reverse some of the damage the human race has wrought on the planet. No one, of course, can be truly self-sufficient, but we can all do more to lessen our impact on the environment by following some basic tenets. The principles of permaculture, introduced in chapter 1, provide a good foundation, but we need to translate them into specific types of actions that individuals can take. For example:

- Cook from scratch.
- Grow as much of your food as possible.
- Learn to store abundance against times of scarcity.

These actions all flow from the permaculture principle, "Obtain a yield." Similarly, the catchphrase, "Reduce, reuse, and recycle," embodies several of the permaculture principles. No individual can make the machines we rely upon today. In fact, even making a flashlight battery is impossible for one person to do. But we can all choose to accumulate less stuff, to make the things we own last as long as possible, and to eliminate waste wherever we can.

The new American homesteading movement is emphatically not a rejection of technology. Rather, it embraces the wise use of technology to obtain a greater level of self-sufficiency. As the future brings technological improvements, such as solar panels that install like roofing shingles, urban homesteaders will be deploying them to achieve their goals.

# Native Plants and Permaculture

Another permaculture principle is "Use and value diversity." The ideal way to put this principle into practice in the homestead garden involves utilizing native plant species when possible instead of overused exotics that can in some circumstances become weeds. Some gardeners go so far as to devote a special area of the yard to native plants, creating a wildflower garden. Others insist on using *only* natives for ornamental plantings. One can also integrate local species into the landscape alongside traditional vegetables, perennials, and annuals. This latter option is the one most gardeners will probably choose.

## Native Plants for Food and Forage

The plant species that were growing in your area prior to the arrival of Europeans in North America provided all the forage needed for dozens of bird and mammal species. Although large mammals, with the exception of deer, are generally not prevalent in urban or suburban areas today, numerous small mammals and birds undoubtedly thrive near you, no matter where you live. Plant fruit-bearing native shrubs to attract birds. In my region an example would be *Euonymus americanus*, the strawberry bush. Its bright red seeds, enclosed in a spiked, purplish fruit, look great in the early winter garden and feed the local birds. Sunflowers and various types of seed-bearing plants, such as native grasses, also feed birds and small mammals.

With enough growing space, you can produce a surprising amount of livestock food with perennial native grasses. Panick grass (*Panicum virgatum*) reaches about 4 feet in height and is topped with attractive seed heads. The name *panick* comes from the Celtic term for "fodder" or "forage." Cultivated varieties of panick grass are widely available. Other native warm-season grasses such as big bluestem (*Andropogon gerardii*) and Indian grass (*Sorghastrum nutans*) are being increasingly utilized as cultivated grasses in the hot summer regions. Native warm-season grasses provide forage when cool-season grasses are unproductive.

Native plants of all kinds provide forage and nectar for insects, in turn attracting predators that will help keep bugs from eating your garden. Growing native plants also encourages the development of a complex system of invertebrates, root fungi, and soil microbes unique to the local area. These, in turn, can provide benefits for crop plants. That is why high plant diversity results in a healthier, more productive garden.

North American native plants also helped to feed the Native Americans. East of the Mississippi, persimmon (*Diospyros virginiana*) and pawpaw

(*Asimina triloba*) supplied tasty fruit in winter and summer, respectively. In autumn, hickory, American chestnut, and black walnut dropped bushels of edible nuts. Blackberries, huckleberries, strawberries, and muscadine grapes supplied sweetness during the warm months. Summer's corn and squashes are New World natives, as are many varieties of beans. Wild greens of all kinds still grow unattended throughout the country. In the southern Appalachian region poke salat (*Phytolacca americana*) emerges in early spring. It is highly esteemed as cooked greens. Another Appalachian favorite is ramp (*Allium trioccum*), a wild leek so esteemed for its pungent flavor that festivals celebrating it are held throughout its range in the spring. In the American West, familiar edibles include Oregon grape (*Mahonia aquifolium*), manzanita (*Arctostaphylos* species), miner's lettuce (*Claytonia perfoliata*), blue elderberry (*Sambucus mexicana*), wild currant (*Ribes aureum*), and California bay tree (*Umbellularia californica*).

Across the continent, cattails (*Typha* species) grow where the soil is wet enough. Different species of cattails live in different regions, but all parts of all species are edible. Cattails were so valued in some Native American societies that the plant was incorporated into important religious ceremonies. Spend some time researching the possibilities in your specific locale. Good garden centers may offer a separate section of natives, but you may have to rely on your own research to discover the edibles among them. With proper siting and care, most native plants will adapt to the garden. Once established, they tend to be carefree.

## Native Plants for Butterflies and Other Beneficial Insects

Plants with showy flowers attract butterflies, along with other pollinators, to the garden. The insects will repay you for growing their nectar plants by pollinating your cucumbers, melons, and fruit trees. A garden spot glowing with bright flowers adds to your property's curb appeal, also.

You can go a step further and grow food plants for butterfly larvae. Providing forage for larvae not only attracts the mating adults, it also helps to ensure that your local butterfly population remains abundant. If this variation on native plant gardening appeals to you, start by investigating your region's butterfly species. Field guides often list both nectar sources and larval food plants. Some of these, such as nettles, can do double duty as edibles for humans; some, such as violets, can do triple duty, producing flowers both showy and edible along with food for butterfly larvae. Even some native grasses can feed certain butterfly larvae while also fulfilling an aesthetic role in the landscape.

## Native Plant Remedies

A quick Internet search will reveal the vast array of herbal remedies attributable to North American plant species. Native plant guides may include explanations of the plant's traditional uses, both by Native Americans and early European settlers. For example, curatives for diarrhea (undoubtedly a common problem prior to the introduction of modern sanitation) include blackberry or raspberry roots, wild cherry bark, geranium plants, and star grass leaves. Common names for many wild plants indicate their traditional uses: boneset, heal-all, pleurisy root.

Despite the fact that many modern pharmaceuticals owe their origin to traditional medicine, not every claim of efficacy is supported by scientific evidence. Where efficacy has been demonstrated, as in the well-known example of aspirin's discovery in willow bark tea, you may find the plant worth including in your landscape. If you are also growing traditional European medicinal herbs, including native plant remedies in the overall plan for your homestead also makes good sense.

> Always beware of potentially poisonous plants! Do your homework and be certain of your identification. Be especially cautious of plants described as having medicinal uses in traditional cultures. This could indicate that the plant contains substances that might be harmful if consumed in significant amounts. Find out *exactly* how the plant was used before preparing it. One way to safely explore the wild plants, edible and otherwise, of your region is to join a wildflower club. Groups devoted to wild food foraging are also organized throughout the country.

## Invasive Species

I devote a lot of words to suggestions regarding what plants to grow on the new American homestead. In this section, allow me to offer a few words on the subject of invasive species, or "what not to grow."

Some plants thrive so well outside their normal haunts that they turn up, whether uninvited or deliberately planted, in landscapes all over the country. Of these highly adaptable plants, a small fraction adapt far too well and become pests. A pest plant is one that can reproduce outside its native habitat, has the ability to out-compete native species, and has the ability to move from place to place via birds, human activity, or the wind.

Good examples of pest plants are

- Kudzu
- Privet
- Purple loosestrife
- Bradford pear

- 🦠 Japanese honeysuckle
- 🦠 Heavenly bamboo
- 🦠 True bamboo
- 🦠 Yellow nutsedge
- 🦠 Paulwonia

- 🦠 Tree-of-heaven
- 🦠 Mimosa
- 🦠 Australian pine
- 🦠 Knapweed

Before including any plant in your garden inventory, check with the appropriate Endangered Pest Plant Council in your region. If you already have a pest species growing on your property, you may want to consider removing it to make room for something more useful and environmentally friendly.

# Beyond the Property Line

One problem that arises in dealing with pest plants is their mobility. Controlling pests on a scale wider than your individual property boundary requires the cooperation of others and provides a good starting point for discussing the necessary extension of the principles of the urban homestead across the property line. Connecting with like-minded individuals in your neighborhood, city, and region allows for information transfer, cooperative action, and (never forget) political strength. The urgent need for change in our stewardship of the planet, in the social and economic structure of our society, and in the way we relate to the rest of humanity can only be met through community effort. Even with the strength of numbers, making the case for sustainability and a saner approach to living remains a challenge. Globalized corporate industrialism, mass media centralization, and corrupt, money-driven politics all strive to move us in the opposite direction, toward ever increasing consumption, further environmental degradation, and the concentration of economic power into fewer and fewer hands. Therefore reach out, share your knowledge, and join hands with those of us who have a different vision for the future.

## Forging Connections

My friend Pat Rakes says he barely knew any of his neighbors until he started growing a native plant garden along the curb at the front of his house. Now he chats with passersby almost every time he steps out to the garden to dig. This morning I answered a knock at my door from a neighbor, a young woman with a little girl in tow, who wanted to take a look at my raised-bed vegetable garden, which is visible from the street in the spring, before my tall hedge of *Miscanthus* grass resprouts. People at work are forever asking for gardening advice. Many plan on growing vegetables for the first time this season. Begin with simple connections like these. If you are a seasoned gardener, welcome garden visitors, and share your experiences and knowledge with anyone seeking help. If a novice, don't hesitate to approach a neighbor for advice, especially if their tomato plants are hanging full. Most people will gladly help others enjoy gardening, because the old hands know the joy and fulfillment that derive from growing food and flowers well.

Beyond the chance encounter at the curb or the water fountain, you can easily find like-minded locals via the Internet. A search on "vegetable gardening Knoxville" produced over 200,000 hits, covering everything from heirloom vegetables at the University of Tennessee public gardens to community groups such as the Knoxville Permaculture Guild, which offers workshops on a variety of sustainability topics. Organizations like these exist in every part of the country. You could even start your own group. Invite a few friends for coffee and a garden tour and see where the afternoon takes you. Not since folks planted Victory Gardens during World War II has there been such widespread interest in home food production and self-reliance. Then, the goal was to offset shortages produced by war and rationing; today, the aim is to slow down the pace at which humanity is consuming or degrading planetary resources.

## Community EAB Eradication Efforts

A good example of how action at the community level can help solve regional problems can be found in efforts to eradicate the emerald ash borer (EAB). This imported insect pest is destroying native ash trees throughout the Midwest and Upper South. This pest, which probably arrived in wood packing material from Asia, has caused such significant damage that firewood cannot now be moved among any of the states, from Michigan to Tennessee, that have infestations. Control and eradication programs have been geared toward community awareness, with information posted on the Internet, community meetings, and printed materials to alert anyone who might own an ash tree of the need to inspect and treat the tree for EAB. Because the borers will kill every ash tree that is not treated and each infested tree provides a source for more insects the following season, the importance of reaching every tree owner cannot be overestimated.

Even urban apartment dwellers can participate actively in the sustainability movement. Food growing in containers, from sprouts to tomatoes, is possible anywhere the sun shines. By connecting with the larger community, other options become available. These include community gardening and community supported agriculture.

## Community Supported Agriculture

Community supported agriculture (CSA) arrangements generally work like this: you contract with a grower who supplies a certain amount of food each week for the duration of the season. In exchange for this service, you pay an agreed-upon sum in advance. The up-front payment supplies the capital the grower needs for seeds and supplies, and you reap the benefits of home-grown produce without all the work. Besides being a good deal for a household with too little space or time for a full-scale garden, a CSA agreement benefits the local economy and the local environment in all the same ways that a backyard garden does. Some CSA growers also allow a reduced payment in exchange for labor during the growing season. This provides a wonderful opportunity for the novice to gain valuable hands-on experience before tilling up a plot of his or her own out back.

## Community Gardening

Community gardening is the utilization of a single large garden plot by a community of individuals. The classic community garden space is a vacant lot cleaned up and converted to food gardening by a group of people living nearby. Under the typical arrangements, each family has its own plot and makes its own crop plans. The group might also share tools, trellises, and the expenses for fencing or irrigation. Within the bounds of this basic concept lie nearly as many variations as there are communities across America. Some groups, for example, practice *guerilla gardening*, swooping down upon unused urban space to plant vegetables, herbs, and flowers for anyone who happens by to enjoy. Others focus on utilizing city rooftops, harvesting the abundance from fruit and nut trees growing in public parks or bringing window box herb growing to inner city neighborhoods. All these approaches provide ways to bring the opportunity to produce some of their own food to people living anywhere, and especially to those living in low income neighborhoods. Even if you live in an apartment with one window, you can participate in a community effort. Chances are, one already exists near your home. If not, why not scout the neighborhood for some likely growing space? You have nothing to lose but the time, and you and your neighbors could potentially gain healthy local food.

In the suburbs, another approach to community gardening has become a trend. Neighbors whose yards adjoin one another join together to grow food in the entire area, sharing costs and labor. Most important, the time demands a large garden places on the gardener can be shared collectively. A corollary to this approach is the "one gardener, many gardens" variation on the CSA arrangements described in the previous section. One full-time gardener cultivates the gardens of several neighbors, sharing some of the produce with those who provide the land. These examples will serve to show that endlessly variable ways to garden collectively can be devised by anyone. All it takes is a willingness to work with others and to think creatively.

As a general rule, community gardening efforts will reward participants who make an effort to establish ground rules (pardon the pun) up front. Particularly where expenses or other resources are to be shared, it is important to answer in the beginning questions such as:

- Who will collect, deposit, and disburse funds?
- How will records of transactions be maintained?
- How will community tools be kept securely?
- Who is responsible for sharpening, repairing, or maintaining tools?
- Are local permits required, for example, for a fence?
- How will disputes be dealt with?

You may find that organizing a formal group with by-laws works best for a larger number of people, while one or two friends can manage the same thing with a nod and a handshake. The beauty of this approach is that you can tailor it to any situation.

## Other Community Efforts

Endless possibilities exist for communities to come together to enjoy a wider variety of food and other products than an individual family can manage alone. One of the most interesting community projects I've heard about recently involves constructing an oven, from local mud, for community bread baking. This kind of group effort reminds me of old-fashioned quilting bees and corn shuckings, events that I remember with pleasure from my rural childhood. Threshing the soft summer wheat that my grandmother transformed into marvelous biscuits was a community effort, too. A mechanical reaper and threshing machine represent a major investment. In those days, every member of my grandfather's extended family teamed up to thresh wheat. One guy owned the threshing machine, which was towed from farm to farm. On a given day, neighbors gathered at one of the farms, arriving on tractors, wagons in tow, to cut and thresh the crop. Men and boys worked the fields and ran the machinery, women and girls cooked both lunch and dinner back at the house. By sundown, we were exhausted, though sumptuously fed, and ready to go to sleep to the sound of the crickets. The next day, everyone moved to the next farm, and again the following day until the harvest season was done.

On the new American homestead, not only grain threshing but canning, soapmaking, beer brewing, wine pressing, sauerkraut chopping, and numerous other projects can be accomplished more quickly and efficiently as a group effort. As a rule, any home activity that requires bulk processing fits the profile.

Community activities like those mentioned here bring people of like mind together. This has benefits beyond stocking the pantry. Probably more than anything else in the America of the twenty-first century, we citizens need to learn how to talk to one another again. Cellphones, Facebook, Skype, and Twitter are all great, but any businessperson will tell you there is no substitute for a face-to-face conference when you want to build trust, gain cooperation, and develop shared goals. Even the most cursory examination of media reports clearly shows that civil discourse is threatened with extinction. Political rhetoric has sometimes gone so far over the top as to prompt calls—in a land that cherishes free speech—for curbs on the hostile tone of public deliberations. When public figures talk about Second Amendment solutions to political problems, we are teetering near the edge indeed.

Coming together to talk about growing food or making soap inevitably leads to talking about other matters. Every community activity need not be a call to political action, but community activities by definition are also "political" events, involving members of the body politic. Over the years, I have learned that the desire to live more sustainably and self-reliantly is not confined to members of one or the other political party or persuasion.

Another motivation—survival as a species—cuts across all political lines. We have but one planet, we have already degraded its resources alarmingly, and we must change our behavior or our own extinction is inevitable. The scientific evidence of widespread problems that threaten our survival has been accumulating for decades. The conclusions are inescapable. If we act now, we have a chance, albeit a slender one, to remake our society so that all Earth's people will have enough food, water, shelter, and other necessities to live decent lives in reasonable comfort. We can accomplish this without resorting to further degradation of planetary resources and without significant economic disruption, provided we act prudently and soon.

The suburb of today can become the village of tomorrow, with just about anything one really needs accessible via a short stroll down the street. I might brew the best beer in the area, and you might grow the finest potatoes. We can trade. My grandfather used to walk two miles to the local grocer, carrying a bucket filled with fresh eggs. He returned home with the bucket filled with the imported staples for my grandmother's kitchen: coffee, sugar, vanilla extract, ginger, and sometimes rice. Already many local food cooperatives purchase produce from their neighbors who garden, and of course the gardeners can buy seeds from the co-op, or vanilla extract, or coffee, just like Grandpa did.

> We need more co-ops and farmers' markets and fewer "super" markets. Walk through your nearest supermarket and estimate the amount of space devoted to actual food: fresh produce, uncooked meat, seafood, bakery, and dairy products. Subtract all the processed food, the freezers filled with pizza, and the aisles of nonfood items and soft drinks. You will have a much smaller space, a grocery that can easily be accommodated in, say, that old two-story house at the end of your street.

From the suburban village, we can look toward the city where rooftops bloom with vegetables, fruit, and herbs. Vacant lots that once housed piles of garbage and old tires now sprout lettuce and tomatoes. Boulevard medians grow apples or oranges (depending on the latitude) that anyone can pick. And out there, away from the city, natural habitats continue to thrive unmolested. Our need to convert wild lands to development will shrink in direct proportion to the degree to which cities and suburbs evolve greater self-sufficiency in food, services, energy, and raw materials. More land, therefore, can be set aside for the species that claimed it millennia before we arrived. Farmland ruined by industrial agriculture can begin to recover, while arable land can receive the proper stewardship to remain fertile and productive for generations. Regional needs will be met by food-craft cooperatives, much like some organic food mass production is managed today. That way, we avoid increasing the risk that in growing the "amber waves of grain" we will not degrade the "purple mountains' majesty." This is the hope and promise of the new American homestead.

# Appendix

# Resources

The resources that follow include general references and specific resources. The first section of general references is arranged by type and author. The more specific listings are arranged by chapter and topic.

## General References

### Books

Adams, Barbara Berst. *Micro Eco-Farming: Prospering from Backyard to Small Acreage in Partnership with the Earth*. Auburn, CA: New World Publishing, 2005.

Barr, Tracy L., ed. *Living the Country Lifestyle All-In-One For Dummies*. Indianapolis, IN: Wiley Publishing, Inc., 2009.

Belanger, Jerome D. *The Complete Idiot's Guide to Self-Sufficient Living*. New York: Alpha Books, 2009.

Husarik, Theresa A. *Hobby Farming For Dummies*. Indianapolis, IN: Wiley Publishing, Inc., 2008.

Madigan, Carleen, ed. *The Backyard Homestead: Produce All the Food You Need on Just a Quarter Acre*. North Adams, MA: Storey Publishing, 2009.

### Periodicals

*Mother Earth News*, Ogden Publications, www.motherearthnews.com.

*Urban Farm*, www.urbanfarmonline.com.

# Introduction: The Principles of Permaculture

Holmgren, David. *Permaculture: Principles and Pathways Beyond Sustainability*. White River Junction, VT: Chelsea Green Publishing Company, 2002.

Kellog, Scott, and Stacy Pettigrew. *Toolbox for Sustainable City Living: A Do-it-ourselves Guide*. Brooklyn, NY: South End Press, 2008.

Mollison, Bill. *Introduction to Permaculture*. Sisters Creek, Australia: Tagari Publications, 1997.

"Permaculture," www.permacultureprinciples.com.

# 1. The Earth and You

Pollan, Michael. *In Defense of Food: An Eater's Manifesto*. New York: Penguin Press, 2008.

———. *The Omnivore's Dilemma: A Natural History of Four Meals*. New York:  Penguin Press, 2006.

Agricultural Marketing Service (AMS) of the U.S. Department of Agriculture has a searchable database of farmer's markets, apps.ams.usda.gov/FarmersMarkets.

"Chef-2-Chef" networking website, national farmers market directory, marketplace.chef2chef.net/farmer-markets.

"Farmers Market Dot Com," farmersmarket.com.

Kingsolver, Barbara. *Animal, Vegetable, Miracle: A Year of Food Life*. New York: Harper Perennial, 2008.

National Directory of Fruit Stands and Farmers Markets, www.fruitstands.com.

"Slow Food USA," www.slowfoodusa.org/index.php/local_chapters.

"Sustainable Table," www.sustainabletable.org.

# 2. Earth-Friendly Gardening Basics

Bartholomew, Mel. *All New Square Foot Gardening.* Brentwood, TN: Cool Springs Press, 2005.

Coleman, Eliot. *Four Season Harvest: Organic Vegetables From Your Home Garden All Year Long*, 2nd ed., rev. White River Junction, VT: Chelsea Green Publishing, 1999.

Coleman, Eliot. *The New Organic Grower: A Master's Manual of Tools and Techniques for the Home and Market Gardener.* White River Junction, VT: Chelsea Green Publishing, 1995.

National Campaign for Sustainable Agriculture (NCSA), www. sustainableagriculture.net/site/PageServer?pagename=NCSA_Home.

National Sustainable Agriculture Information Service (ATTRA), attra.ncat.org.

The Rodale Institute, www.rodaleinstitute.org.

Sustainable Agriculture Research and Education (SARE), www.sare.org.

## Composting

www.epa.gov/epawaste/conserve/rrr/composting/index.htm

www.howtocompost.org

www.mastercomposter.com

## Cover Cropping

Clemson University, hgic.clemson.edu/factsheets/HGIC1252.htm.

Cornell University, www.gardening.cornell.edu/factsheets/ ecogardening/impsoilcov.html.

Oregon State University, extension.oregonstate.edu/catalog/html/fs/ fs304-e, includes a table showing how much and when to sow.

## Integrated Pest Management

The Resource Guide for Organic Insect and Disease Management, www.nysaes.cornell.edu/pp/resourceguide/index.

Trap cropping table, www.oisat.org/control_methods/cultural__ practices/trap_cropping.html.

The United States Environmental Protection Agency IPM fact sheet, www.epa.gov/pesticides/factsheets/ipm.htm.

University of Massachusetts at Amherst image library for diagnosis of pests and crop diseases, www.umassvegetable.org/soil_crop_ pest_mgt/disease_mgt/index.html.

## Garden Planning

Interactive Vegetable Garden Planner (user fee charged), www.motherearthnews.com/garden-planner/vegetable-garden-planner.aspx.

## Trellises

National Gardening Association, www.garden.org/foodguide/ browse/veggie/vines_care/642.

"Trellising Tomatoes," www.taunton.com/finegardening/how-to/ articles/pruning-tomatoes.aspx.

# 3 and 4: Vegetables, Part One and Part Two

Hirsch, David. *The Moosewood Restaurant Kitchen Garden: Creative Gardening for the Adventurous Cook.* New York: Simon & Schuster, 1992.

Louisiana State University crop yield table for home gardens, www.lsuagcenter.com/en/lawn_garden/home_gardening/vegetables/ cultural_information/Expected+Vegetable+Garden+Yields.htm.

"Planting a Home Vegetable Garden," Iowa State University, www.extension.iastate.edu/Publications/PM819.pdf.

Searchable database of fruit and vegetable information, www.fruits andveggiesmorematters.org/?page_id=164.

State cooperative extension service local offices, www.csrees.usda. gov/Extension.

Texas A&M University production guides for vegetable crops, including typical yields, aggie-horticulture.tamu.edu/extension/ vegetable/cropguides.

USDA handbook for storage of vegetables and other crops, www.ba.ars.usda.gov/hb66.

# 5. Herbs for Flavor and Health

Smith, Miranda. *Your Backyard Herb Garden: A Gardener's Guide to Growing Over 50 Herbs Plus How to Use Them in Cooking, Crafts, Companion Planting, and More.* Emmaus, PA: Rodale Press, 1997.

The Herb Research Foundation, www.herbs.org.

Chart of edible and nonedible flowers, homecooking.about.com/ library/weekly/blflowers.htm.

## Mushrooms

Mycological Society of America, msafungi.org.

MykoWeb, www.mykoweb.com/articles/cultivation.html.

# 6. Fruits

"Blueberries in the Home Garden," www.ces.ncsu.edu/depts/hort/ hil/hil-8207.html.

"Growing Apple Trees in the Home Garden," www.ces.ncsu.edu/ depts/hort/hil/hil-8301.html.

"Growing Bramble Fruits in West Virginia," www.wvu.edu/~agexten/ hortcult/fruits/brambles.htm; includes information applicable to other parts of the country, as well.

"Growing Strawberries," www.hort.purdue.edu/ext/ho-46.pdf.

Kansas State University table for planning small fruit growing space, www.oznet.ksu.edu/library/hort2/mf352.pdf.

Virginia Tech, www.ext.vt.edu/pubs/envirohort/426-840/426-840.html.

# 7. Food from Animals

## Bees

Blackiston, Howland. *Beekeeping for Dummies.* Indianapolis, IN: Wiley Publishing, 2009.

www.beeworks.com/index.html.

University of Missouri, extension.missouri.edu/explorepdf/agguides/pests/g07600.pdf

## Fish

Sipe, Mike. *Earth-Friendly Food for the Future in Your Backyard: The Hatchery Manual for the Mike Sipe Survival System of Home-Based and Commercial Tilapia Farming.* Palmetto, FL: Harmonic Research Associates, 2010.

## Poultry

Willis, Kimberly, with Rob Ludlow. *Raising Chickens For Dummies.* Indianapolis, IN: Wiley Publishing, 2009.

"Chicken Keeping," www.chickenkeeping.com.

"The City Chicken.com," home.centurytel.net/thecitychicken.

"Home Grown Poultry," homegrownpoultry.com.

"Keeping and Raising Chickens at Home," keepingchickens.blogspot.com.

## Dairy Animals

Amundson, Carol A. *How to Raise Goats: Everything You Need to Know*. Minneapolis, MN: Voyageur Press, 2009.

Hashheider, Phillip. *How to Raise Cattle: Everything You Need to Know*. Minneapolis, MN: Voyageur Press, 2007.

Hathaway, Margaret. *Living With Goats: Everything You Need to Know to Raise Your Own Backyard Herd*. Guilford, CT: Lyons Press, 2009.

American Dairy Goat Association, www.adga.org.

# 8. The Homestead Kitchen

## The Homestead Pantry

Alltrista Corporation. *Ball Blue Book Guide to Preserving,* 100th anniversary ed. Daleville, IN: Alltrista Corporation, 2009.

Brenner, Leslie, and Katharine Kinsolving. *Essential Flavors: The Simple Art of Cooking With Infused Oils, Flavored Vinegars, Essences, and Elixirs.* New York: Viking, 1994.

"USDA Complete Guide to Home Canning," www.uga.edu/nchfp/publications/publications_usda.html.

## The Homestead Bakery and Brewery

Baggett, Nancy. *Kneadlessly Simple: Fabulous, Fuss-Free, No-Knead Breads.* Indianapolis, IN: Wiley Publishing, 2009.

Nachel, Marty. *Homebrewing For Dummies.* Indianapolis, IN: Wiley Publishing, 2008.

Palmer, John J. *How to Brew: Everything You Need to Know to Brew Beer Right the First Time.* Boulder, CO: Brewer's Publications, 2006.

American Homebrewers Association, www.homebrewers association.org.

Fermenters International Trade Association, www.fermenters international.org/about.php.

### The Homestead Vineyard

Cox, Jeff. *From Vines to Wines: The Complete Guide to Growing Grapes and Making Your Own Wine*. North Adams, MA: Storey Publishing, 1999.

Patterson, Tim. *Home Winemaking For Dummies*. Indianapolis, IN: Wiley Publishing, 2010.

Fermenters International Trade Association is a great portal site for home winemaking enthusiasts, www.fermentersinternational.org.

### The Homestead Creamery

Helweg, Rick. *The Complete Guide to Making Cheese, Butter, and Yogurt at Home: Everything You Need to Know Explained Simply*. Ocala, FL: Atlantic Publishing Group, 2010.

Karlin, Mary. *Artisan Cheese Making at Home: Techniques & Recipes for Mastering World-Class Cheeses*. Berkeley, CA: Ten Speed Press, 2011.

Leverentz, James R. *The Complete Idiot's Guide to Cheesemaking*. Tucson, AZ: Alpha Publications, 2010.

# 9. Putting It All Together

Steadman, Todd A. *New Complete Guide to Landscaping: Design, Plant, Build*. New York: Better Homes and Gardens, 2002.

# 10. The Future of the American Homestead

Aubrey, Sarah Beth, *Starting and Running Your Own Small Farm Business*. North Adams, MA: Storey Publishing, 2008.

Avent, Tony. *So You Want to Start a Nursery?* Portland, OR: Timber Press, 2003.

Tullock, John. *Pay Dirt: How to Make $10,000 a Year From Your Backyard Garden*. Avon, MA: Adams Media, 2010.

## Butterflies

National Audubon Society Field Guide to North American Butterflies, 1981.

"The Butterfly Site.com," www.thebutterflysite.com/ gardening.shtml.

"The Butterfly Website," www.butterflywebsite.com/ butterflygardening.cfm.

"Missouri Botanical Garden," www.butterflyhouse.org/butterflies/ butterflygardening.aspx.

Search on "butterfly garden <state name>" to find state-specific information.

Butterfly field guides, www.butterflybuzz.com/page/290622.

## Community Supported Agriculture

USDA Alternative Farming Systems Information Center, www.nal. usda.gov/afsic/pubs/csa/csa.shtml.

University of Massachusetts at Amherst, www.umassvegetable.org/ food_farming_systems/csa.

Land Stewardship Project, www.landstewardshipproject.org/ csa.html.

Directory of CSAs, www.greenpeople.org/csa.htm.

Search "community supported agriculture <state name>" to find state-specific information.

## Emerald Ash Borer

Information about this tree-killing pest can be found at www.emeraldashborer.info/index.cfm.

Indiana's program for ash borer eradication is typical. Learn more about it at extension.entm.purdue.edu/eab/index.php?page= management/nabb.

## Native Plants

U.S. Forest Service, www.fs.fed.us/wildflowers/nativegardening/index.shtml.

Search on "native plant society <state name>" to find the web site of your local organization.

## Rain Gardens

Download a PDF on rain garden design at www.aces.edu/waterquality/nemo/Fact%20Sheets/rain%20garden,%20mg,%20final.pdf.

Find design templates for rain garden construction at www.lowimpactdevelopment.org/raingarden_design/how2designraingarden.htm.

## Water Gardens

University of Georgia, pubs.caes.uga.edu/caespubs/horticulture/watergarden.htm.

Southern Regional Aquaculture Center, www.aquanic.org/publicat/usda_rac/efs/srac/435fs.pdf.

# Index